WRAPPING AND UNWRAPPING
MATERIAL CULTURE

PUBLICATIONS OF THE
INSTITUTE OF ARCHAEOLOGY, UNIVERSITY COLLEGE LONDON

Series Editor: Ruth Whitehouse
Director of the Institute: Stephen Shennan
Founding Series Editor: Peter J. Ucko

The Institute of Archaeology of University College London is one of the oldest, largest, and most prestigious archaeology research facilities in the world. Its extensive publications program includes the best theory, research, pedagogy, and reference materials in archaeology and cognate disciplines, through publishing exemplary work of scholars worldwide. Through its publications, the Institute brings together key areas of theoretical and substantive knowledge, improves archaeological practice, and brings archaeological findings to the general public, researchers, and practitioners. It also publishes staff research projects, site and survey reports, and conference proceedings. The publications program, formerly developed in house or in conjunction with UCL Press, is now produced in partnership with Left Coast Press, Inc. The Institute can be accessed online at http://www.ucl.ac.uk/archaeology.

Recent Titles

Susanna Harris and Laurence Douny, *Wrapping and Unwrapping Material Culture*
Laurence Douny, *Living in a Landscape of Scarcity*
Helen Dawson, *Mediterranean Voyages*
Chris J. Stevens, Sam Nixon, Mary Anne Murray, and Dorian Q Fuller (Eds.), *Archaeology of African Plant Use*
Andrew Bevan and Mark Lake (Eds.), *Computational Approaches to Archaeological Spaces*
Sue Colledge, James Conolly, Keith Dobney, Katie Manning, and Stephen Shennan (Eds.), *The Origins and Spread of Domestic Animals in Southwest Asia and Europe*
Julia Shaw, *Buddhist Landscapes of Central India*
Ralph Haeussler, *Becoming Roman?*
Ethan E. Cochrane and Andrew Gardner, *Evolutionary and Interpretive Archaeologies*
Andrew Bevan and David Wengrow (Eds.), *Cultures of Commodity Branding*
Peter Jordan (Ed.), *Landscape and Culture in Northern Eurasia*
Peter Jordan and Marek Zvelebil (Eds.), *Ceramics before Farming*
Marcos Martinón-Torres and Thilo Rehren (Eds.), *Archaeology, History, and Science*
Miriam Davis, *Dame Kathleen Kenyon*
Elizabeth Pye (Ed.), *The Power of Touch*
Russell McDougall and Iain Davidson (Eds.), *The Roth Family, Anthropology, and Colonial Administration*
Eleni Asouti and Dorian Q Fuller, *Trees and Woodlands of South India*
Tony Waldron, *Paleoepidemiology*
Janet Picton, Stephen Quirke, and Paul C. Roberts (Eds.), *Living Images*
Timothy Clack and Marcus Brittain (Eds.), *Archaeology and the Media*
Sue Colledge and James Conolly (Eds.), *The Origins and Spread of Domestic Plants in Southwest Asia and Europe*

Information on older titles in this series can be obtained from the Left Coast Press, Inc., http://www.LCoastPress.com.

WRAPPING AND UNWRAPPING MATERIAL CULTURE

Archaeological and Anthropological Perspectives

Edited by

Susanna Harris
Laurence Douny

Walnut Creek, California

LEFT COAST PRESS, INC.
1630 North Main Street, #400
Walnut Creek, CA 94596
www.LCoastPress.com

ISBN 978-1-61132-887-5 hardback
ISBN 978-1-61132-889-9 institutional eBook
ISBN 978-1-61132-890-5 consumer eBook

Library of Congress Cataloging-in-Publication Data:

Wrapping and unwrapping material culture: archaeological and anthropological perspectives/edited by Susanna Harris & Laurence Douny.

pages cm. — (Publications of the Institute of Archaeology, University College London; 64)

Summary: "This innovative volume challenges contemporary views on material culture by exploring the relationship between wrapping materials and practices and the objects, bodies, and places that define them. Using examples as diverse as Egyptian mummies, Celtic tombs, Native American ceremonial bundles, baby swaddling, and contemporary African textiles, the dozen archaeologist and anthropologist contributors show how acts of wrapping and unwrapping are embedded in beliefs and thoughts of a particular time and place. These context-specific, cultural, and technical acts offer a new lens on material culture and its relationship to cultural meaning"—Provided by publisher.

ISBN 978-1-61132-887-5 (hardback) — ISBN 978-1-61132-889-9 (institutional eBook) — ISBN 978-1-61132-890-5 (consumer eBook)

1. Wrapping cloths—Case studies. 2. Material culture—Case studies. 3. Textile fabrics—Case studies. 4. Textile fabrics, Ancient—Case studies. 5. Funeral rites and ceremonies, Ancient—Case studies. I. Harris, Susanna, author, editor of compilation. II. Douny, Laurence, author, editor of compilation.

GT2225.W73 2014

306—dc23

2014003438

Printed in the United States of America

Contents

Illustrations

Table

Preface

The idea for this book came from a series of conversations between the editors. Both were at that time employed as postdoctoral fellows at University College London: Laurence Douny was investigating contemporary wild silk textiles in Mali and Burkina Faso at the Department of Anthropology, and Susanna Harris was researching the cloth cultures of prehistoric Europe at the Institute of Archaeology. We were initially brought together through the study of textiles and the wish to understand how their respective disciplines conceptualised these fascinating and complex materials. The idea of wrapping stemmed from these conversations and was seen as an avenue along which to investigate shared interests across the disciplines. The topic also offered the opportunity to extend beyond textiles to related materials and, from there, into a range of new theoretical perspectives.

We believed that the wrapping topic held the potential for a larger collaborative research project; thus we decided to invite researchers to present their response to this theme at two conferences. The first session, Wrapping Objects, was hosted by the Theoretical Archaeology Group (TAG) at the University of Durham in December 2009. The second session was a two-day conference, Wrapping and Unwrapping the Body—Archaeological and Anthropological Perspectives, held at the Institute of Archaeology, UCL, in May 2010. It was clear, from the questions and the discussion, that the presentations opened up a range of ideas that spanned disciplines, time periods, and geographical research traditions.

Once initiated, wrapping as a cross disciplinary investigation by archaeologists and anthropologists took on a shape of its own, and this book is the result. It is not the first research into wrapping; indeed, all the writers in this volume owe a debt to forerunners in their particular study areas. Nevertheless, each has further developed this research in the chapters that follow. These chapters have been selected to represent a broad spectrum of perspectives on the concept of wrapping in archaeology and anthropology. They show just how useful, and how widely applicable, this topic can be in terms of finding more out about people's actions, past and present. We hope that they will inspire interest in, and raise curiosity about, the role of wrapping in human cultures through the ages.

We are especially grateful to the Institute of Archaeology, UCL, Policy Group chaired by Professor Stephen Shennan for awarding us the Annual Conference Fund, which provided the funding to invite speakers and chairs to Wrapping and Unwrapping the Body—Archaeological and Anthropological Perspectives. Thanks also to Professor Susanne Kuechler and *The Journal of Material Culture*, Department of Anthropology, UCL, for providing the reception at this event—and to both these departments for their willingness to collaborate in this way. We are grateful to the organisers of TAG for hosting the first session and the participants for providing an innovative forum through which to explore these ideas. As postdoctoral fellows, we are indebted to our funding bodies, the Leverhulme Trust and the British Academy, for supporting us in the early stage of our careers. A number of individuals have also been particularly supportive. Thanks go to all conference participants and Dr. Marie Louise Stig Sørensen, Department of Archaeology, University of Cambridge; Professor David Wengrow, Institute of Archaeology, UCL; Dr. Graeme Were, School of English, Media Studies, and Art History, The University of Queensland; Professor John Chapman, Durham University; and Dr. Linda Hurcombe, The University of Exeter, for their willingness to chair sessions and contribute to the discussion during the two conferences. Thanks, too, to those reviewers who commented on individual chapters and, in particular, to Professor Michael Rowlands, Department of Anthropology, UCL; Professor Jean-Pierre Warnier, L'École des Hautes Études en Sciences Sociales, Paris; Dr. Margarita Gleba, McDonald Institute for Archaeological Research, University of Cambridge; Professor Ruth Whitehouse, Institute of Archaeology, UCL; Pippa White; and two anonymous reviewers for their useful comments on earlier drafts of the introduction and the full manuscript. Many thanks to Professor Ruth Whitehouse, Institute of Archaeology, UCL, for her unwavering support and encouragement from a bid for funding through to publication; and to Dr. Marion Cutting for her editing support, which was made possible by funding from the Grants Sub-Committee, Institute of Archaeology, University College London. Finally, thanks to the Mildmay Community Partnership for the invaluable life lessons learned during Susanna Harris's employment with them. We acknowledge with regret the absence of Dr. Claude Ardouin's contribution 'Protecting the Family, Protecting the Body: Talismanic Islamic Motifs on the Woollen Weavings from Niger Bend, Mali', which unfortunately remained unfinished at the time of his death.

We look forward to the publication of *Unwrapping Ancient Egypt* (Routledge) by Dr. Christina Riggs, a book that was still in press at the time of writing and could not be included in the discussion in our first chapter.

Susanna Harris
Laurence Douny
May 2014

Part I: Introduction

1   Wrapping and Unwrapping, Concepts and Approaches

Laurence Douny and Susanna Harris

What Is Wrapping?

In everyday English, to *wrap* is to cover or enclose in soft materials (*Oxford English Dictionary*). The term conjures up ideas of gifts wrapped in colourful paper, of fresh towels or loose garments wrapped around the body; of being warmly wrapped up against the cold weather. The action of wrapping creates a relationship between the wrapping materials (or wrappers) and their contents. These contents may be bodies, objects, or places (Hendry 1993, 26). The wrappings that are used to cover and enclose their contents may be made from a wide range of malleable materials, typically paper, textiles, or leather, or thin sheets of plastic. These materials share certain properties: they can all be wrapped, folded, shaped, and tied (Harris 2008, 225–27). However, bodies, objects, or places may also be wrapped in a stiffer material: special items, for example, may be wrapped in boxes to preserve them, or, at the other end of the scale, a person may be, metaphorically, wrapped in love or care through language (Hendry 1993, 21–26, 52–69). Wrapping can be distinguished from other forms of adornment or covering in that it can be removed. Typically, what is wrapped can be unwrapped. It is here that Gell distinguished the otherwise similar practices of tattooing and wrapping the body in cloth; cloth can be removed from the body, whereas tattoos cannot and so provide a contrasting form of wrapping (Gell 1993, 87–91). To unwrap is not simply to reverse wrapping; the act of unwrapping is significant in itself and has its own outcomes. Unwrapping may refer either to a physical or a conceptual revelation

(Wieczorkiewicz 2005), whereby knowledge is gained or secrecy exposed. The removal of wrappings and their application elsewhere may be a device to accumulate and store the power of their contents (Gell 1993, 89). As investigated in this volume, wrapping is the act of covering, enclosing, and containing with a wide range of materials, patterns, and metaphysical or conceptual devices. Unwrapping is seen as equally significant; the removal of wrappings is potentially an arena of revelation and finding out, the exposure of secrets, an act of disclosure of withheld knowledge, or the creation of an emotional response such as surprise or awe. The intention and purpose of wrapping and unwrapping becomes, therefore, the subject of contextual enquiry.

Through covering, enclosing, and containing, wrapping materials have properties and efficacy that act on their contents or the perception of their contents. Wrapping materials are acted on in order to be applied to surfaces, bodies, objects, and places. They may shape, cover, and form their content every bit as much as the contents can be transformed by them. Through texture and surface, wrapping may adorn and decorate. As a cultural and technical act, wrapping is a form of containment that can be used to conceal and reveal, camouflage or highlight, transform and exhibit, conserve and preserve. In Warnier's work the experience and practice of containment are revealed through multiple media such as skins, container forms, and envelopes that are used as technologies of power (Warnier 2007, 154). As intentional acts, wrappings are put in contact with their contents and enable actions to be performed; they may also be perceived as boundaries to create interfaces between objects, subjects, and the world. There is also an ambivalence in the act of wrapping; the relationship between the content and wrapping is questionable. Wrapping may make the contents clearer or conceal them to the extent that they cease to exist. To unwrap may reverse these outcomes or create an entirely new state of existence.

From such a perspective, wrappings bestow specific materialities that are also forged through human agency. Following Ingold's definition, materiality is considered to be a combination of 'the "brute materiality" of the physical world' and 'the ways this world is appropriated by human projects' (Ingold 2012, 435). These materials and processes are worked through techniques. This volume examines wrapping by placing emphasis on the materials, techniques, and processes by which the lived world is created and transformed. From this perspective, materials are acted on (Lemonnier 1992, 5–6) as they are cut, crushed, woven, or assembled before being finally transformed into a wide surface or a structure that can in turn be wrapped and unwrapped. The concept of materiality emerges from material practice, as a transformative potential, and plays a role in the construction of an individual's social and material world (Kuechler 2003, 2008, 266).

Through the chapters in this volume we bring together twelve contributors from archaeology, anthropology, and conservation who develop these concepts to present contextually specific studies of wrapping. The topic has wide applicability as people across the world in the past and present have engaged in wrapping and unwrapping practices as a means of creating and transforming themselves. However, it is also specific, because these wrapping practices are embedded in beliefs and thoughts belonging to a particular time and place. In this introduction, we present wrapping as material action and review the theories and methodologies of investigating wrapping that have developed in archaeology and anthropology. What follows seeks to present the methods and contributions made to a topic that is rooted in excavation, artefact analysis, participant observation, and conservation practice.

Wrapping as Material Action

Through investigating the act and intentions of wrapping, we recognise the subtle yet potent role that wrapping and unwrapping have played in different societies. The addition of a particular wrapper can be used to alter the content it enwraps, to manipulate its perception by others, and to provide a surface with which to contain or convey emotions. Wrappers can take a simple form but convey profound messages, as for example the square Korean wrapping cloths (*pojagi*) of the Chosŏn dynasty between 1392–1910 c.e. (Kumja Paik 2003, 10). Used by royalty and poor alike, and made by women from specially procured silk, scraps of left-over cloth, or oiled paper, these wrapping cloths played a prominent role in the daily lives of the Koreans, who used them to cover, store, and carry objects (Kumja Paik 2003, 11, 14). Whether covering a table of food, an altar, a bridal gift, bedding, cutlery or clothes, there was an "unspoken folk belief that by wrapping an object, *pok* (good fortune) could be enclosed or captured within a *pojagi*" (Kumja Paik 2003, 12–15). Made exclusively by women, who at that time were confined to work alone in the inner court of the household, blessing and happiness were stitched into the *pojagis'* very fabric (Kumja Paik 2003, 20–21; Sŏng-mi 2003, 24). These cloths remind us of the relationships, creativity, intentions, and emotions that are involved in the act of wrapping.

As material action, wrapping may be temporary or permanent; it may also involve psychological, symbolic, and physical transformations of objects, place, and people. For instance, the practice of foot binding in China demonstrates the complex interplay between bandages, skin, flesh, and bones—and emotions. Throughout its long history, foot binding in China had many forms and a rich and varied significance (for details: Ko 2001, 2005; Wang 2000). Young girls had their feet bound with cloth bandages by their mothers, the aim of this painful process being to reduce the size of their feet and to prepare young girls for marriage, sexuality, and reproduction (Wang 2000, 4–20). Small bound feet in tiny socks and shoes were an object of beauty and a taboo for the male gaze and touch; in literature and art, they were portrayed as objects of desire and the centre of erotic symbolism (Wang 2000, 24–28). Through shape and posture, the practice differentiated male and female bodies and, indeed, separated women with bound feet from those with unbound feet (Ko 2005, 136–39; Wang 2000, 32). Resulting in the permanent transformation of the bones and flesh of the feet, binding created social boundaries and opportunities; it was a process through which girls were prepared for their ideological role in life.

While wrapping applies layers, unwrapping takes them off and has its own particular significance. According to studies of Christmas-giving in America, wrapping gifts adds the giver's personal sentiment to the contents; it also acts to transform the shop-bought commodity inside into a personal gift through the act of its wrapping in mass-produced paper (Caplow 1984; Carrier 1993, 60). Unwrapping of gifts, especially from family, is often accompanied by some kind of formal ritual. A gift will perhaps be opened by the recipient on or around Christmas day in the company of friends or family. Before being unwrapped, these gifts may be displayed with other similarly wrapped gifts below a Christmas tree or in a pile in a living room (Caplow 1982, 389). By contrast, on other occasions unwrapping gifts may be a spontaneous act that takes place in front of the giver. The unwrapping process brings an element of surprise and excitement to the act of giving; and it heightens the emotions. An ostensibly similar practice of wrapping and unwrapping gifts is found in Japan. However, there are different signals embodied in what appear to be the familiar materials and practice of unwrapping. In Japan, the intention of wrapping is not so much about concealing followed by unwrapping to create a surprise as about separating the recipient from potential pollution from the donor (Hendry 1990, 1993, 14). Rather than unwrapping the gift immediately, one is supposed to put it aside. Immediate opening is impolite, because it removes the focus away from the sentiment and toward an unseemly interest in the content (Hendry 1993, 14). Indeed, the recipient may not open the gift at all but, instead, make an assessment of its value while it is still wrapped and then pass it on as a gift to someone else. Hendry points out how misunderstandings between Japanese and British forms of gift giving, wrapping, and unwrapping can lead to the breakdown of social relationships (Hendry 1993, 14).

Moving beyond the close relationship of wrapping to malleable textile and paper materials, we recognise the enclosing, covering, and enveloping aspect of wrapping in other media. In his study of body tattoos in the Pacific, Gell recognised the potency of pigment and pattern to wrap the body in social identities and a protective layer (Gell 1993). Although distinct from the cloth wrappings, which can be removed (Gell 1993, 87), there is nevertheless a relationship between clothes and tattoos that is recognised through language. The word *pulu* in Samoa is associated with back tattoos and, used with the compound *ta*, it means to strike or wrap and can therefore be taken to mean that the design is wrapped around the body (Gell 1993, 96). Other verbs associated with tattooing are caulking, a process rather like sealing a canoe with bread-fruit gum or the protective layer of a coconut husk, and interposing, which is associated with the idea of creating a defensive screen between a person and the world (Gell 1993, 96). The relationship between, on the one hand, wrapping as the application of material layers that can be removed and, on the other hand, the metaphorical and metaphysical forms of wrapping is worthy of investigation—and, here, context becomes all important. The concept of wrapping should not be so rigidly defined in the name of academic rigour that it excludes other, interrelated, aspects of a culture.

By covering, enclosing, and enveloping, wrapping can be understood as an act of grouping, a gathering process or a means of quantifying to achieve control over things and people. In Gell's example, for instance, people are grouped together in hierarchies through tattooing (Gell 1993, 300–03), albeit a permanent form of wrapping. In other cultural contexts, grouping is also true for objects. In the North American Plains, ceremonial bundles are made by North American/Plains Indians and are composed of two or more small objects, such as animal or plant parts and mineral or manufactured objects, and these are grouped together through being wrapped in cloth or skins (Zedeño 2008, 363–64). These bundles represent more than a simple collection of objects: they are repositories of knowledge, powerful in their own right and as potentially powerful as people with their own life histories, personalities, and social positions (Zedeño 2008, 364–65). It is through the effect of being in a bundle with other potent objects that the individual collection becomes more than a sum of its parts (Zedeño 2008, 364). In this and other instances we see the role of wrapping to group, gather, and enclose, with the potential to transform the contents within.

Consequently, the concept of wrapping used in this book is based on the principle that wrapping is the act of enclosing, binding, enveloping, or covering. Unwrapping is the act of removing the layers of wrapping. The contents of wrapping may be bodies and objects, places or space, either singly or grouped together. In this volume we consider clothing, for example, as a form of wrapping that is specifically used to cover, enclose, and adorn the body. From this perspective, all clothing is seen as a means of wrapping the body. A distinction is often made, however, between draped clothing (a clothing technique) and tailored clothing (Anawalt 1981, 5). By wrapping, and indeed unwrapping, contents may be gathered together, transformed, hidden, or revealed. The materials used to wrap or unwrap vary. Nearly all the authors in this book deal with textile wrappings. Textiles are investigated as clothing materials, either through wrapping techniques (Johnstone, Chapter 3; Douny, Chapter 10) or through the idea of textile-wrapped bodies, whereby the implication is that wrapping may reveal, conceal, or redefine shape (Malkogeorgou, Chapter 4; Makovicky, Chapter 5). Wrapping the dead body in textiles highlights the concept of layering in materials not only to perpetuate beliefs but also to ensure the appropriate treatment of the dead body (Harris, Chapter 6; Wills, Chapter 9).

Wrapping, however, is not limited to sheets of malleable materials such as textiles. The contributors to this volume also contrast clay and textile envelopes (Garcia Ventura & Lopen-Bertran, Chapter 11), wrapping the dead in layers of leather, wood, and turf in addition to textile (Harris, Chapter 6), and wrapping landscape in images carved in stone (Croucher & Richards, Chapter 12). As a consequence, wrappings constitute units that are designed in such a way as to be filled or to hold people and things. The intention behind these acts is both specific and variable, which is demonstrated directly through the reshaping and restitching of a valuable dress over time to suit changing fashions and concepts of the female body (Malkogeorgou, Chapter 4); the contrasting ways in which a baby is swaddled or carried in different geographical regions (Russell, Chapter 2); and in the questions raised by the textiles used to wrap objects in burials in the Iron Age (Gleba, Chapter 7; Banck-Burgess, Chapter 8). The contributors to this volume draw on a wide range of methodological and theoretical developments in both archaeology and anthropology. The following sections outline the principal ideas from which this volume draws its inspiration.

Disciplinary Approaches to Wrapping

Archaeology

Archaeologists investigate past human societies, many of which are known only from their material remains. Owing to the nature of this archaeological record, one of the principal foundations of their research is the analysis of artefacts. Archaeologists use such analyses in their search to understand more about the people who made, used, deposited, or discarded such material objects. In the quest to understand people, they share the general concern of the humanities to understand the motivation of individuals and groups, both cross-culturally and through time. Archaeology, as a discipline, typically works without texts and oral traditions. For this reason, perhaps, it tends to focus on developing methodologies and theoretical perspectives. It is through these approaches that archaeologists interpret material culture as evidence of the thoughts and actions of past people. They, like many of the contributors to this volume, are concerned with excavation techniques and artefact studies. At the same time, archaeologists also attach great importance to the means by which they arrive at the interpretation of these material remains.

There is no single book on wrapping in archaeology; it has been most closely studied through the discovery of wrapped archaeological artefacts, the identification of the wrappers, and an interpretation of the meaning or intentions of wrapping practices within the context of a given society. Because many of the materials used for wrapping are organic and highly perishable, archaeological evidence for wrapping is often complex, partial, and fragmentary.

Preservation and Identification   Where there are favourable preservation conditions, wrappings may be studied directly through their preserved remains. In ancient Egyptian tombs, for example, the dry, undisturbed chambers provide good conditions for the preservation of complete, or nearly complete, wrapped artefacts and wrapping materials. Here, mummified bodies wrapped in layers of linen bandages survive alongside wrapped statues, rolled papyrus scrolls, and preserved items of draped clothing. Some of the most famous objects and statues from Tutankhamun's tomb were discovered wrapped; the 'treasury' of the tomb was guarded by a sculpture of the god Anubis shaped as a jackal and draped in textiles (Carter 1933, pl. II). For the most part, however, archaeologists have to work with more fragmentary evidence for wrapping. In the burials of temperate Europe, for example, textiles and other organic materials are at times preserved in waterlogged conditions or through their contact with metals that produce salts that create a mineral replacement or pseudomorph of the original material (Bartel 2002, 163–66; Bender Jørgensen 1992, 11–13; Chen, Jakes, & Foreman 1998; Good 2001; Masurel 1992, 65–66). In this and other situations, such fragmented archaeological remains may not provide clear enough evidence to show whether the material was wrapped around the artefact or simply put under or over it. Wrapping can be researched only on a case by case basis according to the circumstances of its preservation.

Even where there are no wrappings preserved, archaeologists may be able to recognise where they were once present. The position of bones in a burial may suggest that the body was originally bound (Bradley 1994, 63; McAnany, Storey, & Lockard 1999, 132; Richter et al. 2010, 327–28). At Hemp Knoll, near Avebury in Britain, for instance, the central inhumation of a Beaker grave was recovered in a tightly flexed position with the knees pulled up against the chest, suggesting it had originally been bound in wrappings that have since decayed (Robertson-Mackay 1980, 140–41). The temporal implications of binding the dead are demonstrated in the Late Formative deposits of the Maya site of K'axob, Belize, where tightly wrapped bodies in seated and flexed positions are believed to represent the prolonged display of the corpse as part of its transformation into an ancestor (McAnany, Storey, & Lockard 1999, 131). Where organic materials do not survive, wrapped clothing may also be identified through the position of fastenings. In Anglo-Saxon graves on the British Isles, paired shoulder brooches in female graves may have held up a wide tube of fabric that was fastened on either shoulder, a suggestion supported by iconographic evidence (Owen-Crocker 1986, 28; Walton Rogers 2007, 144).

For archaeologists, faced with materials transformed by the environment in which they have been preserved, the challenge is to apply detailed and careful scientific analysis to identify the original materials and the features that identify examples of wrapping. Such identification is, of course, a key principle in the study of any archaeological material and not exclusive to wrapping. Excavation and examination methods need to be sympathetic to the properties of wrapping in order to record the type of information relevant to the identification both of the material used and how an object was wrapped. They record a range of information on the type and sequence of single or multiple layers, their inward or outward faces, their association with ornaments or fastenings, and their location within the excavated archaeological context. There are a number of examples of Iron Age (Celtic) princely burials from Central Europe where archaeologists have been able to record wrapping practices despite the complex decayed nature of their evidence (Banck-Burgess 1999; Bartel 2002). For example, fragments of organic wrappings have been identified on two Iron Age bronze vessels found in burials at Glauberg, Hesse, Germany (Bartel 2002, 163–66). The sequence of wrapping on one of the vessels reveals layers of textile, inward-facing stitched fur and crisscrossing bands lined with a patterned textile. These wrappings raise questions about what the vessel might have looked like in the funeral procession and its significance for the afterlife (Bartel 2002, 163–66).

The fact that so many forms of ancient wrappings fail to survive in all but the most favourable conditions emphasises the ephemeral nature of many of them. Their vulnerability to decay seems somewhat ironic, given that wrappings were probably added in an attempt to care for, protect, and preserve their contents, at least in the short term. The presence of fragments of textiles on copper alloy mirrors from burials from the Ninth Dynasty to the First Intermediate Period (late third millennium) in Egypt suggests that they were coverings intended to protect both the material of the polished reflective surface and, in a cosmological sense, the appearance and soul of the deceased (Price & Gleba 2012, 10). Examples such as these demonstrate how even the smallest traces of preserved remains not only strengthen the evidence for wrapping but also raise questions relevant to the interpretation of the site and the beliefs of past societies.

The Wrapped Body   There are many ways in which the body can be clothed and that, as already outlined, can be considered to be a type of wrapping. One question that arises in archaeology is the distinction between draped and tailored clothing traditions. Draped garments are those 'obtained by wrapping a piece of material around the body' (Anawalt 1981, 9); these can also be referred to as wrapped clothing and are technically distinct from tailored garments. In the case of the latter, the cloth is cut, stitched, and shaped into limb-encasing garments. Complete garments from early periods are rarely preserved. As a result, both wrapped and tailored clothing techniques are often analysed through a combination of their representation in statues, paintings, and illustrated manuscripts; preserved garments; fragmentary textile evidence; and experimental reconstruction. Early technical studies of Etruscan, Roman, and Greek clothing used an analysis of statues carved in relief to understand the technique of draped garment styles such as the toga, cloak, tunic, and veil

(Bonfante 1975; Wilson 1938). In New Kingdom Egypt, wrapped garments were predominantly made using rectangular pieces of textile, as is known from preserved textiles and representations (Kemp & Vogelsang-Eastwood 2001, 438–40; Vogelsang-Eastwood 1992). In later periods in Egypt (as in Rome), evidence shows that some garments were not rectangular textiles cut or wrapped to shape but, instead, woven on the loom with curved edges, a technique unlike that used in modern cutting and tailoring (Granger-Taylor 1982, 14–16; Pritchard 2006). Through studying the figurative paintings of the Mesoamerica codices, Anawalt investigated regional clothing traditions according to five principles of garment construction: draped garments, slip on garments, open-sewn garments, closed-sewn garments, and limb-encasing garments (Anawalt 1981). Through identifying these techniques of draped and tailored garment construction, Anawalt distinguished variations in costume and regional identities (Anawalt 1981, 193–205). Such studies demonstrate how close observation of wrapped and tailored techniques can be used to understand both expressions of identity and changes in style through time.

As an example or a wrapped garment, the Roman toga has long fascinated researchers. It was a highly symbolic garment of status. It was the legally required dress in the forum and theatre and was worn only by male Roman citizens (and, somewhat surprisingly, by female prostitutes) (Croom 2002). It was also rather impractical and hence unpopular, because it had constantly to be rearranged on the body (Croom 2002, 41–49; George 2008, 95–96). Attention to the folds and drapes of the toga was essential; there was a proper way to put on, fold, and wear its various fashions (Croom 2002, 42–48). Studies of such examples of wrapped clothing extend beyond the documentation of wrapping techniques to question how wrapped garments were used to investigate a person's characteristics—for example, their gender and sexuality—or to consider their role in concealing and revealing parts of the body such as female breasts (Bremmer 1991; Dalby 2002; Lee 2005; Llewellyn-Jones 2003; Stafford 2005). In the classical world, draped clothing influenced everyday bodily behaviour such as styles of walking, sitting, and standing. In Athenian comedy, for instance, men whose long tunics reduced their walking speed were taunted as being passive homosexuals (Bremmer 1991, 19); and Greek statues, gods, and heroes were portrayed in a standing position, wearing short tunics, a stature and dress considered to be synonymous with physical power (Bremmer 1991, 24). From these studies, we can understand something of what it meant to wear this wrapped clothing in the ancient past and recognise the embodiment of gender and the self through dress.

Wrapping also serves as a way to care for the body either by protecting a vulnerable or wounded body part or by changing its appearance in response to certain beliefs. The stitched hand-leathers (palm protectors) and finger bandages preserved in the Bronze Age salt mines in Hallstatt, Austria, provide an example of this usage: they were intended to protect the miners' hands when they were hauling ropes (Reschreiter & Kowarik 2009, 56–57). The fact that bodies were once wrapped can also be detected from bone deformation: skulls, limbs, or other body parts, especially those of young children, become permanently altered in shape if tightly bound (for example, Duncan & Hofling 2011). Bones may also be 'wrapped' after death. A Near Eastern Neolithic mortuary practice, for example, involved removing skulls that were subsequently revitalised, using clay and paint, so that they might to be displayed inside houses (Garfinkel 1994; Wengrow 1998, 785).

Not only the living or dead flesh-and-bones bodies were wrapped; statues of human or animal forms were, too. In addition to the (already mentioned) jackal draped in textiles in Tutankhamun's tomb, statues and statuettes of rulers and divinities were also found clothed or wrapped in textiles (for instance, Carter 1933, pl. XI, XIIb). It is nearly impossible for archaeologists to detect whether statues were once wrapped or dressed when all physical trace of perishable materials has decayed. A case for accessorised statues has been made at the Pre-Pottery Neolithic B (PPNB) site of 'Ain Ghazal, Jordan, where plaster statues are believed to have been dressed in wigs and clothing (Grissom 2000, 43–44). Here, smoothed plaster body parts contrast with the unsmoothed plaster on the chest (which is presumed to have been covered by clothing), and brows are recessed where the hair would once have been. On other statues, the white face surface ends in a v-shape on the chest, suggesting that at this point it met a v-necked garment (Grissom 2000, 43). While such interpretations are subject to debate, they do show that it is important to consider the possibility that statues that we are used to seeing unwrapped may once have been dressed. If this was indeed the case, then their appearance and, no doubt, their impact would have been much altered. Such examples reveal how the living, the dead, and the represented body can be curated, cared for, and transformed through the act of wrapping.

Unrolling, Conservation, and Museum Display   In their quest to understand the past, archaeologists are more often concerned with unwrapping rather than with wrapping, with getting deep inside past contexts and artefacts in order to understand date, origins, and meaning. In the nineteenth century, mummies were unwrapped, or 'unrolled', in front of an audience (Granville 1825). During these displays, the mummy case, ornaments, layers of linen bandages, and wadding were removed in the quest to find the actual body (the skin, the bones, the face). The body itself was then dissected to find more out about the treatment of the internal organs during mummification and about gender and race. Finally, the hieroglyphics painted on the case were deciphered in an attempt to discover the mummy's name (Dawson 1934). Today, composite artefacts such as mummies are conserved whole and explored through computer tomography (CT scan) and X-radiography (X-ray) rather than scalpel (Parkes & Watkinson 2010, 58–61; Taylor 2004). The development of these methods has been fuelled both by ethical considerations about the treatment of human remains and by the growing appreciation that the wrappings are meaningful in themselves (Cortes 2012, 85–97; Taylor 2004). Non-invasive methods have the potential to explore delicate materials that might otherwise be destroyed through unwrapping or unrolling (for example, Taylor 2004). New methods such as these are being applied to, for example, the delicate carbonised rolls of papyri from the Villa of Papyri, Herculaneum, Italy. These rolls were charred when the eruption of Vesuvius in 79 c.e. destroyed the town, and attempts to unroll them to read their text have so far had limited success, owing to their extremely delicate condition. The development of virtual methods of analysis, such as CT scanning will, it is hoped, allow the scripts to be read without unrolling, and thereby destroying, either them and or their rolled form (Seales, Griffioen, & Jacops 2011, 84). Thus archaeologists are increasingly moving beyond simply wishing to preserve the wrappings and wrapped artefact as they come to recognise that the layers, wraps, and rolls are as important a means to understand the complexity of past material culture as are the artefacts themselves. This importance is further illustrated by the ancient Egyptian mummies, whose linen wrappings offer insights into the preparation of the body for the afterlife. Yet the debate about what it means to unwrap these bodies to be put on museum display remains multivocal and controversial (Wieczorkiewicz 2005, 67–68). And so the act of unwrapping becomes, in this context, a metaphor for the process of investigation, interpretation, and public display.

Archaeology is interested not only in the wrapping techniques practiced in ancient cultures but also, equally, in the process of wrapping and unwrapping artefacts for conservation and display in the present. In 2008 the Manchester Museum decided to cover several of the mummies that were on public display in its Egyptian Collection (O'Neill 2011). The covers used consisted of sheets of modern cloth wrapped around the mummified bodies. According to the museum blog, this procedure was 'carried out in order that the human remains be treated with respect and to keep the bodies on display in line with the Manchester Museum Remains policy' (quoted in O'Neill 2011, 130). This unusual display policy produced a heated public debate. Reponses on blogs and web forums, and from the museum's own public consultation, showed that the majority of museum visitors wanted to see the mummies uncovered, with only a few mentioning the ethnical considerations involved in displaying the dead in this fashion (O'Neill 2011, 130–31).

These examples, then, represent the the main perspectives adopted by those archaeologists actively engaged in the study of wrapping and unwrapping. Archaeologists discuss the broader issues, too, of course—materials and technology, production and consumption—alongside the more specific topics such as clothing and burial practices. All these interests, in their different ways, contribute to the rich intellectual origins of this book's chapters.

Social Anthropology

Social anthropology investigates contemporary societies, seeking to understand human practices in everyday life and ritual settings and on a cross-cultural basis. It examines sociocultural meanings that emerge from the relationships between individuals and the natural and material environments in which they live. The role that individuals play in the shaping of cultures through their bodies remains one of the main foci of the discipline. Social anthropologists bring to light, through participant observation, systems of beliefs, knowledge, and representations about a people's world—and about the social, material, and technical aspects of the act of wrapping. From this perspective, cultures are understood through a close examination of the production and consumption of objects and wrappings that themselves constitute material interfaces between individuals and the world, the self and society. Through this approach, wrapping and unwrapping become sociocultural practices that occur through embedded practices of 'making' and 'doing' the material and social world (Naji & Douny 2009). These practices emerge from webs of relationships involving subjects, their bodies, places, materials, and objects. Hence, wrapping and unwrapping as embodied practices are observable, and capable of being experienced, in everyday life and/or ritual settings.

Wrapping as Sociocultural Practice

Anthropologists have investigated wrapping as an embedded social practice used to materialise beliefs, concepts, and social institutions. Two books published in the 1990s have been particularly influential: Hendry's *Wrapping Culture* (1993) and Gell's *Wrapping in Images* (1993). As yet, there is no direct equivalent to these books in archaeology. Hendry's study of Japan starts with observations on the practice of wrapping gifts in paper, straw, wood, and cloth as the proper methods of gift presentation serving to demonstrate the correct level of politeness and care for the occasion (Hendry 1993, 12–51). Her analysis of wrapping soon moves into recognising that such aesthetic presentation is also found in language, space, packaging, the body, and people. The organisation and use of space in Japanese homes, temples, gardens, and work places is interpreted as a form of social wrapping whereby guests penetrate the interior to different degrees (Hendry 1993, 98–100). Like wrapped gifts, the choice of words for formal greeting and well wishes demonstrate care and politeness while they also conceal their contents and mark the occasion as special (Hendry 1993, 52–67). Hendry presents wrapping as a structuring principle in Japanese society and in this way shows how material and metaphorical wrapping is an expression of deeper social values, which both order and organise the social world.

Although Gell presents very different examples of wrapping in his book on tattooing in Polynesia, he shares Hendry's concept of wrapping to construct the social person and social relationships, which he explains as social reproduction (Gell 1993, 4–8). These concepts have been taken forward by other authors. For example, in his study of the Pot-King of the Mankon Kingdom, in the Grassfields of Cameroon, Warnier (2007) describes the body of the king as a container for the living, bodily, and ancestral substances that are necessary to revitalise his kingdom. In Warnier's ethnography, the king has three bodies, which are his physical body as a pot, the palace, and the city, all of which are enclosed by a skin envelope, ditches, and borders. These enclosures are made of openings and closings through which various contents such as life substances, people, money, and commodities transit through time. By being porous, the skin of the king's body and the boundaries of his palace and territory create inside/outside dialectics (Warnier 2007, 186–95) between the king and his subjects through which the king's embodiment and mediation of power occur. The multiple forms of containers as technologies of power enable practices of containment through which the Kingdom of the Mankon is reproduced over time.

These anthropological approaches provide an intellectual basis from which to see forms of layering, wrapping, enclosing, enveloping, covering, and containing not simply as symbols of social and political institutions but also as a means to perpetuate identities, political power, and social organisation.

Concealing and Revealing, Protection and Empowerment   As in archaeology, researchers researching from an anthropological perspective have recognised the role of wrappings as material and conceptual devices to engender their contents. In many societies, acts of revealing or concealing different aspects of the body respond to laws, taboos, and prohibitions. Drawing on colonial ideas of dress, undress, and nakedness, Masquelier (2005, 7–10) discusses the cultural specificity of appropriate body covering and its interpretation as moral or immoral. In the eyes of colonialists and ethnographers of the early twentieth century, bodies without sufficient clothing were considered naked, hence immoral and primitive. These Westerners failed to recognise that small items of clothing such as a waist cord or an armlet were sufficient dress to those who knew how to read them (Masquelier 2005, 10). The morality of the concealed and revealed body has been hotly debated in contemporary Europe in terms of Muslim women's veils. Because attitudes to the veil are multifaceted and sometimes contradictory, no single interpretation can represent the full spectrum of attitudes. For example, to some in British Muslim communities, veils, dress lengths, and styles are means of concealing the body by which faith, identity, modesty, and beauty are expressed (Tarlo 2010). From this perspective, the veil by its very concealment reveals that which is internal. Yet veiling the body, especially the face, is often seen by those outside these communities as hiding the identity, as a challenge to the freedom of the individual and a symbol of the submission of women to men (El Guindi 1999,

23–46; Joppke 2009, 107–26). Contrarily, from this perspective, veiling is seen to conceal and confine the internal self. From these examples we understand the potential of wrapping to change radically the perceptions of the wearer through its ability to cover and leave uncovered. These examples provide a reminder both of the complexities involved in reading meaning across cultures and of the potential of reading opposing messages in a single form.

While wrapping through dress is closely associated with expressions of identity that highlight the body through their presence, it may also make visible or invisible the contents it enwraps, create secrecy, and be used defensively. Inspired by nature, military design makes use of disruptive colour patterns to create camouflage on weapons, buildings, clothing, and vehicles. Through camouflage, military design is intended to fuse bodies and objects within their surrounding environment as a means to confound the enemy and avoid recognition from a distance. In nature, numerous animals, insects, and plants species are capable of blending into the landscape in remarkable ways through innate protective and self-defense techniques called *mimesis* (Newark 2007, 12).

In other cases, wrapping to reveal and conceal may lead to empowerment and protection amplified through magic, which metaphysically creates a protective wrapping around the body. For instance, a combination of materials embedded with magic are found in European folk dress. Here skirts, shawls, hats, and metal charms were worn to embody protective power or ensure fertility through negotiations with the invisible world (Welters 1999). Similarly, wild silk embroidered motifs on prestigious Hausa gowns or charm gowns covered with Arabic calligraphy worn underneath Hausa men's robes are imbued with magic and thus act as protective body envelopes. In the meantime, they empower the self through reinforcing the charisma of the Hausa elite (Douny 2011). As Claude Ardouin demonstrated in his lecture 'Protecting the Family, Protecting the Body: Talismanic Islamic Motifs on the Woollen Weavings from Niger Bend, Mali' at University College London, wrappers may be used to close off spaces and to metaphorically or literally protect bodies and space. For instance, the *Fulani Maabube Arkila kerka* serves as mosquito covering that stands in the nuptial room while also protecting against the cold and sandy winds. It may also be treated as a talismanic barrier that prevents malevolent spirits from entering and causing harm (Ardouin 2010). In these examples anthropologists investigate the material and conceptual boundaries created by wrapping that act on many levels of the self, society, and the spiritual world. Such anthropological studies show that while texture, pattern, and physical presence can be intentionally used to conceal and reveal, to protect and empower, the means by which people perceive these effects is contextual and may also be reactionary.

Materialising Identities   Enclosing, covering, and containing with wrappings are used either as means to materialise the identity of the contents or to add identity to an otherwise uninscribed surface. Tilley proposes that the concept of identities refers to the ways by which social and cultural identities materialise through time in objects, cultural transmission, and inheritance (Gosselain 2000; Tilley 2011, 348). These are ongoing processes by which people 'make' themselves, and they describe how social and individual identities are constructed, reproduced, transformed, and passed on to the next generation (Tilley 2011, 350).

Wrapping as a social and cultural practice of materialising identities (Gosselain 2000) and, by extension, social status, gender, and life-cycles is found predominantly in the literature on textiles, cloth, clothing, and dress. Textiles constitute a vast domain of research in social anthropology and other disciplines that focus on the body as the articulation of cultural meaning (Femenias 2010; Hansen 2004; Schneider 1987; Schneider & Weiner 1989). Clothing can be put on and taken off at a different frequency, whether changed through a day, a season, or over a lifetime. This process of wrapping and unwrapping the body through the addition and removal of clothing allows different aspects of the person to be revealed and concealed according to the situation, which changes through time. Through this clothing materialise aspects of a person, whether these are aesthetic, economic, and moral values or aspects such as charisma, power, or gender. Such wrappers may reveal the true nature of the contents or may be so integral to the contents that the wrappers' removal changes the contents' nature entirely. Attire made of selected materials, bearing motifs and colours and designed to be worn in a specific way, are often meant to achieve political and social goals by disclosing gender roles and status (Allman 2004; Eicher 1995; Kuechler & Miller 2005; Perani & Wolff 1999). Parts or elements of dress may be added or removed while old and new textile traditions, patterns, and styles may be mixed; thus new designs emerge in creative ways. For example, Ghanean *kente* cloth is a colourful and intricately patterned woven fabric that is popular in African American culture. A *kente* cloth pattern may be incorporated into dresses, on shoes, or on Christmas cards. Similarly, the cloth may be made into scarves or hats. It was originally associated with Asante elite, such as the royalty as in wrapping the body of the king. It may also adorn university ceremonial gowns in America (Ross 1998, 232) where *kente* cloth stands as an expression of African-American identity. In many social and historical contexts, the cloth has symbolised pride of origins, cultural heritage, and authenticity (Ross 1998, 196).

As cloth is used to wrap the living, so it is used to wrap the dead. Among the Ebira of Nigeria *Itokueta*, a stripped hand-spun white and indigo cotton cloth is used as a burial cloth that symbolises the continuity between the living and the dead in the context of masked performance and display at funeral ceremonies (Picton 2009, 302). Cloth bears a different design for a deceased man or a woman and is wrapped around his or her body to reveal identity, status, and gender. The entrance of the house of the deceased is draped with *itokueta* as a means to signify a death. This drape is the same cloth used to wrap the body and emphasises the relationship between the body and the house. Later, the cloth is taken down from the wall and used to wrap the deceased for burial. This practice of displaying *itokueta* demonstrates the importance for the Ebira people of establishing a relationship between the deceased and their community. As Picton writes: 'In advertising the fact of a death, the cloth also marked out the transition within the composition and perhaps the status of the household, and it invited the wider community to participate in the grief of the household at least by visiting to greet the close relatives of the deceased' (Picton 2009, 309). Here, through draping, wrapping, and performance, a cloth wrapper reveals Ebira social and individual identities as it brings the life-death continuum into a same symbolic system of meaning.

The materiality of wrappings used to transform a material's surface and texture may also transfer social identities between different media over time. African body arts such as paintings and cicatrised tattoos on men's and women's faces, arms and hands, or chest constitute 'long-standing forms of dressing the body' (Renne 2010, 72). Cicatrised tattoos consist of designs cut in the skin that are darkened with charcoal or lampblack that is rubbed onto the wound before it heals. As Renne suggests, this form of body art provides indications about the wearer's social status—such as wealth and premarital status or ethnic affiliation—as well as meeting the criteria of beauty and attractiveness (Renne 2010, 73). In her examination of the African lace that enjoys a wide popularity across Nigeria, Renne proposes that cicatrised tattoos, as 'lace-like patterns' on the skin, display an 'aesthetic of figured, plain and textured surfaces' (Renne 2010, 73). In this sense, the visual and tactile characteristics of these expensive lace textiles recall body art forms such as the cicatrised tattoos (Renne 2010, 72). Here, patterns on skin and/or textures that result from skin incisions that, in turn, thicken and thus produce a relief-effect on the skin are also replicated on embroidered or woven cloth that materialise and reveal an individual's social acuity, status, and, hence, identity (Renne 2010, 74).

The archaeological and anthropological approaches outlined above present the history of wrapping research within these disciplines. The contributors to this volume draw on these themes while also developing them in new directions to bring their own insights into the analysis and interpretation of the acts of wrapping and unwrapping.

Structure of the Book

The chapters that follow are grouped into three parts: Part II, Wrapping and Unwrapping the Living; Part III, Wrapping and Unwrapping the Dead; and Part IV, The Materiality of Wrapping: Materials, Places, and Objects. These parts reflect key areas of interest in the archaeology and anthropology of wrapping.

Part II: Wrapping and Unwrapping the Living

In many areas of the world, both in the past and in the present, the living body is or has been in a constant process of being wrapped and unwrapped. The repetition of dress and undress is reoccurring and cyclical, changing according to factors such as day or night, the passage of time, and the occasion and stages in the life cycle.

Wrappers add to the body as containers, covers, and envelopes. Part II begins by looking at one particular kind of wrapping, the living body, one associated with the beginnings of a life. Russell (Chapter 2) views baby wrapping as an extension, a boundary, and a portal of the mother's and child's bodies. She describes many of the techniques developed by women and men to bring babies to maturity, including swaddling, baby wearing, wrapping, tying, and carrying. Through her comparative approach Russell highlights the emotional, moralising, and didactic notions embedded in such techniques. During the cold war, for instance, baby-wrapping techniques became politically sensitised at a time when the United States was deriding Russian swaddling techniques as being hateful and ineffective, in line with its adopted ideological stance against swaddling.

The next three chapters (Johnstone, Chapter 3; Malkogeorgou, Chapter 4; and Makovicky, Chapter 5) focus on different approaches to wrapping as a form of dress. In the first, Johnstone examines wrapped garments in the New Kingdom of ancient Egypt (the Mid-Eighteenth Dynasty), dated to the middle of the second millennium B.C.E. To investigate her subject Johnstone combines iconographic evidence of clothing styles with preserved textiles and lessons from experimental archaeology to understand the techniques of Egyptian wrapped and tied clothing. This clothing style is time-specific and is a characteristic of the political and religious changes of the period known as the Amarna Period. Through her analysis Johnstone is able to demonstrate how this wrapped clothing, combined with jewellery, served to highlight the face and gesture of the wearer. At the same time she observes how the wrapped clothing was adjusted to show the internal emotional state of the wearer—for example, to reveal grief at a funeral. The knot used to tie the wrapped clothing also served as a form of protection, because it created a magic force to protect the wearer from evil. As a form of individual identity, the wrapped clothing of the Amarna Period aligned the individual with the politics of the time, ultimately bringing about its demise as people actively and visibly sought to disassociate themselves from that era.

Malkogeorgou (Chapter 4) shows, likewise, how the practice of wrapping can be closely linked to a particular time and place and, in so doing, demonstrates how wrapping has the ability to change the very shape of the female form. The author investigates an eighteen-century mantua dress of British design held at the Victoria and Albert Museum in London. Like the ancient

Egyptian clothing of the Amarna Period described by Johnstone, the mantua was a dress of power and politics. Exquisite and representing many hours of work, it was made to be worn just once before becoming redundant when its political role had been played out. Subsequent owners were compelled to change and adapt the luxurious fabric for their own ends. Detailed analysis shows how the fabric of an eighteenth-century court dress was taken apart and restitched by the different owners over many years. Through these processes, the shape of the dress was re-formed and its role redefined to fit the intentions of the new owners. Alterations such as re-stitching allowed conservators not only to understand more about the first owner's body shape and eighteenth-century body aesthetics but also to reconceptualise the dress to re-create a specific and intentional female body shape that could be displayed to the public.

Makovicky (Chapter 5) approaches wrapping from a very different perspective, building on Gell's notion of wrapping as a symbolic technique for protection against, and control of, the supernatural world. The author here examines the role of Polish crocheted lace in rural Poland. She introduces the history of lace in these communities and its use to rub babies at christenings, wrap Christian alters, and dress married women. She examines the controversy caused by lace's most recent incarnation in the form of crochet lace G-strings. This transformation has proved controversial: crocheted lace as a material is too closely related to the spiritual domain to make its use in the making of G-strings anything other than highly contentious. The lace described by Makovicky brings a specific materiality to the body as it is an open, lacy layer and considered to reveal the female body.

Part III: Wrapping and Unwrapping the Dead

The investigation of the dead inevitably plays a special role in archaeology, given that so much of archaeological evidence is gained from burial grounds and burial chambers. Anthropologists are equally concerned with the dead since death is the final rite of passage. As in the Ebira example cited above, cloth often plays a role in the ceremonies and preparations of the body for the grave, whether used as shrouds, bindings, drapes, or clothing—or in the special care of objects placed in the grave. Archaeologists have long-since recognised that the wrapping of both body and grave goods is common practice (for example, Carroll & Wild 2012). The four chapters in this part offer examples from Bronze Age Scandinavia (Harris, Chapter 6); Early Iron Age central and southern Europe (Gleba, Chapter 7); Early Iron Age southwest Germany (Banck-Burgess, Chapter 8); and Egypt (Wills, Chapter 9).

The extreme fragility of archaeological wrapping remains requires careful observation, handling, and recording of the process. The extent of this fragility is emphasised in Harris's exploration of the ordering principles behind the multiple layers of wrapping that covered and enclosed the men, women, and children in burial mounds of the Bronze Age in southern Scandinavia in the latter half of the second millennium B.C.E. Clothed and wrapped in textiles and leather, surrounded by grave goods, enclosed in wooden coffins placed on and within stone platforms, and, finally, covered with thick layers of turf sods, these burials represent multiple layers of wrapping and enclosing. Each layer represents a modification of the dead, from the dressed body whose face was left visible, to the fully shrouded corpse or to the coffin buried deep in the turf mound, the construction of the layers may be seen as a performance involving many members of that society. Repeated over decades, this practice transformed the landscape and, Harris argues, was based on the ordering principles behind the then contemporary beliefs and knowledge. This reinterpretation of the archaeological evidence has only been made possible by presenting the evidence according to the wrapping sequence at the time of burial rather than according to the unwrapping sequence of the excavation.

Gleba draws together early written sources and archaeological evidence from the princely burials of the first half of the second millennium B.C.E. in central and southern Europe, concentrating on Italy and Greece. Here she not only identifies funerary shrouds, wrapped cremation urns, and cloth-wrapped cremation bundles but also observes specific wrapped objects, such as weapons and wagons, which were carefully covered in fabric before being laid in the burial. How can these wrappings be best interpreted? Were they meant to protect the objects they enwrapped? Were they intended to make their contents visible or invisible? Or did they provide a material means to control the dead? In Chapter 8, Banck-Burgess provides a detailed insight into one such tomb, the early Iron Age (Celtic) princely grave from Hochdorf, in southwest Germany, dated to the end of the seventh century B.C.E. The methodology used to study the wrappings from this tomb provided a landmark in the investigation of fragile and fragmentary textile remains in burial contexts. Through analysis of fibres, dyes, micro-stratigraphy, and their position in the tomb, Banck-Burgess and the team working on the objects in this burial chamber were able to reconstruct the position of numerous textiles in the tomb and to reveal their full splendour. This painstaking work established the wrapping sequence: the man's body was first wrapped with a simple undyed wool cloth; this cloth was then used to wrap every facet of the wagon placed with him; and, last, the body was laid on top of coloured and decorated textiles that were quite unlike the plain wool cloth that lay right next to his skin. Banck-Burgess, like Gleba, questions the concept of visibility and invisibility, thereby suggesting that the act of wrapping may have been either a means of drawing boundaries between the living and the dead or a way of communicating between the living and the dead—or both.

Through excavation and artefact analysis, archaeologists examine how the dead were prepared for burial in the past. Conservators, on the other hand, are faced with how to present the dead in the present. Wills (Chapter 9) describes the wrapping practices involved in the conservation of Egyptian mummies destined for museum display. She shows how current practices in museum conservation are designed to reduce the impact of conservation techniques by stitching invisible layers of wrapping onto the decaying surface in such a way that they pass unnoticed by the museum visitors who believe that they are gazing on the surface of the original artefact. The selection and application of this wrapping treatment respects current ideas about the appropriate treatment of human bodies stored in museums. It also demonstrates the ongoing role of wrapping as a way of maintaining the integrity of the body while at the same time handling it in line with current good practice.

Part IV: The Materiality of Wrapping: Materials, Places, and Objects

At the heart of the idea of wrapping lies the great diversity of available materials, each with very different materialities. In this volume, *materiality* is envisaged as the physicality of wrappings as shaped through human agency and belief. The contributors to this final part of the book suggest that wrappings acquire meanings that become embedded in their materiality through both the transformative processes of specific materials and their relationships with the places, bodies, and objects with which they are in contact. In Parts II and III, the idea that wrappings possess particular physical, chemical, or ideological properties derived from the matter and materiality of objects has already been touched on—for instance, in Makovicky's study (Chapter 5) of semitransparent crochet lace and the studies of different kinds of wrapping in the Iron Age graves (Gleba and Banck-Burgess, Chapters 7 and 8). In Part IV, the contributors focus on the associations between certain material expressions and their contexts. They thus address the relationship between material and its meaning.

Douny (Chapter 10) examines the cultural significance and use of wild silk indigo wrappers as produced by the Dogon of the Tengu and Tommon kan areas of Mali. By focusing on the material properties of this insect-produced substance, and on its processing as well as its culturally determined modes of self-display and performance, the author demonstrates how this cloth of prestige materialises and legitimises regional, collective, and individual identities. Here wild silk is perceived as living and active. As a material of power, silk requires complex techniques and knowledge to transform cocoons into cloth. Douny proposes that this material practice constitutes a Manden heritage that the Dogon share with the neighbouring Marka-Dafing community. As part of an enduring tradition, *tome toun* wrappers legitimise the Dogon's Tengu and Tommon identity while at the same time marking women's social status and personal worth in the context of everyday life, weddings, and funerals. Through the use of wild silk, with its remarkable properties and elaborate manufacturing processes, such wrappings have come to be used as a form of self-display; they legitimise tradition, cultural identities, and social status, and they reaffirm both a shared heritage and an ancestral affiliation.

Garcia-Ventura and López-Bertran (Chapter 11) further develop this theme of materiality. They explore Mesopotamian figurines and cuneiform tablets dating to 2100–2000 B.C.E. These figurines and tablets were concealed with textile and clay wrapping under the foundations of temples and other public buildings. The first stage of their investigation was to catalogue the figurines that had textile wrappings still adhering to them at the time of the original excavation—that is, before these fragile traces were destroyed, as so frequently happened, in the cleaning and exhibiting process. They then used their knowledge of the material properties of clay and textiles to question the role of, and meaning behind, these wrappings. Through exploring the foundation context of these figurines and tablets, and the actions of those performing these rituals, they reflect on the relationship between the contents and the wrappings as packaging, protection, and concealment. Given that many of the wrapped figurines represent kings, they question whether these wrappings were intended to divest the body of corporality and/or to offer a form of magical protection, symbolising institutional powers and acting as a protection for the buildings that lay above them.

Finally (Chapter 12), and on a different scale, Croucher and Richards use the concept of wrapping to trace the way that the Rapa Nui Island landscape is mapped out with stone. Gigantic *Moai* heads stand astride *Ahu* stone platforms as living cosmological constructs that both physically and symbolically contain the landscape. These authors explore the relationship between covering the body in tattoos and wrapping liminal areas of the landscape. They do this by contrasting the tattooing of facial orifices with the positioning of petroglyphs at openings in the geological and spiritual landscape. These practices are, they argue, a measure to control dangerous boundaries and to channel *mana* (power) between realms. Tattoos thereby provide a means to wrap bodies and petroglyphs to wrap the land. Archaeological fieldwork, interpreted with the help of anthropological studies, has allowed the systematic interlinking of evidence on two such different scales.

These contributions in Part IV embrace the materiality of wrapping either for its transformative potential or for the technical, social, and ideological processes involved in the very act of wrapping. In these chapters the materiality of wrapping plays a role in the shaping of the individual's social and material world through materialising cultural identities (Douny, Chapter 10), reaffirming institutional power and presence (Garcia-Ventura & López-Bertran, Chapter 11), and embodying a cosmology (Croucher & Richards, Chapter 12).

We hope that the vibrant chapters on wrapping and unwrapping in this volume will provide an in-depth analysis and evaluation of this topic's potential to enhance our investigation into, and understanding of, human cultures. We are grateful to the contributors for their time and effort in researching this subject and hope that you enjoy their efforts.

References

Allman, J. 2004. *Fashioning Africa: Power and the Politics of Dress*. Bloomington: Indiana University Press.

Anawalt, P. R. 1981. *Indian Clothing before Cortés: Mesoamerican Costumes from the Codices*, foreword by H. B. Nicholson, charts prepared by Jean Cuker Sells. Norman: University of Oklahoma Press.

Ardouin, C. 2010. Protecting the Family, Protecting the Body: Talismanic Islamic Motifs on the Woollen Weavings from Niger Bend, Mali, lecture delivered at Wrapping & Unwrapping the Body, Archaeological and Anthropological Perspectives May 20–21, 2010, Institute of Archaeology, University College London.

Banck-Burgess, J. 1999. *Hochdorf IV. Die Textilfunde aus dem späthallstattzeitlichen Fürstengrab von Eberdingen-Hochdorf (Kreis Ludwigsburg) und weitere Grabtextilien aus hallstatt- und latènezeitlichen Kulturgruppen*. Mit Beiträgen von Lise Raeder Knudsen, Karl Heinzmann, Penelope Walton Rogers, Wener Hübner. Stuttgart: Konrad Theiss.

Bartel, A. 2002. Untersuchungen der Organischen Reste. In H. Baitinger, ed., *Das Rätsel der Kelten vom Glauberg*. Stuttgart: Theiss, pp. 163–67.

Bender Jørgensen, L. 1992. *North European Textiles until AD 1000*. Aarhus: Aarhus University Press.

Bonfante, L. 1975. *Etruscan Dress*. Baltimore: Johns Hopkins University Press.

Bradley, M. 1994. Preliminary Assessment of the Medieval Christian Burials from Tel Jezreel. *Levant* 24, pp. 63–65.

Bremmer, J. 1991. Walking, Standing, and Sitting in Ancient Greek Culture. In J. Bremmer & H. Roodenberg, eds., *A Cultural History of Gesture from Antiquity to the Present Day*. Cambridge: Polity Press, pp. 15–35.

Caplow, T. 1982. Christmas Gifts and Kin Networks. *American Sociological Review* 4(3), pp. 383–92.

———. 1984. Rule Enforcement without Visible Means: Christmas Gift Giving in Middleton. *American Journal of Sociology* 89(6), pp. 1306–23.

Carrier, J. G. 1993. The Rituals of Christmas Giving. In D. Miller, ed., *Unwrapping Christmas*. Oxford: Clarendon Press, pp. 55–74.

Carroll, M., & Wild, J.-P. (eds.) 2012. *Dressing the Dead in Classical Antiquity*. Stroud: Amberley.

Carter, H. 1933. *The Tomb of Tut-Ankh-Amen Discovered by the Late Earl of Carnarvon and Howard Carter*, Vol. 3. London: Cassell.

Chen, H. L., Jakes, K. A., & Foreman, D. W. 1998. Preservation of Archaeological Textiles through Fibre Mineralization. *Journal of Archaeological Science* 25, pp. 1015–21.

Cortes, E. 2012. Recovering Contexts: The Roman Mummies Excavated by The Metropolitan Museum of Art at Dahshur, Egypt. In M. Carroll & J.-P. Wild, eds., *Dressing the Dead in Classical Antiquity*. Stroud: Amberley, pp. 74–88.

Croom, A. T. 2000. *Roman Clothing and Fashion*. Stroud: Tempus.

Dalby, A. 2002. Levels of Concealment: The Dress as *hetairai* and *pornai* in Greek Texts. In L. Llewellyn-Jones, ed., *Women's Dress in the Ancient Greek World*. Swansea: Duckworth & The Classical Press of Wales.

Dawson, W. R. 1934. Pettigrew's Demonstrations upon Mummies: A Chapter in the History of Egyptology. *The Journal of Egyptian Archaeology* 20(3/4), p. 170.

Douny, L. 2011. Silk-Embroidered Garments as Transformative Processes: Layering, Inscribing and Displaying Hausa Material Identities. *The Journal of Material Culture* 16(4), pp. 401–15.

Duncan, B., & Hofling, C. A. 2011. Why the Head? Cranial Modification as Protection and Ensoulment among the Maya. *Ancient Mesoamerica* 22, pp. 199–210.

Eicher, J. B. 1995. Introduction: Dress as Expression of Ethnic Identity. In J. B. Eicher, *Dress and Ethnicity: Change across Space and Time.* Oxford: Berg, pp. 1–6.

El Guindi, F. 1999. *Veil: Modesty, Privacy and Resistance.* Oxford: Berg.

Femenias, B. 2010. In Cloth We Trust. *Reviews in Anthropology* 39(4), pp. 258–87.

Garfinkel, Y. 1994. Ritual Burial of Cultic Objects: The Earliest Evidence. *Cambridge Archaeological Journal* 4(2), pp. 159–88.

Gell, A. 1993. *Wrapping in Images: Tattooing in Polynesia.* Oxford: Clarendon Press.

George, M. 2008. The 'Dark Side' of the Toga. In J. C. Edmondson & A. Keith, eds., *Roman Dress and the Fabrics of Roman Culture.* Toronto: University of Toronto Press, pp. 94–112.

Good, I. 2001. Archaeological Textiles: A Review of Current Research. *Annual Review of Anthropology* 30, pp. 209–26.

Gosselain, O. P. 2000. Materializing Identities: An African Perspective. *Journal of Archaeological Method and Theory* 7(3), pp. 187–217.

Granger-Taylor, H. 1982. Weaving Clothes to Shape in the Ancient World: The Tunic and Toga of the Arringatore. *Textile History* 13(1), pp. 3–25.

Granville, A. B. 1825. An Essay on Egyptian Mummies, with Observations on the Art of Embalming among the Ancient Egyptians. *Philosophical Transactions of the Royal Society of London* 115, pp. 269–316.

Grissom, C. A. 2000. Neolithic Statues from 'Ain Ghazal: Construction and Form. *American Journal of Archaeology* 104(1), pp. 25–45.

Hansen, K. T. 2004. The World in Dress: Anthropological Perspectives on Clothing, Fashion, and Culture. *Annual Review of Anthropology* 33, pp. 369–92.

Harris, S. 2008. Textiles, Cloth, and Skins: The Problem of Terminology and Relationship. *Textile: The Journal of Cloth & Culture* 6(3), pp. 222–37.

Hendry, J. 1990. Humidity, Hygiene, or Ritual Care: Some Thoughts on Wrapping as a Social Phenomenon. In E. Ben-Ari, B. Moeran, & J. Valentine, eds., *Unwrapping Japan: Society and Culture in Anthropological Perspective.* Manchester: Manchester University Press, pp. 18–35.

———. 1993. *Wrapping Culture: Politeness, Presentation and Power in Japan and Other Societies.* Oxford: Clarendon Press.

Ingold, T. 2012. Toward an Ecology of Materials. *Annual Review of Anthropology* 41, pp. 427–42.

Joppke, C. 2009. *Veil: Mirror of Identity.* Cambridge: Polity.

Kemp, B. J., & Vogelsang-Eastwood, G. 2001. *The Ancient Textile Industry at Amarna* (assisted by A. Boyce, H. G. Farbrother, G. Owen, & P. Rose). London: Egypt Exploration Society.

Ko, D. 2001. *Every Step a Lotus: Shoes for Bound Feet.* Berkeley and Los Angeles: University of California Press.

———. 2005. *Cinderella's Sisters: A Revisionist History of Footbinding.* Berkeley and Los Angeles: University of California Press.

Kuechler, S. 2003. Rethinking Textile: The Advent of the Smart Fibre Surface. *Textile: Culture and History* 1(3), pp. 262–73.

———. 2008. Technological Materiality: Beyond the Dualist Paradigm. *Theory, Culture & Society* 25(1), pp. 101–20.

Kuechler, S., & Miller, D. (eds.) 2005. *Clothing as Material Culture*. Oxford: Berg.

Kumja Paik, K. 2003. Profusion of Colour: Korean Costumes and Wrapping Cloths of the Chŏson Dynasty. In J. M. White & H. Dong-hwa, eds., *Wrappings of Happiness: A Traditional Korean Art Form*. Catalogue of exhibition held at the Honolulu Academy of Arts, September 4–December 7, 2003. Honolulu: Honolulu Academy of Arts; Seoul: Museum of Korean Embroidery.

Lee, M. 2005. Constru(ct)ing Gender in the Feminine Greek Peplos. In L. Cleland, M. Harlow, & L. Llewellyn-Jones, eds., *The Clothed Body in the Ancient World*. Oxford: Oxbow.

Lemonnier, P. 1992. *Elements for an Anthropology of Technology*. Ann Arbor: University of Michigan/Museum of Anthropology.

Llewellyn-Jones, L. 2003. *Aphrodite's Tortoise: The Veiled Woman of Ancient Greece*. Swansea: Classical Press of Wales.

Masquelier, A. 2005. Dirt, Undress, and Difference: An Introduction. In A. Masquelier, ed., *Dirt, Undress, and Difference: Critical Perspectives on the Body's Surface*. Bloomington: Indiana University Press.

Masurel, H. 1992. Vestiges textiles visibles sur les objects métalliques de Franche-Comté: L'áge du Fer dans le Jura. *Cahiers d'Archéologie Romandes* 57, pp. 65–69.

McAnany, P., Storey, R., & Lockard, A. K. 1999. Mortuary Ritual and Family Politics at Formative and Early Classic K'axob, Belize. *Ancient Mesoamerica* 10, pp. 129–46.

Naji, M., & Douny, L. 2009. Editorial: The 'Making' and 'Doing' of the Material World: French Anthropology of Techniques Revisited. *The Journal of Material Culture* 14(4), pp. 411–32.

Newark, T. 2007. Camouflage Introduction by Jonathan Miller. London: Thames & Hudson.

O'Neill, M. 2011. Images of the Dead: Ethics and Contemporary Art Practice. In B. Garner, S. Pavlenko, S. Shaheen, & A. Wolanski, eds., *Cultural and Ethical Turns: Interdisciplinary Reflections on Culture, Politics and Ethics*. Oxford: Inter-Disciplinary Press, pp. 129–36.

Owen-Crocker, G. R. 1986. *Dress in Anglo-Saxon England with Drawings by Christine Wetherell and Rosalyn Smith*. Manchester: Manchester University Press.

Oxford English Dictionary. 2013. Wrapping. OED Online. http://www.oed.com/view/Entry/230543?rskey=FXeMRA&result=1, accessed August 6, 2013.

Parkes, P., & Watkinson, D. 2010. Computed Tomography and X-Radiography of a 21st/22nd Dynasty Coffin. In J. Dawson, C. Rozeik, & M. Wright, eds., *Decorated Surfaces on Egyptian Objects: Technology, Deterioration and Conservation*. London: Archetype publications, pp. 58–66.

Perani, J., & Wolff, N. H. 1999. *Cloth, Dress, and Art Patronage in Africa*. Oxford: Berg.

Picton, J. 2009. Cloth and the Corpse in Ebira. *Textile: The Journal of Cloth & Culture* 7(3), pp. 296–313.

Price, K., & Gleba, M. 2012. Textiles on Egyptian Mirrors: Pragmatics or Religion? *Archaeological Textiles Review* 54, pp. 2–13.

Pritchard, F. 2006. *Whitworth Art Gallery: Clothing Culture—Dress in Egypt in the First Millennium AD, Clothing from Egypt in the Collection of the Whitworth Art Gallery, the University of Manchester*. Manchester: Whitworth Art Gallery.

Renne, E. 2010. Figured, Textured, and Empty Spaces: An Aesthetics of Textiles and Dress in Nigeria. In B. Plankensteiner & N. Mayo Adediran, eds., *African Lace: A History of Trade, Creativity and Fashion in Nigeria.* Ghent: Snoeck Publishers, pp. 71–89.

Reschreiter, H., & Kowarik, K. 2009. The Bronze Age Initiative—Up to the Surface. In A. Kern, K. Kowarik, A. W. Rausch, & H. Reschreiter, eds., *Kingdom of Salt: 7000 Years of Hallstatt*, Vol. 3. Vienna: Prehistoric Department, Natural History Museum Vienna, pp. 55–57.

Richter, T., Stock, T., Maher, L., & Hebron, C. 2010. An Early Epipalaeolithic Sitting Burial from the Azraq Oasis, Jordan. *Antiquity* 84, pp. 321–34.

Robertson-Mackay, M. E. 1980. A 'Head and Hooves' Burial beneath a Round Barrow, with Other Neolithic and Bronze Age Sites, on Hemp Knott, Near Avebury, Wiltshire. *Proceedings of the Prehistoric Society* 46(123), p. 176.

Ross, D. H. (ed.) 1998. *Wrapped in Pride: Ghanaian Kente and African American Identity.* Los Angeles: UCLA Fowler Museum of Cultural History.

Schneider, J. 1987. The Anthropology of Cloth. *Annual Review of Anthropology* 16, pp. 409–48.

Schneider, J., & Weiner, A. B. 1989. Introduction. In A. B. Weiner & J. Schneider, eds., *Cloth and Human Experience.* Washington, D.C.: Smithsonian Institution Press, pp. 1–29.

Seales, W. B., Griffioen, J., & Jacops, D. 2011. Virtual Conservation: Experience with Micro-CT and Manuscripts. In V. Vahtikari, M. Hakkarainen, & A. Nurminen, eds., *EIKONOPOIIA. Digital Imaging of Ancient Textual Heritage.* Proceedings of the International Conference Helsinki, November 28–29, 2010. Ekenäs: Finnish Society of Sciences and Letters. Commentationes Humanarum Litterarum 129, pp. 81–88.

Sŏng-mi, Y. 2003. Women in Korean History and Art. In J. M. White & H. Dong-hwa, eds., *Wrappings of Happiness: A Traditional Korean Art Form.* Honolulu: Honolulu Academy of Arts; Seoul: Museum of Korean Embroidery.

Stafford, E. J. 2005. Viewing and Obscuring the Female Breast: Glimpses of the Ancient Bra. In L. Cleland, M. Harlow, & L. Llewellyn-Jones, eds., *The Clothed Body in the Ancient World.* Oxford: Oxbow, p. 96.

Tarlo, E. 2010. *Visibly Muslim: Fashion, Politics, Faith.* Oxford: Berg.

Taylor, J. H. 2004. *Mummy: The Inside Story.* London: British Museum Press.

Tilley, C. 2011. Materializing Identities: An Introduction. *The Journal of Material Culture* 16(3), pp. 347–57.

Vogelsang-Eastwood, G. 1992. *Patterns for Ancient Egyptian Clothing.* Leiden: Stichting Textile Research Center.

Walton Rogers, P. 2007. *Cloth and Clothing in Early Anglo-Saxon England, AD 450–700.* York: Council for British Archaeology.

Wang, P. 2000. *Aching for Beauty: Footbinding in China.* Minneapolis: University of Minnesota Press.

Warnier, J.-P. 2007. *The Pot-King: The Body and Technologies of Power.* Leiden, Brill.

Welters, L. 1999. Introduction: Folk Dress, Supernatural Beliefs, and the Body. In L. Welters, *Folk Dress in Europe and Anatolia: Beliefs about Protection and Fertility.* Oxford: Berg, pp. 1–12.

Wengrow, D. 1998. 'The Changing Face of Clay': Continuity and Change in the Transition from Village to Urban Life in the Near East. *Antiquity* 72, pp. 783–95.

———. 2010. Introduction: Commodity Branding in Archaeological and Anthropological Perspectives. In A. Bevan & D. Wengrow, eds., *Cultures of Commodity Branding.* Walnut Creek, CA: Left Coast Press, pp. 11–33.

Wieczorkiewicz, A. 2005. Unwrapping Mummies and Telling Their Stories: Egyptian Mummies in Museum Rhetoric. In N. Porto & M. Bouquet, eds., *Science, Magic and Religion: The Ritual Processes of Museum Magic*, Vol. 23. Oxford: Berghahn Books, pp. 1–70.

Wilson, L. M. 1938. *The Clothing of the Ancient Romans.* Baltimore: Johns Hopkins Press.

Zedeño, M. N. 2008. Bundled Worlds: The Role and Interactions of Complex Objects from the North American Plains. *Journal of Archaeological Method and Theory* 15, pp. 362–78.

Part II: Wrapping and Unwrapping the Living

2 Aspects of Baby Wrappings: Swaddling, Carrying, and Wearing

Nancy Ukai Russell

The first object that touches a newborn is, in many cases, a wrapping material. It may bind, swaddle, cover, carry, or straighten the body, and the object's form and the material from which it is made vary across time and space. Animal skins, bark cloth, and linen bands as well as netbags, shawls, and sarongs are among the objects that can be considered as baby wrappings. It is easy enough to see how a cloth or sling may be used to transport a baby or keep it warm, but other cultural meanings are less easy to discern and are often intertwined with the body. For example, after a prolonged gestational period during which mother and baby are fused, the wrapping material may be perceived as containing elements that carry over from the womb and help to move the infant from a liminal, transitional state to viable personhood. The distinction between inside-the-womb and outside-the-womb is thus blurred. The use of wrapping to extend the transition differs from the American idea that, until recently, conflated the baby's delivery with personhood (Conklin & Morgan 1996, 677). However, there is an increasing effort to link personhood with fertilisation and to accord to the foetus the legal protection of personhood (Schroedel 2000, 5).

In anthropology, the study of baby wrappings has been sporadic, despite its potential importance for topics such as infant care, kinship, gender, morality, the body, and material culture. The Tropenmuseum alone has extensively investigated cross-cultural practices and concepts in its exhibition and catalogue on baby-carrying (van Hout 1993). Baby wrappings, however, have merited close study in other disciplines. Medical studies, for example, have shown that swaddled infants sleep more soundly with fewer arousals (Gerard, Harris, & Thach 2002). Psychologists explore concepts of swaddling and touch (Anisfeld et al. 1990), and textile specialists have analysed the symbols and surface ornamentation on carriers (University of Hawai'i Art Gallery 2009). National practices of swaddling have even been linked to geopolitical behaviour (Gorer 1949; Mead 1954). The existence of baby wrappings has been visually recorded in art (Kloek 2008) and referred to in religious and historical texts since antiquity. Archaeological excavations have uncovered baby wrappings, mummified infants, and Greek votive statuettes of swaddled infants. Some theories hold that a baby sling or similar carrying device may have been one of the first material items made by humans (Ehrenburg 1989; Taylor 2010).

Outside academia, baby wrappings have enthralled and even entertained the public. A century ago, during the heyday of the picture postcard between 1900 and 1915, the practice of using a cloth or an animal skin to tie a child to the body, as observed in Oceania, Africa, Asia, and Latin America, was a source of curiosity in the colonial West. This exotic image of 'primitive types' was popularised by photographers and circulated globally on picture postcards. Such postcard images, alongside the anthropological research of the day, helped to 'define modern Europeans in terms of what they were not' (Edwards, Gosden, & Phillips 2006, 16).

Today, however, the act of carrying a baby on the body using a wrap, which had been a marking of the 'other', has become widely adopted in Western societies. Swaddling, once rejected in Western childcare manuals, is now recommended to parents as a calming method (Sarvady 2005). Interest in 'ethnic' baby-wrapping materials has consequently grown, yet there remains a gap in information about the diverse cultural and historical practices and their meanings.

This exploratory chapter discusses some concepts and practices of wrapping babies. First, the terms *swaddling*, *wrapping*, and other related vocabulary are examined. Different terms used in English imply different material objects, ideologies, and trajectories of caring activities, and they frame references to related practices when translated from other languages. Second, this chapter introduces examples of baby wrappings in the lived experience, as found in ethnographic accounts. A preliminary theory of baby wrappings is proposed using the terms *extension, portal*, and *boundary*.

Swaddling, Wrapping, Carrying, Tying, and Wearing

Terms used in English to describe baby wrapping, such as *swaddling*, are part of a semantic field that forms ways of thinking about particular practices and their materials, techniques, and meanings. This brief examination of lexical terms concludes that swaddling and wrapping lead to other vocabulary clusters related to functions such as carrying and wearing and the manipulation of the material by tying and knotting.

Swaddling

Swaddling is a term familiar to English speakers because of its use in the Bible, yet it is infrequently used in contemporary speech (Hudson & Phillips 1968). Since antiquity it has been part of a ritual and protective activity undertaken soon after delivery. In the Christian religion, the infant Jesus is a gift to humankind, wrapped in 'swaddling cloths' (Luke II: 6–7). Soranus, a Greek medical writer of the second century, described in his text *Gynaecology* how a newborn should be swaddled; his method was followed until the sixteenth century (Temkin 1991, xxv). The Greek Omega (Ω), which has been seen as a symbolic representation of cloth swaddling bands, is similar to the character used to designate the Sumerian goddess of childbirth and fertility, Ninhursag (Adamson 1985).

What does swaddling mean for the body of the baby? Although the winding technique varies, the common feature of a swaddled baby is motor restraint (Lipton, Steinschneider, & Richmondet 1965, 522; van Sleuwen 2007). By limiting the physical ability of the baby to move, the body becomes a compact object whose soft, curled contours are shaped to make a straight, regular, and symmetrical form. Some writings have noted that the swaddled and immobilised baby appears as a loaf of bread (Calvert 1992, 21) or 'a log of wood for the fireplace' to Russian parents (Benedict 1959, 451). In some rural areas of Europe until World War I, swaddled babies were inserted in sacks and hung on pegs while caregivers worked nearby (Fontanel & d'Harcourt 1997, 176). Different meanings have been attached to swaddling practices, including helping the limbs to grow straight so that the baby would not 'always crawl on all fours like little animals' for the rest of his life (Mauriceau quoted in Hunt 1972, 130) and being a part of the process of 'hardening' a child (Benedict 1959, 454–55). Once made into portable bundles, swaddled babies were laced into narrow cradles, an adjunct to swaddling (Calvert 1992, 28).

In different contexts, however, swaddled babies are wrapped in an additional layer of carrying cloth and tied to the back, such as is practiced in Peru, or placed within a stiff container, such as the cradleboard used by native cultures in North America (Bibby 2004; Hail 2000). The term *swaddling* suggests clothing (swaddling clothes) or the wrapping material (swaddling blankets), and it can be used to modify the object that is wound around the baby (swaddling bands). A swaddle is a wrap or blanket.

Wrapping

Wrapping and swaddling are interconnected: *swaddling* derives from the Old English *swathian*, which means 'to wrap, bandage' (Marshall 2008). But in contrast to swaddling, which is associated with childbirth, babies, and physical restraint, *wrapping* is a broader term that does not imply or require the presence of an infant. Its usage, however, is changing as the term evolves to include babies, following the revival in the late 1970s of baby-carrying and -swaddling practices in the United States and Europe. Wrapping suggests the act of covering as a form of protection and restraint, and it can be applied to many categories of objects, life forms, actions, spaces, and relationships (Hendry 1995).

Baby wrappings can be conceptualised more broadly to include the human body as a covering material. The Japanese verb for 'to wrap' (*tsutsumu*), which is used to describe mundane covering and wrapping activities, such as the wrapping of gifts or boxes, originally employed a Chinese ideograph 包 that depicts a baby inside a womb or the human body as a wrapping around the unborn infant (Fujido, Matsumoto, & Takeda 2007).

Partial or total concealment may result. According to Fred Spier (pers. comm.), when a Peruvian infant is tightly swaddled and placed inside a square carrying cloth that is then tied to the carrier's back, 'it is hard if not impossible to know' what is being carried, a finding that was also reported by Tronick, Thomas, and Daltabuit (1994, 1006) in their investigation of the microenvironment inside a Quecha *manta* pouch. Infant concealment inside a cloth or bag returns to the concept of an infant concealed within a womb, as discussed by MacKenzie. In central New Guinea, women 'carry the produce of their garden and their womb' in the expansive *bilum* looped bag, which is a visual and metaphorical expression of their productive and reproductive work (MacKenzie 1991, 6–7).

Carrying

The diverse materials that wrap babies often serve as tools for transport. In the case where a wrapping material ties the baby to a caregiver, the two are joined into one mobile unit. In this regard, the wrapping material may be seen as an extension of the body or what Allerton calls a 'super skin' in her work on the sarongs of Manggarai (Allerton 2007, 25). Lee points out that in the 'carrying cloth culture' of Korea and Japan (*furoshiki bunka*), babies were traditionally wrapped in carrying cloths and tied to the body, which exemplifies a carrying cloth practice (Ii in Hendry 1995, 34). Whiting (1981) classifies cultures that carry infants on the body as 'sling and shawl' cultures. Given that babies *in utero* are accustomed both to multidirectional movement and, especially, to vertical motion (Schaper 1982), it is interesting to note that neonates are carried—and also fall asleep—in a diversity of directions when carried on the body.

If baby wrappings have a carrying function, does it follow that all infant-carrying devices qualify as wrappings? Does the flat plane of a carry cloth have the same wrapping characteristics as a slender, loop-like sling? The loop may not literally conceal or cover, but it may protect by keeping the baby close; it can be seen as a tool that holds the baby to a carrier. Examples of minimal slings include both the 3-cm-wide *ayĩ* strap woven of palm-leaf fibre by a Kayapo husband for his wife (Turner 1995, 155) and the loop of animal tissue that Taylor hypothesises may have been used by early hominins (Taylor 2010, 123). Perhaps such loops and slings may be likened to the cord that circles the wrapping paper.

Hard carrying devices, if thought of as 'stiff' wrappings, include wooden cradles, cradleboards, and bark and woven containers.

Tying

Tying techniques are integral to a discussion of baby wrappings, because the ends of the material must be secured in some way so that the wrapping does not slip apart or off the baby. Before the invention of fastening devices such as rings, snaps, hooks, and pins, or the more recent zippers and velcro, tying techniques such as twisting, looping, tucking, and knotting were used as binding actions. Symbolically, the act of tying may signify connection, as in the Miao term for the baby fastening cord used in Guizhou: 'tying up life' (Qiyao 2009, 54). Anlo techniques of wrapping a baby to the body using a cloth are referred to in the Ewe language as *vikpakpa* or 'back tying' (Guerts 2002, 98). To the extent that yards of bandage wound around a baby have to be secured in some fashion, a knot or tuck was frequently the solution, although a straight pin was used in the eighteenth century to hold English stomach binders in place. Looping and fastening techniques, used with cord and needle, are part of the sewing repertoire.

There are many books devoted to nautical knots that illustrate the sequence of tying, but the myriad ways of winding swaddling bands or attaching babies to humans is not similarly documented. Even in medical articles that discuss swaddling, a baseline definition of the technique is often not given despite the expectation that the technical details would be germane; the efficacy of a tourniquet, for example, relies in large part on the way it is tied. Tying methods seem to be accepted as a universal and ancient folk practice, but techniques are loosely defined, and written descriptions are sparse (Lipton, Steinschneider, & Richmondet 1965). It may be that tying a baby wrap, an action often performed by women and children, has gone unrecorded both because of the traditionally low research interest in the subject and because it is such a homely and 'natural' activity, rather like tying shoelaces, that it becomes invisible. Knot-tying techniques are often demonstrated and practiced but not described or explained, possibly because they are practiced and learned through physically doing them.

'Babywearing', which refers to the practice of holding a baby on the body using a cloth, sling, or some type of soft carrier, is becoming more widely used in the United States and Europe, as is shown by the proliferation of babywearing online groups, conferences, classes, and an explosion in mass-produced products. But the 'wearing' of babies on the body is merely an old carrying practice given a new name. Babies can be seen cradled in the drapes of clothing in ancient Egyptian friezes, for example (Malek & Miles 1989), and Welsh nursing shawls, Batak sarongs (Niessen 2009), and saris (Bannerjee & Miller 2003) are clothing items that can be accommodated to the holding of a baby on the body. The *wearing* term is an interesting one because, conceptually, it includes the swaddling bands that are the baby's first clothes; the object tied to the wearer, which permits a baby to be 'worn' like an appendage or accessory; and an item of clothing that is specially constructed to hold the baby inside, as in the case of the sealskin hood of the *amaarngut*, once worn by Inuit women on the east coast of Greenland (Robbe 2008). The term in English became popularised in the mid-1980s, some twenty years after commercial baby carriers became commonplace. One popular account attributes the coinage of the term to Dr. William Sears, an American pediatrician who is also a well-known childcare expert and bestselling author (Blois 2005). His wife fabricated a sling out of a bed sheet for their sixth child and remarked that it was 'like a piece of clothing' that she put on in the morning and took off at night. 'Hence the "babywearing" term was born in the Sears household' (Ask Doctor Sears 2013), and Sears later patented a sling that is now sold in his online store. In the context of a capitalist, consumer society, 'wearing' babies supports fashion and consumption practices: mothers speak, for example, of having multiple carriers for different occasions, even comparing them to their shoe collections (Netburn 2010).

Inside and around baby wrappings, there is potential for much cultural variation. There may be layers and combinations of materials, such as green leaves, moss (Robbe 2008), and dung. Precious objects may be attached or inserted, such as amulets, the umbilical cord (Hilger 1952, 23), or a coin— or practical, mundane objects such as car keys and cup holders. Wrappings, therefore, can be seen as protective coverings of varying thicknesses and number that may also contain sedimentary layers of objects and ornamentation as well as bodily excretions and cosmological beliefs. When they are worn on bodies, they form an integral part of the sensory experience of the wearers and the worn (Allerton 2007).

Meanings in Ethnographic Accounts

A survey of ethnographic work finds that baby wrappings take on an intriguing shape-shifting quality, appearing variously as moving bed, artificial body part, house, portal to ancestry, and a visual text. Miller (2005, 13) refers to the *pallu* end portion of the sari, which babies cling to or play with while nursing, as a sort of 'third hand', and Gottlieb (2004, 179) calls the back-tying cloth a type of 'moving bed' owing to the long hours Beng babies spend sleeping within it. The *bilum* netbag (MacKenzie 1991, 7) and the Maori cloak (Henare 2006, 129) appear as an external 'house' for the baby during the first year of life.

Various themes emerge from these accounts. There are three preliminary categories suggested here, none of which are mutually exclusive, for thinking about baby wrappings: an extension of the body, a portal, and a boundary-setting device. These are general categories that need further development but are offered as one way of thinking about different aspects of wrappings. The examples that follow must be treated carefully, since the ethnographic research is often a glimpse rather than a focused examination, and abstracting a single example from its cultural context is notoriously problematic.

Extension

The wrapping can be thought of as an extension of the human body, materially, visually, temporally, and metaphorically. Unlike most other mammals, human babies are dependent for their survival on external caregivers and a long nurturing period after leaving the womb; the brain of a newborn is only twenty-five percent of its eventual adult size. If the period of postnatal dependence is thought of as completing gestation outside the womb (McKenna 1996), the wrapping can be seen as a transitional material that covers and protects the baby until it grows stronger and more viable.

In this regard, it is intriguing to find instances of baby-wrapping cloths that contain in their names or gestures references to childbirth or the bodily materials of the gestation process. In East Flores, for example, people speak of *wéngko molé* or 'making a blanket' around their shoulders on a chilly evening (Allerton 2007, 33). The term *wéngko* also refers to the placenta, so that when babies are wrapped in their mothers' sarongs, the wrapping becomes an 'artefactual skin' (Gell 1993, 38) that substitutes for the amniotic sac and placenta. A Maori term used to describe a birthing hut used in the early twentieth century, *whare kahu*, is translated as 'foetus house', but *kahu*, which refers to the amniotic sac, is also used as a generic word for garments and, in particular, for the woven cloaks that were important objects at the time of delivery in the early twentieth century, in terms of both the materials on which the baby arrived and in which it was then wrapped (Henare 2006, 128–29). Kaluli people in Papua New Guinea do not seem to have a specific term for 'childbirth' but use a phrase that means 'to put (a child) in a netbag' (Schieffelin in MacKenzie 1991, 20). In Luwu, South Sulawesi, after the birth of a baby, the newborn and placenta, still connected by the umbilical cord, were wrapped in a sarong. When the placenta, considered the 'older sibling' of the infant, was separated and ritually buried by the father, it was put into a container and 'carried out of the house in a sling, just like a baby' (Errington 1983, 549–50).

A wrapping may be used to bind both mother and newborn together, prolonging their mutual fusion symbolically and physically. This fusion is exemplified in Hmong minority baby carriers that are seen as artificial extensions of the umbilical cord (Suntop 2007). In cultures where babies are wrapped to caregivers' bodies, 'it is as though the infant is not yet born' (Whiting 1981, 174).

According to Astuti's fieldwork in Madagascar, childbirth leaves potentially dangerous openings both on the Vezo mother at the location of her loss of placenta and on the baby at its navel wound. Both must therefore for the first few weeks after birth be kept facing each other and hot and wrapped securely by layers of clothes and blankets, creating a bundle of heat and sweat. The baby is 'hardly visible' as the continued symbiosis of mother and child is extended by wrappings.

> The separation which has occurred at the moment of birth is also the cause of this prolonged symbiosis, for it is the lack of strong and clearly defined bodily boundaries (which the baby never had, and which the mother has lost as a result of giving birth) that requires mother and baby to remain fused with each other. (Astuti 1998, 36)

A baby carried on the body may also visually and physically suggest the continuance of the rounded shape of pregnancy. An Anlo-speaking mother in Ghana said that the newborn's position was shifted from her front side during pregnancy to her back after birth. With the use of a cloth, this shift in location helped to straighten out the mother's posture, returning her to a balanced somatic state (Guerts 2002, 98–99).

Wrappings have been successfully used to attach premature infants 'skin-to-skin' on the bare chest of the mother, in a marsupial-like pouch, as an alternative to incubator care. The Kangaroo Mother Care (KMC) method was first developed in Bogotá, Colombia, in 1978, in a hospital that lacked enough incubators to help indigent mothers. It is now used worldwide. The method calls for the naked infant to be placed in an upright position between the mother's breasts, facing her, with exclusive breastfeeding. The wrapping can be a blouse, a towel, a blanket (Kirsten, Bergman, & Hann 2001), or other specially made wrap, and the benefits of this practice include thermal regulation, maintenance of a regular heart rate, weight gain, and deep sleeping with less crying. Fathers and others also hold the baby skin-to-skin (Anderson 1991; Kirsten, Bergman, & Hann 2001). An important feature of KMC is that the mother's sensitivity to the baby's cues is enhanced owing to proximity (Nyqvist et al. 2010).

Portal

Wrapping cloths can be conceptualised as a symbolic portal or social and material channel between the baby and other places, concepts, or kin. *Porter* means 'to carry' in French; a baby might be thought of as being carried to a port in the social, ancestral, or spirit landscape. Henare (2006, 125–30) describes how Maori cloaks embody a pathway to ancestral lineage, for example, in the weaving of the cloth made using techniques handed down by ancestors to future descendants; in the examples of shared vocabulary pertaining to cloaks, human reproduction, and ancestry; and in the important role that a cloak played at the time of childbirth in the early 1900s for high-born Maori women. Such cloaks continue to possess an 'abiding presence' of ancestors (Henare 2006, 12) and are objects that are valued not in legal terms as cultural property, for example, but as embodiments of ancestors.

The swaddling process itself can be seen as an opportunity for the renewal or reinvigorating of life chances. An archaic custom in Kosovo practiced by some Serbians in villages in the Mount Kopaonik region held that if young adults reached maturity and remained single, a 'do-over' of the swaddling process would be enacted in which the young people in question would each be wrapped in a pack saddle (the cradle) and tied to it using a horse girth (swaddling bands) by the mother or, if she were no longer alive, an old female relative or village woman: 'The unmarried person is liberated by the same woman and the person lying in the saddle imitates a newborn baby. The ceremony is celebrated with dancing, singing and laughter. . . . [It] should be performed in the same way as if it were a question of a real newborn baby' (Vukanovic 1980). In this ceremony, an appeal is made, using food and the mock-swaddling, to any devils and spirits that have not been propitiated at the original lying-in period after birth. The horse girth, which is seen to have phallic properties, is presumed to transmit the sexual potency of the horse to the unmarried persons.

The importance of the materiality of the wrapping object as a portal to the infant is also seen in an example of Bantu pregnancy aprons (*isidiya*), made by the father using the skin of a duiker or specific type of antelope. This apron was then worn by the woman over her belly in the hopes of passing on the qualities of speed and surefootedness to the unborn baby. After the baby was born, the apron was used as a baby carrier (Brodie 2006, 55).

Wrapping cloths also can be seen as an instrument through which babies connect to their ancestral heritage and absorb a cultural style. Anlo-speaking women of southeast Ghana carry their babies on their backs using a *vikpakpa* back-tying cloth. The cloth ensures a firm connection to the mother, and through her, to the ancestors as well. Such strong bonds cannot be made in the front of the body, in the arms, or in a rag. The wrapping is also part of an ensemble of clothing and bodily movements that communicate moral characteristics. The sense of balance is counted as one of the main bodily senses that define how one is in the world for the Anlo-speaking population, and the *vikpakpa* permits the carrier to walk flexibly, with grace and good comportment. The wrapping is an integral part of the successful transmission of these valued qualities to the baby (Guerts 2002).

Boundary

Physical Boundaries   Within the vocabulary of wrapping and swaddling, babies also can be *bound* using linen *binders*. The English noun derives from verbs that describe the action 'to bind, roll, swathe' (Marshall 2008, 63). That such binders create physical and visual boundaries around the body can be seen in images of tightly swaddled babies. In medieval Europe it was believed that the bindings held 'nourishing juices' inside the wrappings, but criticisms were also made as late as the 1860s that the baby's fluids and infrequent changing made the infant fetid, smelly, and unsanitary (Tucker 1985). The bound baby is spatially separated, unlike the naked baby wrapped to the body, where there are no physical barriers between infant and carrier. Among the Beng in Cote d'Ivoire, it is believed that newborn babies have recently emerged from the previous life and are in a tenuous state, still longing to return. By keeping the baby close to the warm human body using cloth wrappings, and thus luring it to stay, the chances of its remaining and becoming a full-fledged Beng person are strengthened (Gottlieb 2004, 183).

The physical boundaries created by swaddling drew criticism from Enlightenment philosophers who saw in the windings a restriction on movement and personal liberty. In *Emile* (1761), for example, Rousseau discouraged moving a newborn from one 'envelope' to another.

> From the moment that the child breathes on leaving its envelope, do not suffer his being given other envelopes which keep him more restricted: no caps, no belts, no swaddling. . . . When he begins to grow stronger, let him crawl around the room. Let him spread out, stretch his little limbs. You will see them gaining strength day by day. Compare him with a well-swaddled child of the same age; you will be surprised at the difference in their progress. (Rousseau 1979/1761, 60)

Such thinking, amplified by physicians in Europe and followed later in the United States, laid the foundation for future ideological positions against swaddling. The *Oxford English Dictionary* cites a late nineteenth-century reference to swaddling as a form of 'incarceration'. Respected pediatricians in Europe criticised the practice, which led to a retreat from swaddling among the upper classes. Public debate about swaddling entered political discourse in the United States during the Cold War when Gorer's 'swaddling hypothesis' suggested that swaddling practices created in Russian babies a 'free-floating hate' and 'destructive rage' against the tight bindings that, when undone, gave rise to gratification, guilt, and the 'violent' release of emotions (Gorer 1949, 156–62). It is interesting that the insignia of the American Academy of Pediatrics (AAP) features a swaddled baby based on a fifteenth-century terracotta roundel taken from a historic Italian foundling hospital in Florence. Out of ten renditions of upright swaddled babies (Figure 2.1), the AAP eventually settled on the only one in which the feet are unbound and the swaddling bands are coming off, suggesting perhaps a freedom from illness or, for modern pediatricians, a liberation from ignorance of medical science (Kahn 2002, 179).

Figure 2.1 One of the ten terracotta roundels by Andrea della Robbia on the facade of the fifteenth-century foundling hospital *Ospedale degli Innocenti* in Florence. One of the roundels is the insignia of the American Academy of Pediatrics. The bands are coming off at the feet, suggesting freedom from illness or liberation from ignorance. (drawing by Jasmine Parker)

Symbolic Boundaries   The baby-wrapping cloth may also be seen as a canvas or signpost on which ornaments and symbols are attached, establishing barriers against malevolent spirits that wish to steal the infant away. In the Yunnan-Guizhou plateau region of southwest China (Figure 2.2), where clothing is an important marker of ethnic identity, Qiyao (2009, 52) was told that 'when a child is born, if they aren't quickly wrapped in the clothing of the group, the baby will be claimed by the devil.' The wrapping may also permit ancestors to recognise the infant as one of their own. The Miao history of forced migration is recorded on clothing, and some Nankai Miao back carriers feature embroidered geometric designs that are thought to reference the walled cities of the ancestral homeland, placing the baby safely within the protective symbols of ancestors (Qiyao 2009, 258, 279). It is also interesting that swaddling bands have been seen as instruments to guard and shape the boundaries between what was considered human and what was seen as animal-like. In colonial America, snug swaddling was used to keep the body straight and unlike the animal crawling on all fours (Calvert 1992, 25).

Conclusion: Wrappings as an Index of Physical Contact

This research suggests that one can think about baby wrappings using the abstract categories of extension, portal, and boundary. The practical aspects of baby wrappings and their place in child-raising activities must not, however, be neglected. A critical distinction may be whether a baby is wrapped in a shawl or sling and carried on the body or whether it is swaddled and placed away

Figure 2.2   Gejia mother wearing her child in an indigo-dyed batik carrier at a wedding in Matang Village, Guizhou Province, China, 2008. (photograph by Pamela Najdowski)

from the body, in cradles, perambulators, and other objects that keep the baby spatially separated. Whiting (1981, 162) coded different infant-carrying practices and concluded that this dichotomy is the best single index for measuring the amount of physical contact between the mother and the infant. If a baby is tied to another's body, intimate signals between baby and carrier are immediate, physical, sensory, and intimately communicated. According to fieldwork in West Africa, a mother who is carrying a naked infant on her back knows when a bowel movement is imminent by the shifting movements of the baby on the body, which she has grown to recognise (Menzel 2006). Feeding is facilitated by having the infant close by—one reason that the La Leche League was an early supporter of baby carriers when they first appeared on the scene in the United States in the late 1960s. Sleeping habits, moreover, are closely connected to the type of baby wrapping used. Further investigation is needed on the web of nurturing activities that are contingent on the type of wrapping that is used.

The important topic of the implied connection between gender and baby wrappings has not been explicitly addressed here. Women—not always mothers—and children were found in ethnographic reports to be those most intimately involved in the routine daily activities related to baby wrappings, in many cases because they were wearing them. Linguistically, visually, and in terms of childbirth and child raising, baby wrappings and their use are implicated as a gendered object and a marker for femininity. The exception was Aka pygmy fathers in the Congo, who were observed to be within arm's length or actually carrying their young children forty-seven percent of the day (Hewlett 1991, 168), including time spent holding babies face to face using wrapping cloths.

What has been less well examined here is the role of other kin, especially males, in the production of devices, rituals, naming ceremonies, childbirth, and carrying practices. The lack of examination is in part due to the fragmentary ethnographic evidence that can be derived from a survey of fieldwork accounts that are neither systematic nor closely focused studies of baby wrappings. Men may use different methods of carrying, for example, such as in their arms without the mediating tool of a wrapping; or they participate in the social activity of creating a carrier. One of the acts that Wari' fathers in Rondônia, Brazil, perform after birth to establish social paternity is the making of a sling for the new mother (Conklin & Morgan 1996, 673). MacKenzie examines how the looped string *bilum*, which she describes as an external womb for Telefol women in central New Guinea, is also a symbolic and visual expression of gender relations that are complementary rather than distinct. *Bilum* are complex objects with multiple authorship and have lexical analogies to men's ritual houses, which can be viewed as large-scale wombs for the production of social relations (1991, 170–76). To suggest, therefore, that wrappings are an 'either-or' male-or-female object is to deny the complexity of the form and its power as a metaphor of the human condition.

The diversity of practices, devices, and conceptualisations of baby wrappings shows that there is no universal 'baby-wrapping' object. Concepts of the wrapped baby, moreover, are undergoing reconsideration as new reproductive technologies introduce and experiment with new ways of bringing babies to maturity: outside bodies; inside men; within the bodily wrappings of surrogate 'carrying' mothers (Teman 2009); and inside the wombs of transgendered bodies.

References

Adamson, P. B. 1985. Some Rituals Associated with Parturition in Antiquity. *Folklore* 96(ii), pp. 176–83.

Allerton, C. 2007. The Secret Life of Sarongs: Manggarai Textiles as Super-Skins. *Journal of Material Culture* 12(1), pp. 22–46.

Anderson, G. C. 1991. Current Knowledge about Skin-to-Skin (Kangaroo) Care for Preterm Infants. *Journal of Perinatology* 11(3), pp. 216–26.

Anisfeld, E., Casper, V., Nozyce, M., & Cunningham, N. 1990. Does Infant Carrying Promote Attachment? An Experimental Study of the Effects of Increased Physical Contact on the Development of Attachment. *Child Development* 61, pp. 1617–27.

Ask Doctor Sears. 2013. *Fussy Babies, 1.* In Ask Doctor Sears, a trusted resource for parents, http://www.askdrsears.com/, accessed January 8, 2013.

Astuti, R. 1998. 'It's a boy,' 'it's a girl!' Reflections on the Sex and Gender in Madagascar and Beyond. In M. Lambek & A. Strathern, eds., *Bodies and Persons: Comparative Perspectives from Africa and Melanesia.* Cambridge: Cambridge University Press, pp. 29–52.

Bannerjee, M., & Miller, D. 2003. *The Sari.* Oxford: Berg.

Benedict, R. 1959 (1949). Child Rearing in Certain European Countries. In M. Mead, ed., *An Anthropologist at Work: Ruth Benedict.* Cambridge, MA: Riverside Press, pp. 449–58.

Bibby, B. 2004. *Precious Cargo: California Indian Cradle Baskets and Childbirth Traditions.* Marin, CA: Marin Museum of the American Indian.

Blois, M. 2005. *Babywearing: The Benefits and Beauty of This Ancient Tradition.* Amarillo, TX: Pharmasoft Publishing.

Brodie, M. 2006. Southern Africa: The Father Makes the Carrier, but Only after the Birth. In I. van Hout, ed., *Beloved Burden: How Children Are Carried.* Amsterdam: Tropenmuseum, Royal Tropical Institute, pp. 54–57.

Calvert, K. 1992. *Children in the House: The Material Culture of Early Childhood, 1600–1900.* Boston: Northeastern University Press.

Conklin, B. A., & Morgan, L. M. 1996. Babies, Bodies, and the Production of Personhood in North America and a Native Amazonian Society. *Ethos* 24(4), pp. 657–94.

Edwards, E., Gosden, C., & Phillips, R. B. (Eds.) 2006. *Sensible Objects: Colonialism, Museums and Material Culture.* Oxford: Berg.

Ehrenburg, M. 1989. *Women in Prehistory.* London: British Museum Publications.

Errington, S. 1983. Embodied *sumange'* in Luwu. *The Journal of Asian Studies* 42(3), pp. 545–70.

Fontanel, B., & d'Harcourt, C. 1997. *Babies: History, Art, and Folklore.* New York: Harry N. Abrams.

Fujido, M., Matsumoto, A., & Takeda, A. (eds.) 2007. *Kanjigen.* Tokyo: Gakushukenkyusha.

Gell, A. 1993. *Wrapping in Images: Tattooing in Polynesia.* Oxford: Clarendon Press.

Gerard, C. M., Harris, K. A., & Thach, B. T. 2002. Spontaneous Arousals in Supine Infants while Swaddled and Unswaddled during Rapid Eye Movement and Quiet Sleep. *Pediatrics* 110(6), p. e70.

Gorer, G. 1949. Some Aspects of the Psychology of the People of Great Russia. *American Slavic and East European Review* 8(3), pp. 155–66.

Gottlieb, A. 2004. *The Afterlife Is Where We Come from: The Culture of Infancy in West Africa.* Chicago: University of Chicago Press.

Guerts, K. L. 2002. *Culture and the Senses: Bodily Ways of Knowing in an African Community.* Berkeley and Los Angeles: University of California Press.

Hail, B. A. (ed.) 2000. *Gifts of Pride and Love: Kiowa and Comanche Cradles.* Providence, RI: Haffenreffer Museum of Anthropology, Brown University.

Henare, A. 2006. Nga Aho Tipuna (ancestral threads): Maori Cloaks from New Zealand. In S. Küchler & D. Miller, eds., *Clothing as Material Culture.* Oxford: Berg, pp.121–38.

Hendry, J. 1995. *Wrapping Culture: Politeness, Presentation and Power in Japan and Other Societies.* Oxford: Oxford University Press.

Hewlett, B. S. 1991. *Intimate Fathers: The Nature and Context of Aka Pygmy Paternal Infant Care*. Ann Arbor: University of Michigan Press.

Hilger, S. M. I. 1952. Arapaho Child Life and Its Cultural Background. Washington, D.C.: *Smithsonian Institution, Bureau of American Ethnology Bulletin* 148.

Holy Bible. 1952. Revised standard version. New York: Thomas Nelson and Sons.

Hudson, C., & Phillips, H. 1968. Rousseau and the Disappearance of Swaddling among Western Europeans. In T. Weaver, ed., *Essays on Medical Anthropology, Southern Anthropological Society Proceedings,* 1. Athens, GA: Southern Anthropological Society, pp. 13–22.

Hunt, D. 1972. *Parents and Children in History: The Psychology of Family Life in Early Modern France*. New York: Harper Torchbooks.

Ii, O. 1989. *Furoshiki bunka no postomodan*. Tokyo: Chūōkōronsha.

Kahn, L. 2002. The 'Ospedale degli Innocenti' and the 'Bambino' of the American Academy of Pediatrics. *Pediatrics* 110(1), pp. 175–80.

Kirsten, G. F., Bergman, N. J., & Hann, F. M. 2001. Kangaroo Mother Care in the Nursery. *Pediatric Clinics of North America* 48(2), pp. 443–52.

Kloek, E. M. 2008. For Beggars, Musicians, Gypsies and Hippies. In I. van Hout, ed., *Beloved Burden: How Children Are Carried*. Amsterdam: Tropenmuseum, Royal Tropical Institute, pp. 58–66.

Konner, M. 1977. Infancy among the Kalahari Desert San. In H. P. Leiderman, S. R. Tulkin, & A. Rosenfeld, eds., *Culture and Infancy: Variations in the Human Experience*. New York: Academic Press, pp. 287–328.

LeVine, R. A. 2007. Ethnographic Studies of Childhood: A Historical Overview. *American Anthropologist* 109(2), pp. 247–60.

Lipton, E. L., Steinschneider, A., & Richmondet, J. B. 1965. Swaddling, a Child Care Practice: Historical, Cultural, and Experimental Observations. *Pediatrics* 35, pp. 521–67.

Liu Lan, Y., Lan Lin, C., & Lin, B. 2001. *Bonding via Baby Carriers: The Art and Soul of the Miao and Dong People*. Taipei: Les Enphants Co.

MacKenzie, M. A. 1991. *Androgynous Objects: String Bags and Gender in Central New Guinea*. Amsterdam: Harwood Academic Publishers.

Malek, J., & Miles, E. 1989. Early Squeezes Made in the Tomb of Khaemhet (TT 57). *The Journal of Egyptian Archaeology* 75, pp. 227–29.

Marshall, N. 2008. *Dictionary of Children's Clothes: 1700s to Present*. London: V&A Publishing.

Mauriceau, F. 1675. *Traité des maladies des femmes grosses, et de celles qui sont accouchées*. Paris: Gerard.

McKenna, J. J. 1996. Sudden Infant Death Syndrome in Cross-Cultural Perspective: Is Infant-Parent Cosleeping Protective? *Annual Review of Anthropology* (25), pp. 201–16.

Mead, M. 1954. The Swaddling Hypothesis: Its Reception. *American Anthropologist New Series* 56(3), pp. 395–409.

Menzel, B. 2006. Ghana and Nigeria: A Long Tradition. In I. van Hout, ed., *Beloved Burden: How Children Are Carried*. Amsterdam: Tropenmuseum, Royal Tropical Institute, pp. 46–53.

Miller, D. 2005. Introduction. In S. Küchler & D. Miller, eds., *Clothing as Material Culture*. Oxford: Berg, pp. 1–19.

Netburn, D. 2010. Meet the Baby-Carrier Fanatics. In *Los Angeles Times*, March 20, http://www.latimes.com/features/home/la-hm-parentology-20100320,0,983113.story.

Niessen, S. A. 2009. *Legacy in Cloth: Batak Textiles of Indonesia.* Leiden: KITLV Press.

Nyqvist, K. H., Anderson, G. C., Bergman, N., Cattaneo, A., Charpak, N., Davanzo, R., et al. 2010. Towards Universal Kangaroo Mother Care: Recommendations and Report from the First European Conference and Seventh International Workshop on Kangaroo Mother Care. *Acta Paediatrica* 99(6), pp. 820–26.

Qiyao, D. (Mark Hammons, trans.) 2009. The Other Writing of People without a Written Language. In *Writing with Thread: Traditional Textiles of Southwest Chinese Minorities.* Honolulu: University of Hawai'i Art Gallery, pp. 43–57.

Robbe, B. 2008. Greenland: A Wide Sealskin Hood. In I. van Hout, ed., *Beloved Burden: How Children Are Carried.* Amsterdam: Tropenmuseum, Royal Tropical Institute, pp. 124–27.

Rousseau, J.-J. 1979/1761. *Emile or On Education.* Introduction, translation and notes by Alan Bloom. New York: Basic Books.

Sarvady, A. 2005. *Baby-gami: Baby Wrapping for Beginners.* San Francisco: Chronicle Books.

Schaper, K. K. 1982. Towards a Calm Baby and Relaxed Parents. *Family Relations* 31, pp. 409–14.

Schieffelin, E. L. 1977. *The Sorrow of the Lonely and the Burning of the Dancers.* St. Lucia: University of Queensland Press.

Schroedel, J. R. 2000. *Is the Fetus a Person? A Comparison of Policies across the Fifty States.* Ithaca, NY: Cornell University Press.

Suntop, R. 2007. Miao Children's Dress. *Textile newsletter*, spring 2007. Washington, D.C.: Textile Society of America.

Taylor, T. 2010. *The Artificial Ape: How Technology Changed the Course of Human Evolution.* New York: Palgrave Macmillan.

Teman, E. 2009. Embodying Surrogate Motherhood: Pregnancy as a Dyadic Body-Project. *Body & Society* 15(3), pp. 47–69.

Temkin, O. (trans.) 1991. *Soranus' Gynaecology.* Baltimore: The Johns Hopkins Press.

Tronick, E. Z., Thomas, R. B., & Daltabuit, M. 1994. The Quechua Manta Pouch: A Caretaking Practice for Buffering the Peruvian Infant against the Multiple Stressors of High Altitude. *Child Development* 65(4), pp. 1005–13.

Tucker, N. 1985. All Cleanly Wrapped. *History Today* 35(9), pp. 5–7.

Turner, T. 1995. Social Body and Embodied Subject: Bodiliness, Subjectivity, and Sociality among the Kayapo. *Cultural Anthropology* 10(2), pp.143–70.

University of Hawai'i Art Gallery. 2009. *Writing with Thread: Traditional Textiles of Southwest Chinese Minorities.* Honolulu: University of Hawai'i Art Gallery.

van Hout, I. (ed., trans.) 1993. *Beloved Burden: How Children Are Carried.* [PDF provided by van Hout from the Dutch *Lieve Lasten: Hoe Kinderen Gedragen Worden.*] Amsterdam: KIT Publications, Tropenmuseum.

Van Sleuwen, B. E., Engelberts, A.C., Boere-Boonekamp, M. M., Kuis, W., Schulpen, T. W. J., & L'Hoir, M. P. 2007. Swaddling: A Systematic Review. *Pediatrics* 120(4), pp. 1097–1106.

Vukanovic, T. P. 1980. Swaddling Clothes for the Unmarried and for Herdsman. *Folklore* 91(1), pp. 111–14.

Whiting, J. W. M. 1981. Environmental Constraints on Infant Care Practices. In R. H. Munroe, R. L. Munroe, & B. B. Whiting, eds., *Handbook of Cross-Cultural Human Development.* New York: Garland STPM Press, pp. 155–80.

3 Wrapping and Tying Ancient Egyptian New Kingdom Dresses

Janet M. Johnstone

Changes in clothing styles are often a reflection of the individual's perception of the social, economic, and religious shifts in society. Significant stylistic changes occurred in ancient Egypt during the New Kingdom (sixteenth–fourteenth century B.C.E.) culminating in the mid-Eighteenth Dynasty. These changes in style were introduced during the reigns of Tuthmosis IV and Amenhotep II as Egypt expanded its empire and developed new technologies. As Egypt cemented its place as one of the leading political and economic powers in the ancient world under Amenhotep III, styles of hair and dress developed in response (Johnstone 2009; Tassie 2009), reaching their height in the Amarna period under Akhenaten. The wardrobe of simple wrap-around clothes and pull-on garments from earlier periods was augmented with complex-wrapped dresses for women and elaborate sash kilts for men. This new style of clothing characterised the sociopolitical and religious changes experienced during the Amarna era, not just within the city of Akhetaten but also in the Memphite region, as illustrated in the New Kingdom tomb-paintings at Saqqara (Martin 1992). Although pictorial representations of ancient Egyptians from this time are idiosyncratic, the dress details are notoriously difficult to decipher. In general, the majority of Egyptian workers and villagers were little affected by the introduction of courtly dress but shared a basic wardrobe in common with the nobility, which, for a man, comprised a linen loincloth, a wrap-around kilt, and a *mss* (Figure 3.1). Complete examples of items from the basic wardrobe were

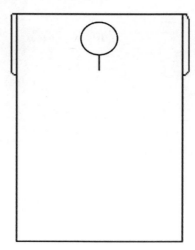

Figure 3.1 A *mss* is a bag-shaped garment constructed from a rectangular length of cloth folded in half across the width and sewn up the side seams, leaving a gap for the arms. A hole was cut in the centre front, just below the folded edge, for the head to go through. (drawing by Janet Johnstone)

found in the tomb of Tutankhamun (KV62) (Carter 2000, 33, 41, 125, pls. 2 and 39; Vogelsang-Eastwood 1997, 7*f*; 1999, 53–58) and the mid-Dynasty 18 tomb of Kha and his wife Merit (TT8) (Hall 2001, 35–38; Schiaparelli 1927, figs. 64, 68, 69).

For women, the basic wardrobe included a loincloth, a range of shawls, scarves, and wraps, and a long *mss*, but the final word in elegance was the complex-wrapped dress. The nobility soon started to emulate the royal court and began to wear layers of garments of often finely pleated linen cloth that were wrapped, arranged, and knotted into place around the body. Achieving the correct mode of wearing this dress was dependent on the skills of a dresser with the ability to drape and arrange the length of cloth on the wearer's body as opposed to the wearer dressing herself, although she may have made minor adjustments as needed. The dress could be worn with or without an under-dress, or *mss*. Scenes from the Dynasty 19 tomb of Sennedjem (TT1) show his wife, Iyneferti, wearing a complex-wrapped dress over a sleeveless *mss* or under-dress denoted by the round close-fitting neckline and the little ties that closed the *mss* neck opening (Shedid 1994, 48, pl. 14). Or, more contro-versially, representations of the royal women of Akhenaten's court are shown naked under their dresses. This has been attributed to mere artistic licence as a means to emphasis the femininity and fecundity of their station, but equally it is feasible that the women really did appear in this form of dress for ritual occasions.

Various versions of the complex-wrapped dress were portrayed in ancient Egyptian art and have given rise to a number of interesting interpretations of their construction by modern scholars (Bonnet 1917, pls. 8 and 9; Bruyère 1937, II, 59, fig. 30; Houston 2002, 91–94; Vogelsang-Eastwood 1993, 107–11; Zoffili 1991, 160–74). As part of an experimental archaeology programme, I followed all these methods of dress construction and found that most of them, with few exceptions, were not wearable or did not resemble the original representation. They came adrift rapidly after very little movement, and, when tested by dressing actresses and models in this style of clothing, the dresses soon looked tired and dishevelled. The interpretation of the construction of ancient Egyptian clothing relies on keeping it as simple as possible and employing methods used by the ancient Egyptians, without resorting to modern tailoring or dressmaking techniques. Equally, where Houston (2002, reprint, 93, figs. 96, 97a, 98a) has based her interpretations of tying complex-wrapped dresses on the method for tying an Indian sari circa 1950s (Banerjee & Miller 2003, ill. 139), she has drawn on an inappropriate cultural reference that does not cross over to ancient Egyptian clothing. Indeed, some of her results are surprisingly close to the originals, but the use of a waist cord and grouping wide pleats into the front of the skirt only gives the Egyptian dress an Indian styling. (See Banerjee & Miller 2003, 167*f*, for sequence of how to wear a modern sari.) Egyptian clothing construction was based on simple shapes of cloth; square, rectangle, triangle, circle, and semicircle either made into pull-on garments (*mss*) or wrapped around the body and tied into place (dresses, kilts, loincloths, sashes, scarves, shawls, wraps, and cloaks). Therefore, New Kingdom dress construction would have followed the same formula and have been practical and relatively comfortable to wear.

Unfortunately, very little extant Pharaonic linen clothing remains for examination. A further complication is the problem of actually recognising a dress from the lengths of textile that are housed in museum collections. One example of a linen cloth possibly used as a dress comes from the Koninklijke Musea, Brussels (E. 6204 Vogelsang-Eastwood 1993, 99, 101, pl. 24, fig. 7.2). Patches of worn or thin fabric coincide with the position of the underarms and hips if the cloth had been wrapped two and a half times around a woman's body like a sarong dress. Linen was reused to the point of destruction in ancient times, and the general lack of regard for it on excavation sites until recently has greatly depleted this resource. Pictorial and textual records become, therefore, the sole source of information. The analysis of these types of evidence is fraught with difficulties. The Egyptians wished to portray themselves to the best advantage, and a vestige of artistic licence is to be expected to achieve this goal. Illustrations of Egyptian men and women sometimes show garments that are technically impossible to construct. But no matter how they were drawn or painted, there must remain an echo of the original garment, as observed by the artist, within the formulised framework of artistic representations.

The Reconstruction Process

All the dress styles discussed here were made and recreated in linen fabric, and some of the styles were hand-pleated (Johnstone In press). A modern equivalent of the finest ancient Egyptian linen (royal linen) is not manufactured today, and there is no comparison between a hand-spliced, tightly spun, and hand-woven ancient Egyptian linen and a modern power-woven commercial linen produced for the fashion market. Examples of ancient Egyptian tabby weave linen, viewed at the Agricultural Museum in Cairo (no accession numbers available), had a silklike quality not dissimilar to georgette or voile and would have been very suitable for making fine dresses. Equally, some examples of complete and fragmentary linen clothing from the tomb of Tutankhamun are made of fine-quality linen including a triangular loincloth (Carter no: 43g, JE 29/3/34/102-b) with a thread count of 112 warp and 32 weft threads per centimetre (Vogelsang-Eastwood 2006, 286). Sourcing suitable linen to reconstruct the ancient Egyptian clothing was, therefore, a slow process. The dress styles were tested, in some cases over a number of years, to make sure that they bore a close proximity to the originals.

Experimental Archaeology on the Film Set

The dresses were supplied as hired costume from the author's stock and were robustly tested by actresses dressed as ancient Egyptians during location filming for several television documentaries on ancient Egypt—thus the clothing reconstructions underwent a lifetime of wear in a matter of days, as the actors attended banquets, performed religious rituals, mourned at funerals, walked, ran, fought, and were marshalled back and forth in processions in the hot sun in addition to a myriad of other activities considered relevant to ancient Egyptian daily life by the TV or film production company (Johnstone 2005, 40–44). Although it was an artificial environment, no other one could have provided such close proximity to the ancient world and the daily activities of its people. Asking a model dressed as a member of the royal Amarna court to walk around the room is hardly a true representation of ancient life and can tell us little about its clothing.

The dresses were wrapped and tied in place with a double knot; no pins or fastenings were used, because there is no archaeological evidence that it was common practice to use an alternative securing system until the Graeco-Roman period (332 B.C.E.–395 C.E.). The knot in ancient Egypt held magical force (Pinch 1994, 83*f*). It could form a barrier to repel evil or mischief and protect the wearer, or it could be used to delay a process or action until the appropriate time when the knot was released. Magic could be bound into the knot if a spell was recited as the knot was tied and then released when the knot was undone. The action of wrapping and tying or tying and unwrapping draws parallels with Anubis preparing the mortal body for the Underworld with linen bandages and wrappings. The statue of Nefertiti wearing a pleated dress resembles the mummified and wrapped body, protected by the gods and safe from bad spirits, evil forces, and mortal corruption. In comparison, a painted scene from the Dynasty 18 tomb of Hormeheb (KV57) shows a seated Osiris wrapped in white mummy wrappings attended by Anubis and Harsiese (Ikram & Dodson 1998, 28, pl. 3). Osiris sits majestically on a throne as if dressed in a white garment with long sleeves rather than in mortuary wrappings.

Back on the film set at the end of each day, the dresses were hung to air and then laid flat on the floor (in the style of Tilke's method of recording folk costume, Tilke 1990) and photographed. Thus it was possible to record areas of wear patterns, rubbing, creasing, and sweat-marking, which may be used as a comparison with ancient textiles and lengths of cloth in museum collections that might originally have been worn as dresses. The actresses on the film set were accessorised with long, black, plaited wigs, hair and body jewellery, including a broad collar necklace, leather sandals, and clothing accessories such as fans, musical instruments, and flowers—all designed to enhance the ancient Egyptian 'experience'. By making observations of the women wearing the dresses while filming and in periods of rest between scenes when their behaviour was more natural, it was possible to see how the dress moved and behaved on the body; how often the wearer or her dresser needed to adjust or rearrange the dress; and the wear, crease, and sweat-patterning on the length of cloths when they were removed from the body. And, finally, the wearers were interviewed regarding their personal experience, both practically and emotionally, of wearing an ancient historical garment. From these data the following dress constructions were made.

Complex-Wrapped Dresses

The style of complex-wrapped dress examined in this chapter is seen in five variations (Figure 3.2):

1. The basic wrap-around dress and a shawl
2. The complex-wrapped dress constructed from one length of cloth
3. The open-front dress
4. The late new Kingdom dress—*mss* and shawl
5. The Third Intermediate to Late Period dress—*mss* and shawl

The Basic Wrap-Around Dress and Shawl

This dress is epitomised by representations of the Amarna royal women, especially the red quartzite statue of Nefertiti in the Louvre, Paris (E25409) (Figure 3.3). Although described as 'basic', this style has been one of the most

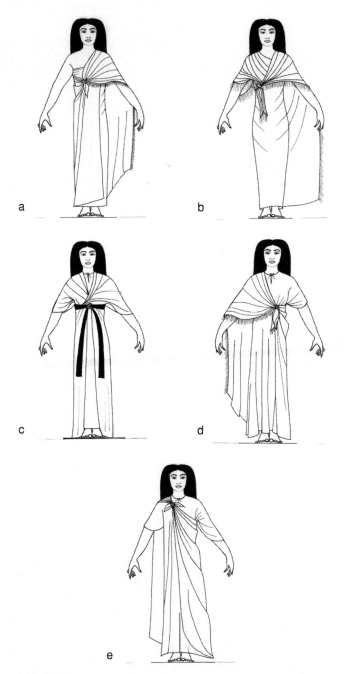

Figure 3.2 (a) Basic wrap-around dress with shawl; (b) complex-wrapped dress; (c) open-fronted dress with sash; (d) *mss* and shawl, Dynasty 19; (e) *mss* and shawl, Dynasty 22. (drawing by Janet Johnstone)

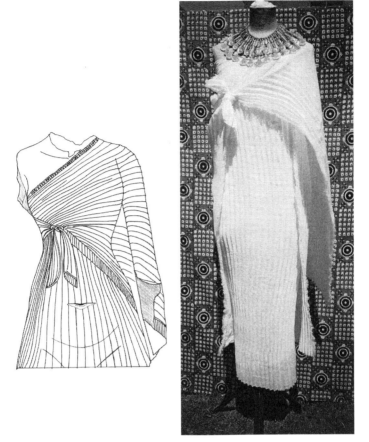

Figure 3.3 *Left*: Red quartzite statue of Nefertiti wearing a simple dress and shawl, Dynasty 18, Louvre Paris E25409. Note the weft or selvedge edge along the top edge of the shawl close to the neck and the longer warp fringe running from the knot to the left arm. *Right*: Reconstruction of a wrap-around dress and shawl made from pleated fine Sarunda linen. (drawing and photo by Janet Johnstone)

difficult dresses to interpret. Trying to tie this dress from one piece of cloth and to follow the pleating direction or fold lines was certainly challenging; the best result was achieved with a length of cloth (2.30 m long × 1.22 m wide) wrapped twice around the body like a sarong, with the top two corners knotted tightly together. A shawl (1.50 m long × 1.50 m wide) was then draped over the right shoulder and knotted below the left breast (Figure 3.4). A wall painting from the tomb of Horemheb (TT 78) (Brack & Brack 1980, pl. 29–31) of women making offerings provides close detail of the combination of an under-dress and a shawl. The shawl was painted in a darker colour to differentiate it from the lighter coloured under-dress.

Figure 3.4 *Left*: Basic wrap-around dress made from a length of cloth wrapped twice around the body like a sarong and secured with a knot at the top. *Right*: A shawl is placed over one shoulder, and the two corners are tied together below the breast. (drawing by Janet Johnstone)

The Complex-Wrapped Dress Constructed from One Length of Cloth

This style of dress was very close-fitting and appears almost impossible to wear. The Egyptians used a clever wrapping and draping technique (Figure 3.5), which was achieved only by using a finely woven linen cloth that was soft and had a good drape. The painted images of the royal court of Amarna show only the frontal perspective, and no back view is visible. The construction of the dress was devised by using Harry Burton's photographs of the four independent, free-standing statues of the goddesses Isis, Nepthys, Neith, and Selkis associated with Tutakhamun's golden canopic shrine (No. 266, Carter 2000, pl. 5; Houston 2002, 93; Reeves 1994,119*f*). These statues are housed in the Egyptian Museum, Cairo, where they are positioned as they were originally found and intended to stand, facing the golden shrine with arms outstretched to protect the canopic contents.

Harry Burton's photographs give a unique 360-degree view of the figures and in particular their mode of dress. The dress was wrapped using one long cloth measuring in the range of 3.5 m long × 1.37–1.52 m wide. It is apparent that the dress was very close-fitting and figure-hugging, which was achieved by crossing over the cloth around the back of the body, drawing the dress closely around the legs and tapering to the ankles—a flattering way to emphasis the figure without restricting movement. The tightness of the dress was deceptive: the crossing-over of the cloth at the back (Figures 3.6 and 3.3), as would be seen in a modern wrap-over tulip skirt, was covered by the end of

Figure 3.5 Statue of Isis (Burton 1148) and Neith (Burton 0938d) from tomb of Tutankhamun (copyright Griffith Institute, University of Oxford)

the cloth (B). It hid the exposed view of the back of the legs when the wearer was walking or sitting (Figure 3.6).

The other notable feature of the back view of the goddess statues was the chevron pleating running down the centre of each statue's back (Figure 3.5, back view of Neith, Burton 0938d). Whether it was in practice possible to make the pleats lie in V-shapes down the back or whether it was merely artistic licence and a means to show the change in direction of the pleating at the end of the cloth as corner B passed to the front of the body (Figure 3.6, models 5 and 6) could be discovered only through experimentation. To this end, a 3.5 m length of linen cloth was dampened and hand-pleated with accordion pleats across the width of the fabric (Johnstone In press). The diagonal pleating was made by folding one end of the cloth firmly to 45 degrees (Figure 3.7). The double thickness section was accordion-pleated in the same manner as the rest of the cloth. Once the damp cloth had dried completely, it was shaken out and arranged into a complex wrapped dress on a dress stand.

Unfortunately, the chevron effect pleating did not sit down the centre back of the dress as hoped, because the cloth was nearly on the straight grain at

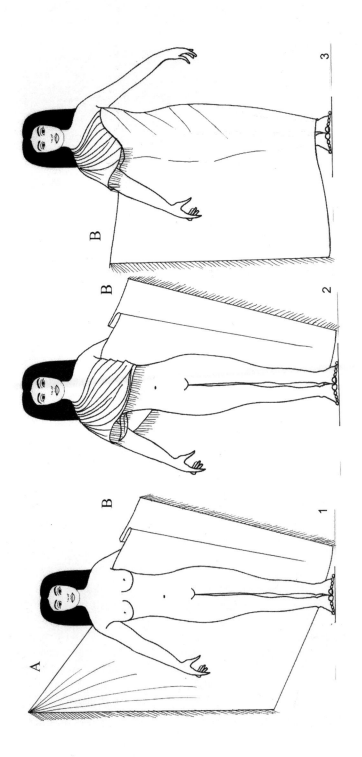

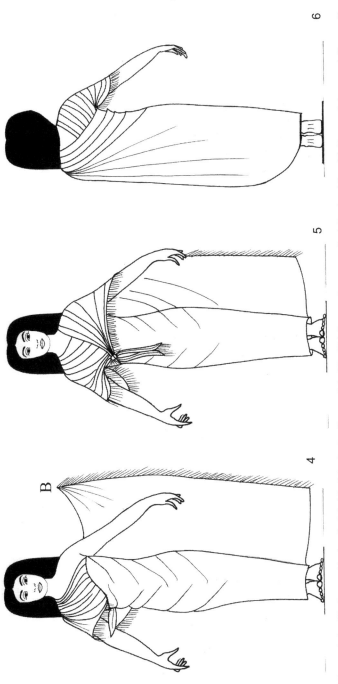

Figure 3.6 (1) Start with the cloth behind the body. Corner A is lifted high over the wearer's right shoulder. (2) Corner A is passed diagonally across the front of the body to the left armpit. It passes around the back so A is visible, sticking out at the right-hand side of the waist. (3) Corner B is pulled across the front of the body over the left breast and slips down to the right waist. (4) Corner B is swept up and backward around the back of the neck and over the left shoulder to the front. (5) Corner B is pulled down over the left breast to meet corner A. The two ends are knotted into a double knot. (6) Back view. (drawing by Janet Johnstone)

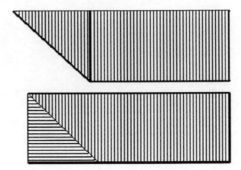

Figure 3.7 Pleating diagram. The bottom left corner was laid on top of the cloth at 45 degrees to make a double layer. The cloth was dampened and hand pleated. When dry it was shaken in to shape creating a pleated chevron on the left side. (drawing by Janet Johnstone)

this point. If the diagonally pleated section was omitted and the cloth was completely accordion-pleated in the weft direction, the pleating lay diagonally across the back of the body, which must have been artistically unacceptable to the composition. The chevron-pleated effect seen on the statues accentuates the shape of the back of the goddesses' bodies; the V shape runs down the spine, between the buttocks and where the two legs meet. This effect compliments the strict vertical and horizontal lines of the canopic shrine and canopy when the four statues stand in position. It was noted that, when the complex-wrapped dress was worn by an actress playing a priestess during a day's filming of a documentary on ancient Egypt, the back of the dress slumped into natural chevron-shaped folds as the linen relaxed on the body. Artists in ancient Egypt may have observed the same effect and translated the random fold lines into a more formal chevron pattern that pleased their artistic eye.

The Open-Front Dress

A third style of complex-wrapped dress is introduced here, and it is specifically different from the previously mentioned variations. It could be worn as an open-front over-dress (Figure 3.8) with or without an under-dress (Vogelsang-Eastwood 1993, 109–11). It is sometimes referred to as a cloak or mantel (Donovan 2003, 28), but over-dress is probably a better description of the garment as explained in the method for tying the dress in a fashion that makes it wearable (Figure 3.9). Both the previous dresses, unlike the open-fronted one, were portrayed in ancient Egyptian art as clothing that covered the body without actually revealing naked flesh. The woman's body (Figure 3.3, Nefertiti) was drawn or modelled as if the dress was semitransparent, but any details of nipples or pubic area were smoothed over to imply that a suitable garment was worn underneath (Robins 1997, 150). The open-front dress was different. This form of dress was worn in celebration by young women attending sumptuous

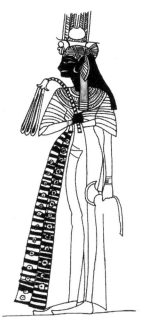

Figure 3.8 Queen Ahmose-Nefertari, wife of Ahmose and mother of Amenhotep I, shown wearing an open-front dress with very long floral sash. Her cult continued into the Ramesside era; this painting was made 400 years after her death in Dynasty 20. British Museum EA37994. (drawing by Janet Johnstone)

banquets; by women of all ages from the royal household as a sign of their status and position in religious and royal rituals, particularly in the Amarna period (Davies 1906, pl. 31; Green 1992; Westendorf 1968, 141); and by mourning women and girls at funerals. All three examples illustrate the use of clothing as an expression of high emotion. Noblewomen and women from the royal court wore this dress at banquets, ceremonies, funerals, and celebrations in differing degrees of undress as a demonstration of drunkenness, euphoria, religious fervour, and grief. Mourning women undid their dresses, tied them below their breasts, and left them open as an expression of inconsolable grief that cared nothing for physical appearance. The disarrangement of their clothing and hair and the lack of concern for their nakedness exemplified the moments of madness that accompany such profound emotions. It was apparent that their clothing was ruined as they poured dust over their heads and hair and tore at their garments. A scene of the funeral entourage from the Dynasty 19 tomb of Raia shows that all the mourning women have tied their dresses under their breasts with a sash, but only the lead mourner has exposed her breasts (Martin 1985, pl. 20 and 22). The rest of the women have arranged the top of the dress to just cover their breasts, striking a contrast between the lamenting leader and her more reserved companions.

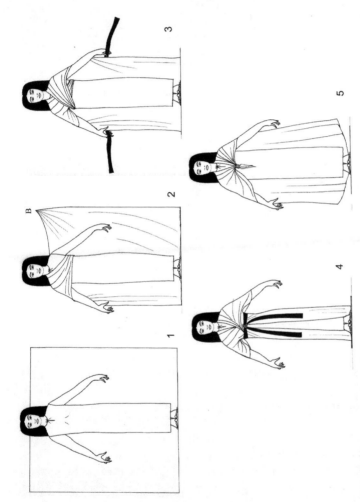

Figure 3.9 Open-front dress. (1) The cloth is placed behind the body. (2) Corner A is passed over the right shoulder diagonally across the front of the body to the left armpit. (3) Corner B is pulled over the left shoulder to the right armpit. Both corners are pulled around to the back and knotted together. (4) A sash is tied under the breasts, and the front of the dress is arranged into shape. (5) The simplest form of this dress was just a shawl tied around the shoulders or top of the arms. (drawing by Janet Johnstone)

The method of tying the dress is obviously very simple (Figure 3.9). In its basic form it is just a rectangle of cloth tied around the neck or shoulders like a cape. But its lack of structure and secured placement proves the dress is out of control. It moves about, it falls backward and flaps forward and looks untidy and chaotic; it is worn as a physical demonstration of the wearer's heightened emotional state, whether she feels elated in party spirit or lost in deep grief. In contrast, the royal women of Amarna tied the shawl around their shoulders or let it slip down to the upper arms (Arnold 1996, *passim*) and controlled its wayward nature with a long coloured sash tied under the breasts with a double knot. The queen or the heiress to the throne alone wore the red sash, and its significance was highly potent and steeped in ritual (Aldred 1991, ill. 72). A wider version of the red sash was worn by the goddesses Isis, Hathor, and Nut as seen on the painted walls of the burial chamber in Tutankhamun's tomb. Similarly, Tutankhamun's queen, Ankhesenamun, wears a double red sash tied around an open-front dress on the little Golden Shrine (Carter no.108, Eaton-Krauss & Graefe 1985; Reeves 1994, 140*f*) from the king's tomb. The sash had a practical and a symbolic purpose that linked the women of the royal family with their counterparts in the realms of the gods (Calvert 2010). Even when the daughters of Akhenaten were shown naked in the tomb scenes from the tomb of Meryre (Davies 1903, pl. 26), the sash was either held in one hand by the princess or an attendant stood close by holding it near to the princess's body (Davies 1903, 11, 13).

The Late New Kingdom Dress—*mss* and Shawl

The complicated New Kingdom wrapped-dress system was supplanted by an elegant but more practical dress that was worn, if representations of women from this time are accurate and not merely artistic license, throughout the Ramesside period—that is, for over 220 years. The dress consisted of two garments; a *mss* or under-dress and a large shawl or over-dress. During Dynasty 18 the *mss* neck-hole was shaped like a key-hole with a slit below it which allowed the head to go through easily. The opening was then closed by two little linen thread or cord ties so that the *mss* neckline sat closely around the wearer's neck (Figure 3.1) (Johnstone 2009, 538*f*; see Kemp & Vogelsang-Eastwood 2001, 202*f*, for cut-out ovals of cloth attributed to *mss* construction found at the Workmen's Village, Amarna). The shawl was usually worn over the right shoulder and the top two corners (A and B) tied in a knot below the left breast (Figure 3.10).

The shawl formed a shoulder drape over the right arm, and the knotted edge drew the left side of the *mss* to the body creating a 'batwing sleeve', or rather a self-sleeve (Kozloff & Bryan 1992, 207) or a sleeve drape on the left side of the *mss*. The variety of dress styles based on the *mss* and shawl combination spans a period of time from Amenhotep II until the Ptolemaic era, a range of

Figure 3.10 Late New Kingdom dress. The shawl is placed over the shoulder and tied in a knot below the breast. (drawing by Janet Johnstone)

over a thousand years. In general there were three variations of the *mss* and shawl dress (Johnstone 2009, 539):

1. Dress with one arm covered and a shoulder drape
2. Dress with both arms covered and a shoulder drape
3. Dress with one or both arms covered, no shoulder drape

Vandier makes the distinction between the shawl covering the left or right arms or both arms (Vandier 1958, 501), a distinction that is supported by the clothing analysis undertaken by the author on clothing represented on stelae from the Salakhana Trove (Duquesne 2009). The cache of over 600 stelae and other objects from the tomb of Djefaihapy III in the necropolis on the Western mountain, Asyut, afford an unparalleled source of information of clothing styles worn by the people of Asyut from mid-Dynasty 18 into the Ptolemaic Period. The majority of the stelae are Ramesside and display many variations of the *mss* and shawl dress style under discussion here (Figure 3.11).

The complex-wrapped dress style of the Amarna period was truly a display of conspicuous consumption (Bell 1976, 29), flaunting layers of expensive fine linen as a manifestation of wealth and social power. It also reflected the

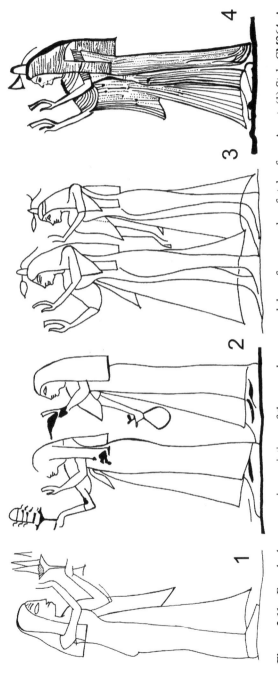

Figure 3.11 Female donors wearing variations of the complex-wrapped dress from a cache of stelae from Asyut. (1) Stela CM264. A chantress in a dress with a shoulder drape, Dynasty 18. (2) Stela CM200. Both women are chantresses and sisters; their dresses are tied under the breasts to control the fabric, and only one arm is covered, Late Dynasty 18. (3) Stela CM039, *nbt-pr*. Both women have both arms covered, Late Dynasty 18. (4) Stela CM018. The Chantress of Upwawet dedicated this stela in her own right; her pleated dress and shawl cover both her arms, and she has a shoulder drape, Late Dynasty 18. Taken from The Salakhana Trove (Johnstone 2009, 540, 551, 548, 546). (drawing by Janet Johnstone)

iconography of the Aten, wherein the rays fanned out and descended from the solar disc like the sunray pleating of the dresses; the wearers were imbued with the spirit of the god. The complex wrapped-dress style and iconography of the Aten are shown on a limestone slab in the Egyptian Museum, Cairo (Cairo RT.10.11.26.4), of Akhenaten, Nefertiti, and two daughters as they make offerings to the Aten as it streams down its rays to them (Robins 1997, 148, fig. 172). With the demise of Akhenaten and the return to the ancient belief system of a pantheon of gods, the clothing had to change both to rid the nobility of the stigma of any connection to the heretic king and to denounce the presence of the Aten from their lives. For women of all classes, the *mss* and the shawl style now came to reflect a simplified variation that combined archaising elements of the *mss* worn by both sexes pre-Amarna with the addition of a large shawl as a nod to the flattering shoulder drape seen on the flamboyantly styled Amarna complex-wrapped dress. The Amarna royal court and nobility's exclusion of themselves from society with their extreme dress had placed them farther outside the 'real' world of the majority of Egyptians. The adoption of the *mss* and shawl dress by the people, the wealthy, and the workers alike proved to be a visual means by which they were drawn into a closer identity. This dress, in its small way, helped to unify and solidify Egyptian identity both within Egypt and on the world stage. It was worn by the wealthy and the less privileged, as demonstrated by the array of donors from the Salakhana stelae. This very Egyptian style of clothing held prominence into the Ptolemaic period.

The Third Intermediate Period to Late Period Dress—*mss* and Shawl

The *mss* and shawl dress underwent a significant change during the Third Intermediate Period (1069 B.C.E.) into the Late Period (747–525 B.C.E.) (Figure 3.12). Pictorial representations of women's dress from the Third Intermediate Period indicate that a large, floor-length *mss* with sleeves was worn similar in look to the dresses of Dynasties 19 and 20 (Figure 3.13). The dress style shortened to mid-calf length rather than floor length during Dynasty 25 and was sometimes decorated with wide, dark-coloured borders around the hem and down the side seams of the *mss* and on the edge of the shawl (Figure 3.12, right). The shawl was still worn with the dress, but its position was moved from the right shoulder to the left side. It was tied diagonally across the body going under the left arm and over the right shoulder (Johnstone 2009, 553).

This method of tying a shawl is unusual and does not appear to be an Egyptian mode of dress; it may indicate some foreign influence. Similarities with the Kushite cloak discussed by Hallmann (2007) would indicate a Kushite origin to this style. The simple relocation of the shawl imbued the classic Egyptian dress with Kushite dress styling echoing the foreign influence

Figure 3.12 *Left*: Third Intermediate Period dress comprising a *mss* and a shawl. *Right*: Painted stela of Hotepamun. The lines of the painting are stylised, but the top edge of the shawl can be seen diagonally across the chest from the left armpit to the right shoulder, where the two top corners of the shawl meet and are tied together. British Museum, Dynasty 25, BM8453. (drawing by Janet Johnstone)

on the sociopolitical status in Egypt at the time. Men's clothing from Dynasty 25–26 returned to the short wrap-around kilt and belt sometimes worn with a longer transparent kilt over the top with strong archaising elements from the Old Kingdom. Interestingly, men sometimes wore a wide shoulder sash, which went over the left shoulder with the ends tucked into the right front and back of the kilt waist (Taylor 2003, 101, figs. 1, 6, 7, 8). Occasionally, this sash was shown worn very high under the left armpit so that it encircled the chest and right shoulder. This wrapping technique follows the same line as the placement of the top edge of the women's shawl when tied into position over the *mss*.

The Experience of Wearing a Complex-Wrapped Dress

A number of points emerged from the experimental work conducted while the author was working on film sets and observing ancient Egyptian replica clothing worn in production:

- All the complex-wrapped dresses were very flattering to wear. They suited all ages of women; all sizes and shapes and were easy to wear.

Figure 3.13 Painted stela of Djeamunesankh before Re-Horakhti, Dynasty 22 (Egyptian Museum Cairo © Egyptology Picture Library)

- The dresses needed only some adjustment after the wearer had exerted herself through energetic movement—that is, running, dancing, and walking. The complex-wrapped dress (2) needed more attention, but it stayed stable for longer if it was arranged on the wearer by a good dresser and tied tightly in place. None of the dresses came completely undone or fell off!
- The broad collar necklace worn with the complex wrapped dress (2) (Figure 3.3) acted as a weight and stabiliser controlling the top of the dress and keeping the shoulder drape from slipping down the arm. Similarly, the open-front dress needed the weight of the broad collar to anchor the

fabric in place especially around the back of the neck, where it was quite bulky.

- When I was dressing the wearer, the make-up was put on first followed by the dress, then the jewellery, sandals, and hand-held accessories. The dress alone had little visual impact and was initially disappointing when the wearer stood waiting for her hair and jewellery to be applied. Only when the woman was fully dressed was the full effect realised. The white linen dress was merely a vehicle to carry all the body decoration and ornaments; it was the perfect white canvas.
- The women found the dresses comfortable, but they were conscious of the elegance and feel of the dress at all times. Most of the wearers stood tall and walked gracefully, thereby modelling the dress to its full potential.
- When asked to describe their experience of wearing an ancient Egyptian dress, wearers used comments such as 'feeling otherworldly', 'do not recognise myself in the mirror', 'powerful', 'removed from my surroundings', 'beautiful'.
- The combination of the white dress, long black hair, polychromic jewellery, and gold, strong black eye make-up and red lips focused the viewer's attention solely on the wearer's face. Every expression that played on the wearer's face was amplified and became a dramatic statement.

The study of ancient clothing construction opens many paths for further research. This chapter has focused on the practical interpretation of recreating New Kingdom dresses and has touched on other issues of importance. Ancient clothing systems or dress are an accessible means to how one sees the past. Because of film producers' need to create the past in the present, ancient clothing has been adapted as period costume for television and film productions. The combination of archaeology and theatre in the dramatic reconstruction scenes that accompany many ancient history documentaries opens a narrative with the past that may engage one audience while equally disengaging another. Knowing how an ancient civilisation dressed draws that civilisation closer to our own experience, but our knowledge is based on a few scant remains of ancient clothing, literary accounts, and a wealth of pictorial representations, which may or may not be a truthful representation of the individuals portrayed.

'Dress produces constant connection between the past and the present, but not in order to justify the relevance of the past to the present, or vice versa: rather, it founds its linkages upon such arbitrary and anachronistic premises that we are impelled to recognize a fundamental discontinuity between the two temporal dimensions and hence the gap between what we know, or think we know, and what we actually experience' (Cavallaro & Warwick 1998, 99). The New Kingdom dresses demonstrate that ancient dress had a theatrical character. The modern experience of wearing such clothing assumes a theatricality of its own whether the wearer is on a film set or standing quietly alone.

The final image should be of a group of ten young women dressed as members of the royal court of Akhenaten waiting on set for their next scene, each one dressed in exactly the same manner except for a touch of individualism in their jewellery. Their individual attire became a uniform; they looked at one another and saw a reflection of themselves and were bolstered by their beauty. The group dynamic was electric—this was true power dressing.

Acknowledgements

The author would like to thank Dr. Susanna Harris, Dr. Laurence Douny, Dr. Geoffrey Tassie, Rosalind Janssen, Dr. Susanna Thomas, and Janet Picton for their expertise and many discussions on areas raised in this chapter; Gill Pegram for her editorial skills; and Laura Holland for her extensive knowledge of clothing construction and inspiring discussions over many years. Thanks are due to the Griffith Institute, University of Oxford, for permission to publish Harry Burton's photographs and the staff and Friends of the Petrie Museum of Egyptian Archaeology for arranging the original demonstration of Wrapping and Tying New Kingdom Dresses as part of the Wrapping and Unwrapping the Body: Archaeological and Anthropological Perspectives conference, May 2010. All illustrations were drawn by Janet Johnstone.

References

Aldred, C. 1991. *Akhenaten, King of Egypt*. London: Thames and Hudson.
Arnold, D. 1996. *The Royal Women of Amarna: Images of Beauty from Ancient Egypt*. New York: Metropolitan Museum of Art.
Banerjee, M., & Miller, D. 2003. *The Sari*. Oxford: Berg.
Bell, Q. 1976. *On Human Finery*. London: Hogarth Press.
Bonnet, H. 1917. Die ägyptische Tracht bis zum Ende des neuen Reiches. Part of K. Sethe, ed., *Untersuchungen zur Geschichte und Altertumskunde Aegyptens 7*. Leipzig: J. C. Heinrichs'sche Buchhandlung.
Brack, A., & Brack, A. 1980. *Das Grab des Haremheb: Theben Nr.78*. Mainz am Rhein: Philipp von Zabern.
Bruyère, B. 1937. *Rapport sur les fouilles de Deir el Médineh (1934–1935) IIéme partie: la nécropole de l'est*. Fouilles de l'Institut français d'archéologie orientale du Caire 15. Cairo: Institut français d'archéologie orientale.
Calvert, A. 2010. The Red Looped Sash: An Enigmatic Element of Royal Regalia in Ancient Egypt, *http://artofcounting.com/2010/08/11/the-red-looped-sash-an-enigmatic-element-of-royal-regalia-in-ancient-egypt-part-1*, accessed November 18, 2010.
Carter, H. 2000 [1933]. *The Tomb of Tut.ankh.Amen: The Annexe and Treasury*, reprint. London: Duckworth.
Cavallaro, D., & Warwick, A. 1998. *Fashioning the Frame: Boundaries, Dress, and the Body*. Oxford: Berg.
Davies, N. de G. 1903. *The Rock Tombs of El Amarna, I*. London: Egypt Exploration Fund.

―――. 1906. *The Rock Tombs of El Amarna, IV*. London: Egypt Exploration Fund.

Donovan, L. 2003. Representations of Costume in New Kingdom Offering Bearer Scenes. *Bulletin of the Australian Centre for Egyptology 14*, pp. 7–37.

Duquesne, T. 2009. *The Salakhana Trove Votive Stelae and Other Objects from Asyut*. London: Darengo Publications.

Eaton-Krauss, M., & Graefe, E. 1985. *The Small Golden Shrine from the Tomb of Tutankhamen*. Oxford: Griffith Institute.

Green, L. 1992. Queen as Goddess: The Religious Role of Royal Women in the Late-Eighteenth Dynasty, *Amarna Letters: Essays on Ancient Egypt 2*. San Francisco: KMT Communications, pp. 28–41.

Hall, R. 2001. *Egyptian Textiles*, revised edition. Princes Risborough: Shire.

Hallmann, A. 2007. The 'Kushite Cloak' of Pekartor and Iriketakana: Novelty or Tradition? *JARCE 43*, pp. 15–27.

Houston, M. G. 2002 [1954]. *Ancient Egyptian, Mesopotamian and Persian Costume*, reprint. New York: Dover Publications Inc.

Ikram, S., & Dodson, A. 1998. *The Mummy in Ancient Egypt*. London: Thames and Hudson.

Janssen, J. J. 2008. *Daily Dress at Deir el-Medina—Words for Clothing*. London: Golden House Publications.

Johnstone, J. M. 2002. Clothes for the Living—Linen for the Dead: A *mss* Garment from the Egyptian Museum, Cairo. In M. Eldamaty & M. Trad, eds., *Egyptian Museum Collections around the World. I*, Cairo: Supreme Council of Antiquities, pp. 595–605.

―――. 2005. Dressing Nefertiti. *Ancient Egypt* 5:7.31. Manchester, pp. 40–44.

―――. 2009. Clothing Represented on the Salakhana Stelae. In T. Duquesne, S. A. Razek, E. S. Meltzer, J. M. Johnstone, & G. J. Tassie, *The Salakhana Trove Votive Stelae and Other Objects from Asyut*. London: Darengo Publications, pp. 537–601.

―――. In press. Practical Dressmaking for Ancient Egyptians: Making and Pleating Replica Ancient Egyptian Clothing. In C. Graves-Brown & K. Szpakowska, eds., *Experiment and Experience: Ancient Egypt in the Present*. Swansea: Classical Press of Wales.

Kemp, B. J., & Vogelsang-Eastwood, G. 2001. *The Ancient Textile Industry at Amarna*. London: Egypt Exploration Society.

Kozloff, A. P., & Bryan, B. M. 1992. *Egypt's Dazzling Sun: Amenhotep III and His World*. Cleveland: Cleveland Museum of Art.

Martin, G. T. 1985. *The Tomb-Chapels of Paser and Ra'ia at Saqqara*. London: Egypt Exploration Society.

―――. 1992. *The Hidden Tombs of Memphis: New Discoveries from the Time of Tutankhamun and Ramesses the Great*. London: Thames and Hudson.

Pinch, G. 1994. *Magic in Ancient Egypt*. London: British Museum Press.

Reeves, N. 1994. *The Complete Tutankhamun*. London: Thames and Hudson.

Robins, G. 1997. *The Art of Ancient Egypt*. London: British Museum Press.

Schiaparelli, E. 1927. *La Tomba intatta dell'architetto: Cha nella necropoli di Tebe*. Turin: R. Museo di Antichità.

Shedid, A. G. 1994. *Das Grab des Sennedjem: ein Künstlegrab der 19. Dynastie in Deir el Medineh*. Mainz am Rhein: Philipp von Zabern.

Tassie, G. J. 2009. The Hairstyles Represented on the Salakhana Stelae. In T. Duquesne, S. A. Razek, E. S. Meltzer, J. M. Johnstone, & G. J. Tassie, *The Salakhana Trove Votive Stelae and Other Objects from Asyut*. London: Darengo Publications, pp. 459–536.

Taylor, J. H. 2003. Theban Coffins from the Twenty-Second to the Twenty-Sixth Dynasty: Dating and Synthesis of Development. In N. Studwick & J. H. Taylor, eds., *The Theban Necropolis: Past, Present and Future*. London: British Museum Press.

Tilke, M. 1990. *Costume Patterns and Designs*. New York: Rizzoli International Publications.

Vandier, J. 1958. *Manuel d'Archéologique Égyptienne III*. Paris: A. and J. Picard.

Vogelsang-Eastwood, G. M. 1993. *Pharaonic Egyptian Clothing*. Studies in Textile and Costume History 2. Leiden: Brill.

———. 1997. *Tutankhamun: Textiles and Clothing in the Egyptian Museum, Cairo*. Rotterdam: van Doorn.

———. 1999. *Tutankhamun's Wardrobe: Garments from the Tomb of Tutankhamun*. Rotterdam: van Doorn.

———. 2006. Textiles. In P. T. Nicholson & I. Shaw, eds., *Ancient Egyptian Materials and Technology*. Cambridge: Cambridge University Press, pp. 268–98.

Westendorf, W. 1968. *Painting, Sculpture and Architecture of Ancient Egypt*. New York: Harry N. Abrams. Inc.

Zoffili, E. 1991. *Costume e Cultura dell'Antico Egitto da Narmer a Cleopatra*. Milan: Fabbri, Visual Books, Libri d'immagine.

4   Reconceptualising Shapes and Bodies: Conservation of an English Eighteenth-Century Court Mantua for the Victoria and Albert Museum Galleries

Titika Malkogeorgou

Textiles and bodies have, historically, been significantly and intricately linked with wrapping. Unfolding such practices can allow us to examine social relationships and to achieve a better understanding of the interplay of aesthetic choices, social conventions, and the body's physical transformations. When dealing with historic garments, one is able to project oneself back into the different 'ideal' body, a changing social construct, and fashions in movement. Bodies can be wrapped in textiles either for protection or display, or to preserve or alter the human shape. But it is the ephemeral, fragile nature of the body's survival, and the damage caused by the wrapping itself, that renders the possible connection between wrapping body practices and social practices vague and elusive. The eighteenth-century mantua, colloquially known as the Christie dress, provides an insight into dressmaking and its significance for both the female body and for social practices. Its conservation story offers us an insight into the way that bodies have been transformed through the centuries via their relationship with garments, a process that is practically documented on the garments themselves. And through them can come insights into how social conventions have been conceptualised, reconceptualised, and made visible.

The mantua, one of the most exquisite objects on display in the British Galleries of the Victoria and Albert Museum (the V&A), is remarkable because of its survival. A court mantua is a woman's formal dress developed

Wrapping and Unwrapping Material Culture: Archaeological and Anthropological Perspectives by Susanna Harris & Laurence Douny, 83–96 © 2014 Left Coast Press, Inc. All rights reserved.

in the seventeenth century that reached its peak in terms of elaboration and design during the eighteenth century. It typically served to demonstrate the distinction and wealth of women of, or associated with, the court. The court mantua consists of a gown and petticoat made of cream silk, embroidered with colour silks and silver metal thread in a floral rococo design. The gown is pleated from the upper back to the waist and has embroidered robings, cuffs, and a border to the train, which drapes upward to form basques and a tail. Mantuas, and especially mantuas in their authentic state, are extremely rare. What has survived together with the dress are the shapes and the bodies of its previous owners—and a biography that can be traced back through what has been learned from descriptions of its conservation treatment. By learning about the mantua's journey and tracing its original shape during conservation, past relationships and practices of covering, shaping, and displaying the body are reexamined. A connection is made to its original wearers through the aesthetics of display, in terms not only of a connection to a past way of life but also through the subsequent reconstructions of the one same dress, of the changing body through time (Figure 4.1).

The mantua was constructed on the body of the person it was made for originally and was intended for a specific celebration or event. The mantua reveals, conceals, enhances, artificially alters, and displays the body of someone

Figure 4.1 Front view of the Christie dress after the 2001 conservation treatment and remounting (© Victoria and Albert Museum, London)

participating in either a special ceremony or a formal social event. Everyday activities such as movement and positioning oneself in space and time have a social meaning and are socially constructed. The mantua's power as a luxurious garment is that it offers a material link with social identity and, in its construction of identity and in its various transformations, highlights what is valued in social interactions with others.

Hansen writes about 'the special power of clothing' (Hansen 2003, 303) and the sensation of the dressed body that can be unique—a quality, however, that is hard to pin down, because sensation is a product of the moment, and, as such, it vanishes as soon as it is experienced, because it is context-dependent. As expressions of the individual and of social identity, dressmaking and dress-wearing mediate collective identities and desires (Hoskins 1998; Turner 1980). Between Appadurai's *Social Life of Things* (1986) and Friedman's argument that 'things do not have social lives. Rather social life has things' (1991, 161) lie the properties of clothes and the strategies that people use to present themselves in the social domain and to achieve advantages in the way they interact with others; all these activities are linked and take many forms: 'the softness and ultimate fragility of these materials capture the vulnerability of humans, whose every relationship is transient subject to the degenerative process of illness death and decay' (Weiner & Schneider 1989, 2).

The experiential dimension to dress, in making, wearing, and viewing—and how meaning and value are ascribed—is a material process that, by being ephemeral, is inevitably connected to the 'social death of things' (Hansen 2003, 303). This is the kind of death that conservation practices try not so much to reverse as to transcend in order to recreate something that otherwise would be lost (Brandi 2005; Munoz-Vinas 2005; Stanley-Price 1996).

Mauss, in his famous essay 'The Notion of Body Techniques', describes how mundane bodily activities, as well as the use of everyday things, are historically and socially constructed (1979). In the 'anthropology of technology' there is a further exploration of the ways that bodies and the related material around them are extensions of each other (Lemonnier 1992). Reconceptualising and reconstructing a historic dress through conservation is a reliable method to use to unpick those very relationships and hence to discover how wrapping the body is documented both in the fabrics themselves and in the changing effect that those fabrics have on bodies.

The Mantua and the V&A Museum Collections

The Christie dress has been on display since its acquisition. But in 1971 and 1983 it was taken back into the textiles conservation studio to be reassessed and reassembled, and in 2001 it was conserved with the express purpose of being redisplayed in the British Galleries. It was, in the mid-1990s, the biggest project that the V&A had undertaken in fifty years.

Figure 4.2 Front view of the Christie dress, 1971 reconstruction and mounting (© Victoria and Albert Museum, London)

The mantua was purchased in 1969 for the highest recorded price (1,300 pounds) paid for an item of English dress at the time. It became part of the very rapidly expanding Furniture, Textiles, and Fashion Department (known as the Textiles Department until 1986, when it became Textiles and Dress), which currently holds more than 62,000 objects (Figure 4.2).

The history of dress, however, was not among the list of recognised disciplines when the V&A was founded, and so the fashion and textiles collection developed in a sporadic fashion. Therefore, the mantua became a rare yet popular piece of clothing forming part of a collection that is still being developed. The mantua is both of historical importance and of the highest quality in terms of its material and manufacture. 'It is of great beauty and of aesthetic significance, it contributes to the history of arts, crafts and design, and very importantly it sheds light on other objects in the collections' (V&A Museum Acquisition Plan 2003).

Surviving eighteenth-century garments are extremely unrepresentative, because clothes performed such different roles, and their survival is rare for a variety of reasons. In his book *The Dress of the People* John Styles writes about the clothing of the poor, the working class, and the servants of the eighteenth century. For evidence of what that material was like, one has to look mainly to literature, the paintings of the time, and the criminal records of the theft of clothes (Styles 2008). Such surviving costumes are rare, because they were worn, reworn, and adapted until they fell apart into rags.

By contrast, the mantua is believed to have been created to be worn just once, at a specific court event, possibly by Isabella Courtenay (Kite and Cogram 2006, 111)—yet it was remade over time. It was all about being seen and about participating in and performing a social role. Most early acquisitions of dress at the V&A were made because of the importance of the textiles used. And only in the later 1970s did the collection of fashion and accessories come to be seen as one of the department's major responsibilities. It is difficult, too, to pinpoint precisely how such a dress would once have looked, given that garments and organic material deteriorate easily and that the different parts of composite objects decompose at different speeds.

But in the eighteenth century, clothes were made on the body of the specific person for whom the garment was created, rather than on a flat surface, as is the case with later clothes, though patterns were used (interview with textile conservators, June 2008). Moreover, eighteenth-century dresses were not expected to be worn directly next to the body but on top of a corseted body. Such a body was already shaped rigorously by a corset and therefore already transformed to perform a social function in which it would serve as an almost static representation of wealth and social significance.

Aesthetically, although a dress may transform the body in an artificial way as it wraps around it, it has evolved from the body itself, contrary to the mass-produced objects created in a way divorced from actual bodies, only later fitted onto them. But it is significant that the mantua dress survived and was acquired by the museum without its corset: there is a link missing between the original shape of the dress and the way the eighteenth-century body was shaped by the garment. Instead, the dress was purchased in its nineteenth- or early twentieth-century reconstruction, when, it is believed, it was worn as fancy dress, loosely and nonchalantly reconnecting its wearer to ancient wealth and the rituals of power and exclusivity. Museum conservators explained to me that, although the Christie dress lacked certain documentation, there are a number of other mantuas in the V&A collections that are documented through pictures showing their owners wearing them at fancy dress parties.

Therefore, when conservators saw the round shape that the mantua had when purchased, they were able to make an informed assessment that the mantua was an original eighteenth-century garment reshaped into a nineteenth-century dress, and one that would almost certainly have been used with additional accessories. It is not known whether any original or later accessories survived. What is certain is that the dress, when purchased, was as it is now displayed. It is possible that this was a dress that had once been created for a formal occasion but was later refashioned for use in a less formal but nevertheless exclusive setting. The mantua had been transformed and by that act had transformed the very bodies that inhabited it, thus creating a direct link between one body and another. Moreover, it retained a physical connection to someone who created, or aspired to create, a powerful social presence through the legitimacy it provided.

Wearer, context, and manufacture all contribute to the creation of meaning and the transmission of legitimacy. The conservators who worked on the mantua explain that the dress shows evidence of having been embroidered by a number of apprentices, whose different hands can be detected in the changing technical standards, while the design of the drawing appears in places to have evolved rather than to have been consciously created. The cloth was not painted before the embroidery was done; instead, the pattern evolved, alternating colour and design with the stitching. These are the sort of details that can be unearthed only through physical engagement with the garment, an engagement enhanced through the conservation treatment and its hands-on approach.

Approaches to Treatment in Relation to Body Techniques

The mantua, acquired in a relatively good condition but already altered extensively, was among a group of objects that were being reassessed as a result of the gallery refurbishment when the Court Dress Galleries were turned into the V&A British Galleries. During the mantua's first treatment in 1971, it was necessary to tidy up some of the earlier conservation measures, and when the conservator looked at the dress she decided that alterations were also needed to its shape. The dress was altered once again in 1983 before going on display in the Court Dress Galleries. Details of this second intervention are not documented either in the Textiles Conservation studio or in the V&A database system, but it is safe to assume, from photographic evidence, that the structure and appearance of the dress were changed once again (Figure 4.3).

Dore describes the approach to the early conservation treatment as a quest to return to an earlier condition using the material evidence available. This process would link the dress as it was when purchased from Christie's to the original owner and to the social context that produced both the dress and the body of the original wearer: 'In the Victoria and Albert Museum the rule is that, if at all possible, the garment will be returned to its earliest condition—providing there is sufficient left to make a reasonably complete whole, and the alterations are not in themselves of historical importance' (Dore 1978, 2). This process also involves an interpretation and a verification of the subsequent interventions and of the social conditions that created them. Because the dress had already been altered a few times before it reached the museum, the conservator and curator found themselves with a very different object from the original on their hands.

Figure 4.3 Front view of the 1983 reconstruction and mounting (© Victoria and Albert Museum, London)

> Now remember the thing had been altered several times before it came here . . .
> they would have come to a conclusion then when they would have looked at it
> again, 10–12 years later different conclusions would have come to. I think they
> would look at it again from the point of view of the evidence and the accuracy
> of the interpretation looking at the pleat marks, trying and get it back to what
> it was: 1745? Its earlier date. (interview with textile conservators, June 2008)

At this stage, the focus of the treatment was still to uncover the mantua's
original state. At the same time, it was also acknowledged that the dress would
always resist interpretation, both because of its physical condition and because
it had once belonged to another time and place.

The approach that guided treatment in the 1971 interpretation of the mantua was based on the idea of revealing a more authentic object, according to
the original thread and stitching and 'ignoring any subsequent threads used'
(Dore 1978, 4). The overall shape of the dress was changed from round to
oval based on the relationship between pocket slits and the back opening; the
various horizontal waist lines; and stitch marks, rub-marks, and the various

pleat marks. The conservator tried to smooth out the creases without losing sight of the pleat lines 'to support damaged and weak areas of the petticoat and gown, to make them safe for redisplay; and to reconstruct and remount the mantua as accurately as possible to its deduced original 1740s form' (Kite & Cogram 2006, 117). Dressmaking knowledge and conservation ethics, which are mainly concerned with the condition of an object and the information that can be gained from an understanding of the materials and any damage present, are both part of a conservation practice that painstakingly tries to rediscover the earliest form of a dress.

Redundant creases and folds hold a great deal of information that risks being eliminated in the process of conservation, thereby weakening the idea of connectedness that is evoked by the dress. Throughout the smoothing-out process, conservators had to be careful about not removing pleats and crease marks, in order not to lose the evidence about the mantua's original shape or later remodelling. These processes were repeated sufficiently enough to improve the overall condition of the dress without affecting its creases and lines.

When the dress came into the conservation studio in 2001 for treatment, the conservators involved say that they had no preconceived ideas about which approach to use: 'when it came off display we weren't happy at all with the interpretation. We were not happy with the proportions—it had a de-lined element. It was too stretched and the proportions weren't logical for a piece of costume of that date' (interview with textile conservators, June 2008).

Attention was drawn to the front centre of the mantua and to a seam running down through the middle. This made conservators question the overall structure of the dress. The existing stitching would not retain the original thread or sewing technique, even though it might still be based on the original stitch holes. For example, in the 2001 treatment, the sewing threads used to couch were found to be polyester and therefore undisputedly twentieth century in origin. Through the process of unpicking the fabric, it was revealed that the robings would have lain flat against the bodice of the gown, thus allowing the full width of the design to show without the embroidery being interrupted by the fold.

On close examination, it was possible to identify the original turnings and stitch holes on the fabric, because the fold line would not have cut through the embroidery. The fabric would not originally have been entirely embroidered and then covered up by the robings. This latter effect would have been a later reconstruction designed to make the garment fit a different body shaped in a different way. And this transformation of the dress, therefore, would have marked not only a different time, space, and place but also a different wearer and a different social occasion. Understanding the manufacture of the garment can offer insights into fashion and a method whereby one can uncover human relationships.

Only the visible areas of the dress were embroidered. Unlike with contemporary mass-produced fabrics, the design and cut of the dress predetermined the type of material used and how it was arranged. And it was observed that the embroidery had been cut up and recut and that panels had been turned the other way. Although originally made for a specific occasion, the dress was then reshaped for subsequent wearers for different occasions and shaped on different bodies. And therefore not only was the dress transforming the body of the wearer but the wearer was also dictating how the cloth should be rearranged.

The way the embroidered fabric was folded over indicated that the garment had been reassembled in a way that did not match the dress as it had originally been put together. By tracing the fold line and seeing how the pleats matched in the way they had been put back on to the bodice, the conservators were able to spot the mistakes that had been made. They therefore took the decision, in accordance with their conservation ethics, to take these pleats apart. And, indeed, none of the original stitching was found in the process of unpicking the pleats, thus confirming that this work was a later intervention.

In their 2006 article, Kite and Cogram explain how, when deconstructing the gown and petticoat, they could observe three clear lines made by the holes left by the stitching when earlier threads had been removed. They believe that these three lines running through the dress represent three previous reconstructions; and they also think that there may have been more, now no longer clearly identifiable. The dress was unpicked and put on a flat working surface. Thus the dress itself had to become flat in the conservation studio before it could take on its current shape, thereby enabling the reconceptualisation of its original form and thereby also reconceputalising a completely different, original body shape.

The stitch lines demonstrated three subsequent reconstructions probably dating to the 1740s, 1780s, and the nineteenth century; the last reconstruction is believed to have involved turning the dress into a fancy dress that was probably pleated up into a circle. A weave analysis of the panels also demonstrated that they were indeed made of original eighteenth-century fabric. The petticoat consists of seven embroidered panels and a single plain panel. The proposed sequence of creating the dress is as follows:

> First, the plain silk looms widths would be sewn together to give the full width of the fabric that was to be embroidered to make the petticoat . . . a single cut would have been made. . . . The ground fabric would then be folded back to make the V-shaped centre front waist shaping. . . . Once the embroidery was finished, the petticoat would have been removed from the frame, sewn up, draped over a pannier and pleated into the required shape. If a plain silk panel was required at the back of the petticoat, which would be unseen by the wearer and covered by the train, or if a plain silk panel was required to be incorporated . . . it would have been cut and stitched in at the point of making up. (Kite & Cogram 2006, 114)

In the previous reconstructions, the plain panel at the back was not given the same importance as the rest of the dress; thus it was tucked under and joined inside the embroidery, both in the earlier museum intervention and in the nineteenth-century reconstruction. In the two previous conservation treatments, therefore, the plain panel of the petticoat was considered to be a later addition and was assumed to be a replacement for a missing embroidered panel. Neither the 1970s nor the 1980s interventions looked at the weave, the stitch line of the panel, or the selvage, because it was a plain fabric: 'no one had really looked at it technically' (interview with textile conservators, June 2008).

The stitch line is significant because there is only one line of stitching; it had not been remade and was therefore original to the dress. When the curator looked at the selvage (the edge of the fabric), she was able to confirm that it was original and matched the fabric of the rest of the dress. There were no other holes, and there were bits of the original eighteenth-century stitching still left in place. Furthermore, the robings of the bodice went all the way down the back. The conservator said that 'you wouldn't have a glorious embroidery that no one could see' (interview with textile conservators, June 2008).

The whole shape of the dress is determined by the presence of the plain fabric at the back and, it is now therefore known that this fabric formed part of the original design of the dress rather than being a later addition to replace a missing piece (Figure 4.4).

The textile conservators who had to decide how to treat the mantua asked themselves: how would it have been made; how would it have been set up on its frame; how would it have wrapped around the body; and how would it have been constructed in the first place? They used their own physical experience of working with textiles in their own practice to answer these questions. They concluded that, initially, everything would have been drawn out and set up on the frame, ready for the embroidering at the embroidery workshop. Once the embroidery had been completed, all parts would have been cut off the frame. Next, but probably several months later, another bolt of the cloth would have been found, one with the same weave but with (necessarily, because it was a different bolt of the cloth) a different selvage.

According to the conservator, 'it really is important when you're dealing with a historic costume to understand how it was made' (interview with textile conservators, June 2008). The conservators' job is to be able to use the material evidence to understand the original act of manufacture: 'We worked with what was there' (interview with textile conservators, June 2008).

Within this paradigm lies the idea that the material of the object contains all the information you will need to understand it: 'We could look at other mantuas, but they wouldn't necessarily tell us what we need to know about this one. You can only really get information by actually looking at the object in front of you. That gives you all the information you need to know' (interview with textile conservators, June 2008).

Figure 4.4 Side view of the Christie mantua after the 2001 conservation treatment and remounting (© Victoria and Albert Museum, London)

A new mannequin had to be created, too, for every conservation treatment and interpretation of the dress. The mannequin is itself an extension of the dress and a mechanical reconstruction of the body that once inhabited the dress; together, they give the sense of the three-dimensional body. It is important to understand both that the petticoat sits on the hips rather than on the waist, a detail that dictates how the body looks and moves, and that the mannequin had to be made robust enough to carry the full weight of the dress, awkwardly distributed as it was, for a number of years, during which the dress would be handled as little as possible.

The mannequin had also to be adjustable because, until the dress was mounted, conservators could not possibly know precisely how tall each section would have to be in order to fit the whole. But they knew that the dress would have to show the feet. With such a complicated dress, getting the mannequin through the door meant moving it sideways, measuring the legs, and pleating the dress up and placing it over the hips without tripping over it. All these steps were impossible to calculate until the dress was actually 'worn'. Each reconstruction of the mantua called for a new mannequin.

All original 1740s mantuas known anywhere in the world have been altered through time. As far as the Christie mantua is concerned, more information has been revealed each time the dress has been treated by conservators. Furthermore, on each of these occasions, additional stitching marks have been added to parts of the dress. Whenever possible, conservators have used the original stitch holes, but additional sewing was necessary in 1971, 1983, and 2001. And there is a constant reminder of trying to put oneself into a position of understanding not only how the dress was created originally but also its journey from its inception through to the time it reached the museum conservation studio and since. Subsequent transformations of the dress and its wearers are also intrinsically part of the garment, and they need to be preserved as much as possible, and to be examined, in the process of conservation treatment.

The key advantage of considering how an object that lacks full documentation was made is that it becomes possible to start unpicking its appearance with some degree of confidence and without the need to consider too much any aesthetic or literary reference. There are paintings and designs of the period that indicate how such a dress might have looked, and there are also the other mantuas in the museum's collections (and some, not always complete, museum documentation)—but according to the textile conservators, none of these resources seemed to be able to give the kind of information they were looking for, the kind that would help them to reconceptualise this particular dress and, by extension, all that it signifies.

Conclusion

Purchased through Christie's auction house, the eighteenth-century English court mantua in the V&A's British Galleries is one of the most important and complete eighteenth-century embroidered mantuas known. When the Christie mantua came into the V&A Museum in 1969 as part of the Furniture, Textiles, and Fashion Department collections, it had a round shape that encouraged the belief that it was a nineteenth-century reconstruction worn by an English noblewoman for a fancy dress event. Taken into the museum's textile conservation studio, it was conserved and reinterpreted a number of times. In the process, its earlier transformations were revealed, and the different bodies that had once inhabited the dress were rediscovered, together with details of its manufacturing process. Three previous reconstructions were clearly identified from the stitch holes left on the mantua's fabric when the dress was worn by the different wearers; this stitching would have transformed their bodies as they wore the mantua to different events.

Indeed, the point of the 2001 intervention is that for the very first time the focus was on how the dress had been made and, consequently, on how it was worn, rather than on the purely material evidence. Throughout the conservation process, the emphasis was on manufacture and the original social context that had created the dress in the first place.

By virtue of empathy toward the craftspeople who initially made the mantua, conservators are able to feel the effect of the mantua on the body and the way this effect was intentionally produced by the dressmakers. Thus, an understanding of body techniques in relation to making and wearing the mantua adds a new layer of interpretation to the conservators' technical knowledge and experience with the dress's appearance and its survival history.

As a method of finding out about ourselves and about the world around us, the study of a historic dress involves looking into the practice of wrapping the body as well as unwrapping the actual practices that made such wrapping possible. Thus social relationships can be revealed through materials and their properties, opening up explicit ways to connect with the past. The mantua, created as a display of power and importance in a particular sociopolitical sphere, shaped an original body by transforming it in an artificial way. The dress was then reconstructed and used again by subsequent wearers who wanted to draw power and reaffirmation from it. At a different time and in a different space, it was inhabited and reshaped until it reached the V&A Museum display, mounted on a series of mannequins representing those early reconstructions.

Through the conservation of the mantua for the V&A Museum Galleries, a process of reconceptualisation of the role of textiles in relation to the transformation of the body has taken place. Conservation techniques and processes of historic garments allow the creation of different bodies, different shapes, and different relationships. Unpicking the process of conservation unearths a complex relationship between dressmaker, garment, and wearer. And, through that relationship, strategies emerge to connect to the past and to a social context that is both time and place specific, a transmission of the power of earlier peoples.

References

Appadurai, A. (ed.) 1986. *The Social Life of Things: Commodities in Cultural Perspective*. Cambridge: Cambridge University Press.

Brandi, C. 2005. *Theory of Restoration: Cesare Brandi*. Edited by Giuseppe Basile, translated by Cynthia Rockwell, presentations by Giuliano Urbani, Nicholas Stanley-Price, and Caterina Bon Valsassina [Teoria del restauro 1963], Firenze: Nardini.

Dore, J. 1978. The Conservation of Two Eighteenth-Century English Court Mantuas. *Studies in Conservation,* Vol. 23, *The Journal of the International Institute for Conservation*, pp. 1–14.

E.C.C.O. 2003. *European Confederation of Conservator-Restorers' Organisation Professional Guidelines II Codes of Ethics*, http://www.ecco-eu.org/about-e.c.c.o./professional-guidelines.html, accessed July 30, 2013.

Friedman, J. 1991. Consuming Desires: Strategies of Selfhood and Appropriation. In *Cultural Anthropology* 6(2), pp. 154–63.

Hansen, K. T. 2003. Fashioning Zambian Moments. In *Journal of Material Culture* 8(3), pp. 301–09.

Hoskins, J. 1998. *Biographical Objects: How Things Tell the Stories of Peoples' Lives.* New York: Routledge.

Kite, M., & Cogram, A. 2006. Re-evaluation and Retreatment: The Conservation and Remounting of an English Court Mantua. In *Studies in Conservation*, Vol. 51, *The Journal of the International Institute for Conservation*, pp. 111–22.

Lemonnier, P. 1992. *Elements for an Anthropology of Technology.* Michigan: University of Michigan.

Mauss, M. 1979. The Notion of Body Techniques. In M. Mauss, ed., *Sociology and Psychology Essays.* London: Routledge & Kegan Paul, pp. 97–105.

Munoz-Vinas, S. 2005. *Contemporary Theory of Conservation.* Oxford: Butterworth-Heinemann.

Stanley-Price, N. (ed.) 1996. *Historical and Philosophical Issues in the Conservation of Cultural Heritage.* Los Angeles: Getty Conservation Institute.

Styles, J. 2008. *The Dress of the People: Everyday Fashion in Eighteenth Century England.* Princeton, NJ: Yale University Press.

Turner, T. S. 1980. The Social Skin. In J. Cerfas & R. Lewin, eds., *Not Work Alone: A Cross-Cultural View of Activities Superfluous to Survival.* London: Temple Smith, pp. 112–40.

V&A Mission Statement. 2009. *Victoria and Albert Museum Annual Report and Accounts 2008–2009.* http://www.official-documents.gov.uk/document/hc0809/hc07/0790/0790.pdf.

V&A Museum Acquisition Plan. 2003. media.vam.ac.uk/media/documents/legacy_documents/.../26984_file.doc, accessed 2010.

Weiner, A. B. &, Schneider, J. (eds.) 1989. *Cloth and the Human Experience.* Washington, D.C.: Smithsonian Books.

5 Wrapping and Unwrapping the Body: Lace, Magic, and Modernity

Nicolette Makovicky

In October 2003, lace makers from the remote village of Koniaków, southern Poland, found themselves on the cover of the Polish weekly *Wysoke Obczasy*. Although these craftswomen are famous across Poland for their delicate lace doilies, tablecloths, and ecclesiastical textiles, the lead story in the magazine covered a surprising innovation from their ranks—handmade, crocheted G-strings—along with the controversy and schism their success had apparently caused within the community. The cover featured a young lady in tight jeans and a T-shirt, a pair of Koniaków lace G-strings clearly visible against the few centimetres of skin between the top of her trousers and the hem of her shirt (Figure 5.1).

This article was the start-gun for a veritable media frenzy. From *Gazeta Wyborcza* to *Le Monde* and *The Wall Street Journal*, Koniaków's lace makers found themselves the subject of numerous light-hearted articles that pitched older generations of lace makers against a younger, ostensibly more entrepreneurially minded set of artisans. Charting how lace had moved abruptly 'from altars to backsides', the press set on the contrast between, on the one hand, the sexual nature of the new product and its presentation and, on the other, the ostensible counter-moves of conservative social and religious mores in the Catholic village community. One German magazine dubbed the local production of handmade lingerie 'erotic needlework' (Keeve 2006), conjuring a playful image of a virtuous housewife expressing a repressed penchant for sexual vice.

This playful juxtaposition of vernacular tradition and sexualised modernity has come to dominate the image of Koniaków and its lace makers over the

Figure 5.1　Cover of *Wysoke Obczasy*, October 2003 (photo by Jacek Piotrowski AG)

past decade, leading anthropologists to analyse the phenomena in terms of politicised discourses of 'folk' tradition, globalisation, and entrepreneurialism (Grygar, Hodrová, & Kočarková 2004; Kuligowski 2007; Makovicky 2010 a, b). The controversy surrounding the emergence and success of crocheted *stringi* is a perfect illustration of how the changing uses of lace often reflect 'the contrast between conservatism and liberal innovation, and clearly reveal the influence of politics on dress and "good taste"' (Sciama 1992, 127). Other scholars have avoided engaging with recent developments, either by choosing instead to document the early history of the cottage industry (Kiereś 2010; Poloczkowa 1968) or by viewing the phenomenon as part of the morphology of local, traditional costume (Deminiok 2010; Hermanowicz-Nowak 1997; Kiereś 2006). Yet, despite the considerable attention paid to Koniaków's lace and lace makers, none of these approaches has considered the history of the use of lace within the context of Highland village life, or the symbolic efficacy of the material itself. Consequently, they ignore not only a long-standing association of lace with notions of female sexuality and fecundity but also the role of lace in the magico-ritual beliefs and practices involving wrapping, covering, and rubbing the body with textiles that persisted well into the twentieth century.

Drawing on insights from ethnology, dress history, and gender studies, this chapter examines how this history of associations plays a part in creating the contemporary cultural references surrounding crocheted *stringi*. In a deliberate departure from previous work on the subject, I examine crochet lace artefacts as an integral part of the sartorial habits, ritual practice, and domestic material culture of historical Koniaków itself, rather than as a commercial product for an outside audience. Inspired by Alfred Gell's (1993) concept of 'wrapping' as a symbolic technique for the protection and control of sacred or supernatural powers, I show how wrapping the body (literally and figuratively) in lace and other textiles developed in response to a local, folk aetiology that pitched community members against supernatural beings in a struggle over (re)productive powers. With the move from 'wrapping the body' to 'wrapping the interior' under the pressures of (socialist) modernisation in the second half of the twentieth century, I argue that this association of lace with the spiritual became displaced into the domestic setting rather than destroyed. Finally, I suggest that current debates surrounding the production of *stringi* should be understood partly in the light of this complex history of shifting perceptions of intimate boundaries between the flesh and the spirit, the public and the private, and fertility and desire.

Wrapping the Body

Anne Hollander describes the folk costume of Central and Eastern European as 'unfocused and overburdened with visual form', a costume that depersonalises the wearer and looks better 'laid out flat, to display construction and embellishment' than when worn on the body (1975, xiv). Hollander identifies a key aspect of the sartorial style of nineteenth-century rural dress: the apparent lack of correspondence between both the construction of dress and its visual presentation, and the contours of the body. Although the traditional costume of Highland Silesia worn by most villagers until after World War II was markedly plainer than that found in the Polish lowlands, it largely conformed to this stereotype. An ensemble of a short, boxy, white linen or cotton blouse worn together with a black, woollen, pleated skirt and an indigo, wax-resist dyed apron, female costume effectively comprised a collection of

Figure 5.2 An elderly lady in festive Highland dress (photo by Nicolette Makovicky)

rectangular pieces of cloth gathered, wrapped, and tied around the torso and limbs. This layering of unstructured textiles was complimented with a kerchief wrapped tightly around the head, where a lace-fronted bonnet or matron's cap (*czepiec*) already occupied the forehead, giving women a nun-like appearance (Figure 5.2). Obscuring the natural contours of the body, this costume rendered the female form as padded and rotund, with angles and peaks protruding at the breasts, elbows, and the back of the head.

This use of wrapping as a principle for dressing the body reflected an archaic technology of domestic weaving and hand-sewing that was gradually abandoned during the first half of the twentieth century as sewing machines and urban-style tailoring became more prevalent. At the same time, certain textiles and the action of wrapping them around the body also played an integral part of ceremonies marking major life-cycle events throughout life: a bride covered her head with a ceremonial sheet (*łochtuszka* or *uobrus*) in which she would later wrap her newborn as it was taken to church to be christened (Malicki 1956). At this time, the baby's godmother would tuck a length of linen inside the christening set so that it became, so it was thought, imbued with magico-religious powers during baptism. This baptism linen (*krcielne płotno*) was subsequently sewn into an underskirt or a shirt to be worn at the baby's future wedding and, later, buried together with its owner (Lehr 1999, 123). And just as textiles played an important role in rites of incorporation, so they were vital for controlling the spiritual dangers associated with bodies in a vulnerable or liminal state. Thus, the early ethnographer Longin Malicki

(1947, 1956) reports that corpses were dressed for burial in shirts sewn with no knots, presumably to prevent them from being 'bound' to the world of the living. The ritual significance of wrapping and covering the body was, in other words, connected to the belief that it was permeable to the spiritual forces inhabiting the domestic, social, and natural environment and, consequently, to the belief that textiles themselves could become imbued with the potency and magical efficacy of the human body itself.

Crocheted matrons' caps with their lace frontispieces were no exception. An obligatory part of a married woman's attire, the nineteenth-century matron's cap was made of plain cloth with a strip of machine-made lace sitting low over the forehead. In about 1900, however, caps began to be made using the crochet technique: the cloth body of the cap was now made as a flexible, plain net, while the frontispiece contained ever-more elaborate motifs that imitated the floral machine lace that had previously been used. This eventually led to the development of an indigenous repertoire of motifs with names such as *listki* (leaves), *winogrono* (grapes), *sowy* (owls), and *wiatraki* (windmills) (Kiereś 2010). Presented to the young bride at the wedding feast by older, married female wedding guests (Malicki 1956, 60–61), it was wrapped around what was considered to be her most sexually potent and alluring attribute— her hair—and tied firmly at the back of the neck behind her ears. So strongly associated was the cap with the marital state that leaving the house without it in place was to appear shamefully naked in public. As a symbol of sexual modesty it also became an instrument of social control: unwed mothers were also required to don the cap without being honoured with a ceremonial welcome into the rank of village matrons (1956, 59). Thus, as Patricia Williams shows for communities in neighbouring Moravia, the 'primary function' of the cap 'was once related to fertility, rather than marriage. The cap protected the women from evil forces that threatened her fertility and that of the community' (1999, 139). Failure to wear it was thought to bring misfortune to the individual and the community: as one elderly informant told me 'we were always told that wearing the cap kept lighting and thunder away from the house' (see also Taylor 2004).

Yet, as this quotation suggests, the matron's cap served just as much to protect the community from the potentially disruptive force of unbridled female sexuality: the female body, as the site of reproductive powers and sexual desirability, itself functioned as a powerful spiritual force that could offer protection from malevolent influences. Along with the matron's cap, the tubular shift (*ciasnocha*) worn by women was believed to offer protection from supernatural powers and disease. People and domestic animals rubbed the hem of such a chemise to ward off the evil eye and wrapped it around an unbaptised newborn to protect it from malevolent spirits. Not only did local folklore abound with stories of nymphs and demons tormenting women in childbirth or replacing newborns with changelings, but the agents of this misfortune were themselves imagined to be female (Lehr 1995, 2009a). While elderly women with knowledge of herbs and healing practices could find themselves being accused of being witches (*strzyga*), diseases such as the plague and scarlet fever were personified in the form of sickly, thin fair-haired maidens; 'crying-nymphs' (*płaczki*) would plague young children, and noon-witches (*południca* or *żytnia baba*) could cause muscle pains and sunstroke (Lehr 2009a, 11–13). Common to all these anthropomorphisations of illness and malevolence was the explicit choice of a female form in which fertility and sexuality were latent (the virgin or maiden) or completely spent (the old woman). In short, peasant society saw the female body and its reproductive powers as part of a hidden economy of fecundity played out between the world of human beings and a restless spiritual realm.

Writing on tattooing in Polynesia, Alfred Gell (1993) described the decoration of the body as a form of 'wrapping in images', the presentation of a 'social skin' that simultaneously acted to contain the contagious sacredness (*mana*) of the body. Although his case study is not comparable geographically, his observations provide a useful analogy for understanding the manner in which folk beliefs about the human body and the spiritual world gave the lace *czepiec* its double role as an indicator of marital status and wealth and as a potent magico-ritual tool. Indeed, as the comment on the protective powers of the matron cap quoted previously illustrates, in the syncretic worldview of traditional village life the two were inextricably linked: folk aetiology cast normative behaviour and morality in terms of the spiritual well-being of the individual and the community by linking human behaviour to an extrasensory, supernatural world in a zero-sum struggle over (re)productive powers. Like Gell's Polynesian tattoos, lace and the sartorial elements to which it was attached provided not only a 'social skin' signalling social conformity and belonging to the community but also the simultaneous protection of the potent body and its control. Rather than simply constituting a technique for protecting the body (and its fecundity) from the potentially harmful effects of spiritual forces beyond human control, wrapping—as ritual practice and aesthetic regimen—constituted the visible frontline in this ongoing battle.

As I show in the following section, the house and the domestic space were also implicated in this metaphysical economy through the actions of their inhabitants. The belief in the permeability and susceptibility of the human body to sorcery and malevolent spiritual influences was matched by a concern about the spiritual integrity of the household: the threshold of the peasant cottage not only formed the physical boundary between outside and in but also demarcated the invisible limits of a space protected by benevolent supernatural forces and the dangers of the outside world.[1] Indeed, although the magico-spiritual significance of lace was all but forgotten with the parallel abandonment of vernacular costume under the pressures of post–World War II socialist modernity, I argue that it found refuge in the continuing influence of a spiritually informed custom in the arrangement of the domestic interior.

Wrapping the Home

The typical nineteenth-century wooden Highland cottage (*chałupa*) had only two rooms and a hayloft, of which the first, 'black' room (*'czarna'* or *'wielka' izba*) was the space of communal living and the second, unheated 'white' room (*'biała' izba* or *'świetnica'*) was reserved for ritual and ceremonial occasions, such as weddings and christenings. Dominated by a large, white-washed brick stove with no chimney, furnishings in the black room were generally kept to a wall-mounted plate rack, one bed for the heads of the household, a single table, and several benches used for sitting, sleeping, and as a work-surface. The most important (and often only) decoration of this room would have been a crucifix and, perhaps, a religiously themed print or an agrarian calendar hung directly over the one table on the eastern-most wall. Indeed, together with the stove, this 'holy corner' (*świąty kąt*) formed the spiritual nexus of the home: whereas ancestral spirits were thought to reside in or near the stove, the decorated holy corner formed the site of prayer and religious ritual in everyday life (Benedyktowicz & Benedyktowicz 1990a, b; Bułat 1990). Until the nineteenth century, the table itself was used only on special occasions. In everyday life, it functioned as a domestic altar, covered with a white tablecloth and decorated with a cross, paper flowers (*bibułki*), and other religious paraphernalia (Sulima 2008). Apart from covering the table under the *świąty kąt*, lace tablecloths and doilies had no place in the traditional, peasant home, where textiles were stored in the unheated white room in large, painted dowry chests.

Like the technique of crochet lace itself, lace doilies were not an indigenous invention but arose from the meeting of local aesthetics and peasant craft with urban, bourgeois tastes and bourgeoning industrial modernity. Ethnographer Małgorżata Kiereś (2010) has traced the inception of the Koniaków lace doily to the inter-war period, when shopkeepers and hotel owners in the nearby spa-towns of Wisła and Ustron began collaborating with a number of artisans in the village to produce small items that met not only the aesthetic criteria of their metropolitan guests but also their romantic conceptions of Highland peasant life as the very essence of Polish national culture (Crowley 1992, 2001). By the outbreak of World War II, there existed a lively cottage industry supplying Wisła's haberdashers and hotels with tablecloths and doilies, affectionately named *różićki* (rosettes) by local lace makers because of their round form. Following the end of the hostilities, and the establishment of the Communist regime, lace continued to be made 'for bread' (*za chlebem*) under the auspices of the Polish Art and Handicraft Foundation *Cepelia* and was sent 'into the world' (*do świata*) to become the foil for romanticised notions of peasant culture and political propaganda.[2] And yet, while lace making continued with the support of the authorities, the post-War period did see an unprecedented sociocultural change in Koniaków. Improved infrastructure, generous social policies, increased levels of education, and a steady income from jobs in the mining and heavy industry in Upper Silesia (for men) and local tourism (for women) meant that the 1960s saw the first full integration of the village within the Polish state and economy. Small-holding gave way to biprofessionalism as the inhabitants became 'farmer-workers' (*chłopo-robotniczy*) (Mezga 1993), combining blue-collar jobs with agriculture and semilegal or illegal private enterprise (for example, hosting tourists, selling lace or home-made cheese, or smuggling goods across the nearby border with Czechoslovakia).

It was not until the late 1970s that lace doilies first appeared in village houses, at a time when a combination of new-found prosperity and the modernisation enforced by the socialist authorities saw an explosion in the number of large, multistorey brick and concrete family homes being built—and traditional cottages were used merely as storage spaces or left to decay. However, just as Frances Pine (1996) has observed for the homes of the Górale in the neighbouring Podhale, the interiors of houses in Koniaków continue to be strongly associated with older customs of ritual and the everyday uses of domestic space. As such, they are homes to large, extended households in which multiple siblings cohabit with their families and their elderly parents; rooms across several floors of these houses are parcelled out so that each nuclear family has its own kitchen and living room, often in complete disharmony with the original structural design and with no attempt made physically to separate the units one from another. The aim appears to be to supply each family unit with a hearth and a representative space in an attempt to imitate the traditional *czarna-biała* split rather than to promote privacy. The living room has taken over many of the symbolic and representative functions of the *biała izba*; this is where life-cycle events and holy days are celebrated and where a bride and groom are blessed by their parents before the church wedding. One wall is decorated with religious iconography in the form of oil paintings depicting biblical scenes, with perhaps a crucifix. Lace doilies, edgings, and covers are heavily involved in the decoration of the areas beneath and around such religious icons. On lace-covered shelves underneath these pictures, statues of the Virgin Mary join plastic flowers and pictures of deceased relatives, creating a space resembling a small domestic altar (Figure 5.3). This arrangement suggests that the *święty kąt*, too, has found its way into the contemporary interior, albeit in a changed form.

Yet, while homes continue to reflect the 'practical and symbolic ordering of space' of the traditional Highland *chałupa* (Pine 1996, 447), they have also become an artefact of consumption and feminine domesticity. As lace makers pragmatically observed, the building of new homes in the 1970s and 1980s not only created a space for display; it was also simply the first time that the lace makers could afford to labour on doilies and tablecloths for their own homes. As the idea of the domestic sphere as a site of leisure, taste, and creativity took hold, so lace began to play an important role as part of the elaborate displays to be found on sideboards and in display cabinets. Today, strips of

Figure 5.3 A typical interior in Koniaków reminiscent of the *świąty kąt* (photo by Nicolette Makovicky)

lace form crenellations on the edges of shelves, and doilies droop over the sides of the furniture, framing vases, statuettes, and candles. Semitranslucent, these lace covers manipulate the visual impression of hard wooden and glass surfaces; they manipulate our visual impression of wooden and glass surfaces by half obscuring and half revealing what lies underneath and soften the hard edges of the living room furniture with fringe, reframing both the items on display and the structure of the furnishings themselves. According to Elaine Freedgood, the fringe and its use in interior decoration can be seen to reflect the positive valuation of 'being able to imagine and construct limits as variable, permeable, and attenuated structures, rather than as hard edges at which one must stop' (2002, 257). In this case, the wish to construct permeable borders seems related to older anxieties about the boundary between the clothed (protected) and unclothed (exposed) body that led to the concentration of sartorial decoration on the hems and edges of outer garments (Welters 1999; Williams 1999). However, rather than providing apotropaic protection, the framing and reframing of religious icons and the contents of the display cabinet—where family and genealogy are objectified in the form of collections of photographs and precious objects (Makovicky 2007)—suggest a wish to patrol and nurture those spaces in the home that continue to be of spiritual and cosmological significance.

The apparent instinct to pad the interior and soften the hard edges of furnishings visually as well as physically, however, is also reminiscent of what Walter Benjamin identified as the urban, bourgeois penchant for creating an *etui* for private life using covers, plush furnishings, and velour (1999, 20). Indeed, the migration of lace from the female body to the interior of the home in the second half of the twentieth century mirrors the late nineteenth-century fashion for 'dressing' furnishings in lace doilies, hangings, and curtains, thereby creating a spatial and visual analogy not only between domestic space and the female body but between the corseted lady and her undergarments (Finch 1991; Gordon 1996). As Casey Finch notes, however, this eroticisation of domestic space emerged with the loss of any 'explicit articulation of the female body as a site of (re)production' and its reclassification into an 'erotic field' referred to through a system of 'covert representational methods—visual puns, tropes, and uncanny confrontations' (1991, 346–47). The power of the metaphorical analogy between the house and the body (the doily and the undergarment) relied on the masking of raw fertility within a discourse of genteel homemaking. To what extent, then, might the adoption of lace doilies by lace makers themselves simply constitute an embourgeoisement of village life and aesthetics?

Finch's analysis of the Victorian aesthetic as an ontology of sexuality masquerading as a regime of taste suggests that the wrapping of furniture with lace in the homes of Koniaków might be seen as more than either aesthetic emulation or an adoption of urban, intellectual notions of folklore and 'folk art'. Behind the visible changes in the decoration of domestic space might lie a change in the relationship between sexuality and the female body, as well as spirituality and domesticity: while traditional costume made explicit references to the fecundity of the female body (the lace matron cap), the adoption of urban dress in everyday life meant that female sexuality slipped from public fact circumscribed by the normative conventions of village life to being a private truth harboured by the individual body. Together with these changes in the perception and the regulation of the body came the loss of the previously overt association of wrapping or covering the body in lace and other textiles with spiritual protection and—I would argue—its displacement into a domestic sphere where symbolic and cosmological references persisted. Rather than being covert references to femininity in an 'eroticised' space, then, doilies and tablecloths in the Koniaków continued to perform the function once played by garments such as the matron's cap and sartorial embellishments by binding normative human action to the realm of the spiritual, a realm that had, by the end of the twentieth century, increasingly become monopolised by Catholic teaching. The continued association of lace and lace artefacts with the sacred domain, as well as with normative behaviour, is the key to an alternative reading of the debate surrounding the phenomena of lace *stringi*.

Unwrapping the Body

Although *stringi* continue to enjoy the aura of novelty today, nearly a decade since their appearance on the cover of *Wysoke Obczasy*, lace makers in Koniaków continually point out that lace has been made to edge lingerie at different periods ever since women in Koniaków had started making lace for the market in the 1930s. A new emphasis on the collaboration of crafts-people and industrial designers during early socialism also facilitated the use of local lace for the production of industrial quantities of underwear. Thus, under the direction of the staff of the Institute of Industrial Design (*Institut Wzornictwa Przemysłowego*) in the 1950s, the designer Lidia Buczek reinter-preted Koniaków lace designs to create templates for decorative lingerie that was later mass-produced in the textile factories of Łódź (Taylor 1990). By the time Koniaków's lace makers began turning out *stringi* in 2003, however, not only did these precedents appear to have been forgotten, but Koniaków lace itself had also become firmly associated with the decoration of the domestic interior. The second half of the twentieth century had seen both a 'petrifica-tion' of form and style and the emergence of a class of certified folk artists pro-ducing a highly circumscribed range of products approved by the socialist-era cooperative *Cepelia*, an organisation that dismissed 'all the artistic expression of village inhabitants that did not fit into the category of folk art' as defined by its own formal criteria (Klekot 2010, 79).

Given this climate, it is hardly surprising that the emergence of lace lingerie should cause such vigorous debate in the community. The image of *stringi* as they appeared from behind the beltline of a hooded young lady on the cover of *Wysoke Obczasy* may have been relatively playful, but in the village commu-nity itself their sexually provocative nature caused considerable controversy. According to media reports, women who made *stringi* risked being named and shamed at Sunday sermons, and others were unsure about whether they were obliged to admit to their production of skimpy underwear at confession. Although none of the women I spoke to mentioned such ecclesiastical oppro-brium, several who had started producing *stringi* in the early days told me that they had initially concealed their work from others in the community, fear-ing reprisals and moral condemnation. Others regarded the rapid turnover and commercialism of *stringi* as the antithesis of traditional artisanship and called for the G-strings to be labelled Koniaków *lingerie*, rather than Koniaków lace. The essential difference between the doily and the G-string lay not in technique or form but in the blatant functionalism and commercialism of the G-strings. As one prominent member of the community put it: 'They are just such thin strips, how can they show your virtuosity?' And another: '*Stringi*—who sees them? If one makes *stringi*, it is so that one can buy bread' (*za chlebem*).

What is striking about these statements is both their conflation of virtue and virtuosity and their focus on the evident tension between the visible and the unseen—literally and figuratively speaking. The worries of some lace makers that *stringi* were insufficient media for the demonstration of their artistic prowess, or that they would be entirely concealed under the wearer's clothing, indicate not only that these lace makers associated the material and aesthetic efficacy of lace with a certain demonstrative visibility but that they were reluctant to engage with the fact that this public display of their labour and creativity was now inextricably linked to the baring of the body. *Stringi* not only challenged what could (or should) be made under the label 'folk art' but, just at the moment when they had reestablished a long-lost association between lace and the female body, they also redefined this association in terms of youth, sexuality, and consumerism. In the marketing material of the local lace retailers, where shots of female bottoms and midsections showed off various designs of lace *stringi*, the women have all the appearance of living mannequins parcelled out into a set of anonymous body parts. Other retailers took a different approach by emulating the conventions of current fashion photography. On their sites, professional models showed off bra and panty sets, arching their backs provocatively and putting on sultry, self-confident expressions. Behind them, green foliage and the glow of the afternoon sun hinted at an exotic location.

The literal undress of the models is accompanied by a figurative stripping of the lace itself from the automatic and well-established association of lace making as folk art and lace makers as folk artists. However, the disembodied midriffs and behinds paraded on websites and brochures also recall Finch's notion of the body as 'erotic field' in reverse: while the Victorian body remained invisible, referred to only through covert visual representations, it is the body that is here exposed and the 'erotic field' rendered flesh, while references to production (and reproduction) remain entirely absent. The body—and sexuality—is once more rendered a public fact but is simultaneously freed from its historical association with the hidden economy of the fecundity of peasant society. Thus, if 'wrapping'—understood in the Gellian sense—once provided a social and material technology for the regulation of the moral and spiritual integrity of the body, then the emergence of *stringi* seems to constitute its literal and symbolic 'unwrapping'—and its disenchantment.

Conclusion

While the press celebrated the emergence of crocheted lingerie in Koniaków as the triumph of a modern, sexually liberated generation over the prudery of their grandmothers, I have suggested here that such references to domesticity and Catholic piety need to be viewed through the prism of a much longer history of religious syncretism that previously bound the use of lace and other textiles to folk beliefs about fertility, the female body, and the household. Drawing inspiration from Alfred Gell's definition of *wrapping* as a technology of containment and protection, I have shown how lace—and particularly the lace matron cap—was seen as playing a pivotal role in both curtailing female sexuality within the confines of normative behaviour and in shielding reproductive powers from malevolent spiritual forces threatening to usurp it. Social order, in other words, was imagined as a metaphysical economy in which balance was maintained through rituals of wrapping, rubbing, and the covering the body with textiles. Furthermore, I suggest that these associations persisted in the home and influenced the eventual adoption of lace doilies by villagers themselves, long after the use of vernacular dress in everyday life (and the magico-religious and moral significance attributed to it) fell out of use.

When one takes this history into account, the consternation from some quarters of the village community about the sexual nature of Koniaków's newest product, as well as questions about its authenticity, take on new meanings. The quip that lace has moved from gracing altars to (hardly) covering backsides summarises a frustration with the loss of its association with the realm of the sacred and its descent to a position that is decidedly profane, alongside the threat that it will lose its status as art and become just a commercial product. At the same time, the *stringi* act as a metaphor for the gradual disenchantment of both the body and the village environment under the pressures of modernisation. In short, the emergence and the popularity of lace *stringi* have not only challenged social norms of aesthetics, authenticity, and sexual morality in the community, they have also challenged the role of lace itself as an artefact both pregnant with meaning and central to the reproduction of social order.

Notes

1. A number of magical and ritual practices were undertaken to ensure the spiritual integrity of the home and its inhabitant: the burial of a blessed loaf of bread in the foundations; a prohibition on passing items through the windows (believed to be access and exit points for spirits); and sweeping dirt across the threshold or carrying it out after dark, lest the spirits of the home be borne away with it (Lehr 2009b; Sulima 2007, 2008).

2. Stalinist cultural policy exploited the double meaning of the adjective *lud* ('folk' or 'the people') to turn vernacular crafts into both 'folk art' and 'the people's art' (both *sztuka ludowa*) (Klekot 2010); it billed folk arts as the politically correct counterweight to cosmopolitan modernism and avant-garde aesthetic movements, effectively conserving prewar Arts and Crafts aesthetic and social ideals (Crowley 1994).

References

Benedyktowicz, D., & Benedyktowicz, Z.1990a. Symbolika domu w tradycji ludowej (cz. I)'. *Polska Sztuka Ludowa* 44(3), pp. 48–68.
———. 1990b. Symbolika domu w tradycji ludowej (cz. II)'. *Polska Sztuka Ludowa* 44(4), pp. 3–16.
Benjamin, W. 1999. *Illuminations*. London: Pimlico.

Bułat, J. 1990. Przestrzeń sakralna domu wiejskiego albo okno i stoł. *Polska Sztuka Ludowa* 44(3), pp. 287–309.

Crowley, D. 1992. *National Style and the Nation State: Design in Poland from the Vernacular to the International Style.* Manchester: Manchester University Press.

———. 1994. Building the World Anew: Design in Stalinist and Post-Stalinist Poland. *Journal of Design History* 7(3), pp. 187–203.

———. 2001. Finding Poland in the Margins: The Case of the Zakopane Style. *Journal of Design History* 14(2), pp. 105–16.

Deminiok, M. 2010. *O Goralech Valaších, Laších a Jaccích na Tešínském Slezsku/O Góralach Wałachach, Lachach, i Jackach na Śląsku Cieszyńskim.* Cieszyn: Muzeum Śląska Cieszyńskiego/Regio Regionální vydavatelství.

Finch, C. 1991. 'Hooked and Buttoned Together': Victorian Underwear and the Representations of the Female Body. *Victorian Studies* 34(3), pp. 337–63.

Freedgood, E. 2002. Fringe. *Victorian Literature and Culture* 30(1), pp. 257–63.

Gell, A. 1993. *Wrapping in Images: Tattooing in Polynesia.* Oxford: Oxford University Press.

Gordon, B. 1996. Woman's Domestic Body: The Conceptual Conflation of Women and Interiors in the Industrial Age. *Winterthur Portfolio* 31(4), pp. 281–301.

Grygar, J., Hodrová, L., & Kočarková, E., 2004. Koniakowská Krajka™. Vyjednávání tradice a lidovosti uměni v Slezských Beskydách'. In L. Hodrová & E. Kočarková, *III Antropologické symposium.* Plzeň: Aleš Čeněk, pp. 56–76.

Hermanowicz-Nowak, K. 1997. *Strój Górale Beskidu Śląskiego. Funkcje Społeczno-kulturowe.* Warsaw: Scientia.

Hollander, A. 1975. *Seeing through Clothes.* Berkeley and Los Angeles: University of California Press.

Keeve, V. 2006. Heilige Höschen. *Stern* 13/2006, http://www.stern.de/lifestyle/mode/tangas-heilige-hoeschen-559450.html?nv=ct_cb, accessed July 21, 2011.

Kiereś, M. 2006. *Strój ludowy górali Istebnej, Jaworzynki, Koniakowa. Etnograficzne osobliwości preobrażenia i zmiany.* Wisła: Muzeum Beskidzku w Wisłe.

———. 2010. *Koronka Koniakowska.* Istebna: Gminny Ośrodek Kultury.

Klekot, E. 2010. The Seventh Life of Polish Folk Art and Craft. *etnološka tribina* 33(40), pp. 55–85.

Kuligowski, W. 2007. *Antropologia współczesności. Wiele światów, jedno miejscie.* Kraków: Towarzystwo Auturów i Wydawców Prac Naukowych UNIVERSITAS.

Lehr, U. 1995. Witches and Sorcery in the Folktales of Polish Carpathian Villages. *Artes Populare* 16–17(2), pp. 521–26.

———. 1999. The Magic of the Time of Death: A Contribution to the Study of Funeral Customs in a Carpathian Village. *Etnolog, Nova Vrstva* 9(1), pp. 117–26.

———. 2009a. Traditional Rural Etiology as a Category of Cultural Phenomena. *Alimori. Journal of Ethnology and Anthropology* 1(3), pp. 7–29.

———. 2009b. Weather Wizards and Contemporary Protecting Resources. *Acta Ethnographica Hungaria* 54(2), pp. 309–18.

Makovicky, N. 2007. Closet and Cabinet: Clutter as Cosmology. *Home Cultures* 4(3), pp. 287–309.

———. 2010a. 'Folk-lingerie' and Other New Traditions: Górale Cultural Entreprenurialism on the Margins of Poland. In R. Pyrah & M. Turda, *Re-Contextualizing East Central European History: Nation, Culture and Minority Groups.* London: Legenda, pp. 126–41.

Makovicky, N. 2010b. 'Erotic Needlework': Vernacular Designs on the 21st Century Market. In A. Clarke, ed., *Design Anthropology*. Vienna: Springer, pp. 154–68.

Malicki, L.1947. *Materiały do kultury społecznej górali śląskich*. Warszawa: Polskiego Towarzystwa Ludoznawczego.

———. 1956. *Strój Górali Śląskich*. Wrocław: Towarzystwa Ludoznawczego we Wrocławiu.

Mezga, D. 1993. Polish Para-Urbanisation: Residential Sprawl in the Urban–Rural Fringe. *Town Planning Review* 64(1), pp. 23–35.

Pine, F. 1996. Naming the House and Naming the Land: Kinship and Social Groups in Highland Poland. *Journal of the Royal Anthropological Institute* 2(3), pp. 443–59.

Poloczkowa, B. 1968. Koronki Koniakowskie. *Polska Sztuka Ludowa* 22, pp. 209–40.

Sciama, L. 1992. Lace Making in Venetian Culture. In R. Barnes, ed., *Dress and Gender: Making and Meaning in Cultural Contexts*. Oxford: Berg Publishers, pp. 121–38.

Sulima, M. 2007. Symbolizne przestrezenie domu. *Zeszyty Naukowe Politechniki Białistockiej* 20, pp. 81–91.

———. 2008. Rola religii w kształtowaniu przestreni domu wiejskiego. *Zeszyty Naukowe Politechniki Białistockiej* 21, pp. 1–10.

Taylor, L. 1990. Polish Design History and the Warsaw Museum of Design. *Journal of Design History* 3(1), pp. 59–62.

———. 2004. *Establishing Dress History*. Manchester: Manchester University Press.

Welters, L. (ed.) 1999. *Folk Dress in Europe and Anatolia: Beliefs about Protection and Fertility*. Oxford: Berg Publishers.

Williams, P. 1999. Protection from Harm: The Shawl and Cap in Czech and Slovak Wedding, Birthing and Funerary Rites. In L. Welters, ed., *Folk Dress in Europe and Anatolia: Beliefs about Protection and Fertility*. Oxford: Berg Publishers, pp. 135–54.

Part III: Wrapping and Unwrapping the Dead

6   Wrapping the Dead: The Bronze Age Mound Burials of Southern Scandinavia through a Wrapping Analysis

Susanna Harris

Bronze Age burials across Europe frequently contain evidence of organic materials such as textiles, leather, and basketry that were used to clothe, wrap, fold around, cover, and contain the inhumed or cremated human remains (Bender Jørgensen 1986, 1992; Bergerbrant 2007; Broholm & Hald 1940; Henshall 1950; Randsborg 2011). Beyond the identification of materials, a key question in the analysis of these organic materials is to identify the sequence of wrappings. Where preservation permits, it appears that the human remains were wrapped in multiple layers of materials. Furthermore, the sequence of wrapping that relates to enclosing the burials often extends beyond these organic layers, because the bodies are subsequently contained in coffins or pots, barrows or cists (Boye 1986/1896; Broholm & Hald 1940). The presence of these multiple layers of wrapping and layering around a central content poses a particular set of questions for archaeologists. Archaeologists recognise individual layers, but more difficult to answer are the questions: Why did people wrap and cover their dead in multiple layers, and what did this form of wrapping do?

This chapter presents examples of the archaeological evidence of the multiple layers of textiles, leather, wood, stone, and earth that wrap and cover an inhumation burial in Bronze Age southern Scandinavia. The method of investigating layers is consciously presented from a wrapping perspective, that is, by describing the addition of layers to the body. The wrapping perspective contrasts to an unwrapping perspective describing the removal of layers, that is, the way archaeologists encounter archaeological evidence through excavation or artefact analysis. Switching to a wrapping method allows the archaeologist to focus on the process by which the dead were buried rather than discovered. From this perspective, one can argue that these multiple layers of wrapping were used not only to protect, contain, and enclose the corpse but also to provide a material expression of the transformation of the contents within. As a commonly reoccurring phenomenon, the wrapping of the corpse represents a reordering of the social world following death.

A Theory and Practice of Wrapping

If one is to consider the wrapped dead body, one needs first to examine theories of wrapping. Archaeologists have recognised clothing and costume as a prime means with which to construct social identity (Gleba 2008; Sørensen 1997; Wels-Weyrauch 1989). The work of social anthropologists Ruth Barnes and Joanne Eicher on dress, ethnicity, and gender has been influential in demonstrating how textiles and skins used as dress are not only both functional and protective but also imbued with social meaning and used to express social identity (Barnes & Eicher 1993, 1; Eicher 1995). In essence, the expression of social identity can be found in nearly all aspect of material culture (Díaz-Andreu & Lucy 2005), so it is not this alone that makes clothing special. What is unique about clothing is that it covers and encloses the body in an act of wrapping. It is therefore this relationship between the centre and the wrapper that is potent as a material form.

The concept of wrapping materials is associated with malleable sheets that envelope, contain, cover, and enclose. In this sense the wrapping materials of clothing (textiles, skins, bark cloth, knitting) seem most appropriate. But the act of wrapping around a central feature can be extended beyond this narrow definition. In his study of tattooing in Polynesia, Alfred Gell saw the inked, patterned skin as a means of wrapping the body and creating personhood through the permanent modification of the skin (Gell 1993, 3). Like clothing in Europe, tattooing was seen to protect and cover, but tattooing was quite unlike clothing in many ways, because, first, it is a permanent skin feature and, second, it is intended as a defence against external threats rather than a protector of modesty (Gell 1993, 38–39). Tattooing in Polynesia, Gell argues, is viewed as a means of enveloping the social persona and of containing and protecting the person, drawing attention to the individual while at the same time being an essential ingredient of major social institutions such as politics, warfare, and religion. Here 'wrapping in images' (tattooing) is integral to the hierarchy, governance, and social institutions (Gell 1993, 3–5).

One of the key aspects of Gell's analysis is the integration of wrapping and the social institutions that are integral to it. This theme is also important in

Joy Hendry's analysis of wrapping in Japan. Hendry drew attention to wrapping as a means of nonverbal communication but also as an ordering principle in Japanese society (Hendry 1990, 18). From gifts wrapped in paper to seaweed-wrapped rice, from individual portions of sugar wrapped in paper to the use of partition in school offices to wrap the headmaster behind his lower-ranking staff, Hendry demonstrated how wrapping in Japan represents politeness, hygiene, ritual care, and social order (Hendry 1993). The combination of material wrappings (paper, seaweed, desk space) with immaterial wrapping (verbal communication, morals, beliefs) demonstrates the depth of wrappings as an ordering principle in Japanese society. One of the important features of Hendry's work for archaeologists is that wrapping is seen as integral to maintaining certain social norms and to knowing how to act correctly. This work does not separate the so-called secular and ritual spheres of activity that can so often blight archaeologists in their attempt to interpret elaborate, seemingly nonfunctional, material acts.

It is useful to question wrapping themes through familiar experiences. Commercial packaging often involves several layers of wrapping materials (net, paper, cardboard, plastic). At the most utilitarian level, these wrappings serve to contain the contents to allow them to be carried home and at the same time to add information about the content, origins, and price. But commercial packaging does more than this. The shape, texture, colour, motifs, and any lettering printed on the layers of wrapping are chosen by designers to enhance the appeal of the product and to convey ideas that the producers want the public to believe about the contents. Subtle techniques, such as the satisfaction created through colours and materials, the use of varied textures on a box surface to appeal to the senses, and unexpected opening mechanisms, are used by designers and marketers to enhance the customer's sensual experience (Burgopak Ltd 2009; Jordan 2000; Zotefoams plc 2009). Specifically, the materials, colour, logo, and form are chosen to represent and promote the ethos of the company (Grasseni 2003). This clever use of materials in packaging is used to persuade the consumer to buy the product and to pay a higher price. It is therefore both a means to influence and enhance perceptions of the contents and to create a form of exchange that is acceptable and expected within the social institutions of commerce.

Superficially similar, but fulfilling a different purpose, is the use of gift wrap in contemporary culture. The practice of wrapping an object inside thin sheets of colourful paper is used to conceal totally the contents, to hide them from the person receiving the gift until they are unwrapped. In this context wrapping is used to create an element of surprise and excitement through unwrapping and therefore to elicit a learned and appropriate cultural response. According to studies of Christmas gift-giving in the United States, this type of wrapping not only adds the giver's personal sentiment to the contents, it also acts to transform the shop-bought commodity inside into a personal gift

(Caplow 1984; Carrier 1993, 60). Gifts wrapped like this are usually distributed between family and friends according to predictable social relationships between the recipient and giver (Caplow 1982, 387–88). The task of wrapping may also be subject to a division of labour: in Caplow's study the majority of the wrapping was performed by women (1982, 388). Like the commercial packaging, gift wrapping is a means of communicating information about both the contents and the associated social exchange, but here the exchange is directed toward quite different social networks. Once unwrapped, the nonverbal ideas in the wrappings have been communicated, and the purpose of the wrapping is fulfilled. The wrapping paper is usually thrown away, because it has little intrinsic value. More enduring are the social relationships formed by the gift exchange, demonstrating how wrapping is a proper and correct manifestation of social order.

These instances of wrapping draw attention to the relationship between the wrapping and the contents; the use of wrapping to transform the content through various means; and the way wrapping is used not only to reflect social order but also to create order through making contents appropriate in particular time and place situations. For an archaeologist, the task is then to apply and explore these ideas in relation to archaeological examples of multiple layers of wrapping.

Method

Wrapping is presented here as the layering and enclosing of a central content through the application of materials, whether textiles, leather, stones, or layers of turf. Using this definition as a starting point, the archaeologist first proceeds with the formal analysis of materials. A formal analysis describes the wrapping materials—their raw materials, colour, shape, and method of application—and is based on what can be said without insider knowledge and focuses entirely on a physical analysis (Taçon & Chippindale 1998, 6–8). This stage of analysis addresses the question of what is being wrapped and how. It is important as the first part of any archaeological investigation, because it focuses on the material and the contents (Wobst 1977, 320). This process is described here from a wrapping perspective—that is, by considering the order in which layers were added, as opposed to an unwrapping one, which seems to be the unconscious result of archaeological research methods. Archaeological methods, by necessity, adopt an unwrapping perspective because this is how excavation is carried out (digging into a burial mound from the top down) and how artefacts are analysed (removing layers to reach the centre). For this reason, this chapter's focus on wrapping provides an original basis from which to reconsider the meaning of the layers as added at the time of construction.

The next stage of this analysis is to make a contextual analysis of wrapping in order to interpret the reason or meaning behind the selection of materials and their role in the wrapping of their contents. This stage addresses the question of what do the wrappings do and how do they do it; it draws on culturally specific knowledge, providing information such as the meaning of motifs, colour symbolism, the social relationships and identity of participants, and the motivation behind each layer. In anthropological research, such a contextual or informed analysis may be based on insights provided by the direct or indirect understanding of those people who made or used the material or objects in question (Taçon & Chippindale 1998, 6–7). For the Bronze Age, as indeed for much of the archaeological time frame, there is no direct insider knowledge. Instead, a contextual analysis can be indirectly drawn both from an investigation of the preserved material remains in their archaeological context and from a wider understanding of the societies who produced them.

The Early Bronze Age in Southern Scandinavia

Now that we have examined something of the complexity surrounding objects wrapped with multiple layers, we can investigate the principles underpinning their use in past cultures. The wrapped bodies in the Bronze Age burial mounds of southern Scandinavia provide a case study.

'Bronze Age' refers to a time when bronze was the predominant material used to make tools and weapons. Across Europe, metalwork (bronze and gold), pottery, amber, woodwork, and textiles were key technologies (Harding 2000, 242–70; Kristiansen & Larsson 2005, 108–41). The desire for raw materials and craft expertise is seen as one of the driving factors for travel through trade and reciprocal exchange, and various models for exchange practices are proposed (for example: Harding 2000, 164–96; Kristiansen & Larsson 2005, 32–61). The production of manufactured goods was important not only for the creation of personal possessions but also for the accumulation of wealth and the expression of social identities. In southern Scandinavia, as elsewhere in Europe, farming societies cultivated plants using the plough and reared domestic animals (Harding 2000, ch. 4; Jensen 1982, 132). People built large, two- or three-aisled longhouses accompanied by outbuildings, a pattern that could represent either single farmsteads or small clusters of independent households (Jensen 1982, 148–49; Rasmussen & Adamsen 1993, 136–38). During the Early to Middle Bronze Age in northwest and Eastern Europe, many men, women, and children were buried beneath large earth mounds (Bergerbrant 2007, 12; Boye 1986/1896; Glob 1974). By recent estimates, around 50,000–85,000 barrows were built in Denmark alone, most of which date to Montelius Period II or III, circa 1500–1100 cal. b.c. (Jensen 2002, 144; Kristiansen 2012, 381). Archaeologists have interpreted the grave goods of these burials as the personal possessions of the deceased, an interpretation sometimes used to argue that this was a time of increasing social inequality (summarised in Jensen 1999, 93–94; Vandkilde 1996, 22–23, 259, fig. 278). Investigating the lives of individuals and past populations through the evidence of grave goods from the burials has been an important focus since the discovery of these barrows in the nineteenth century (Broholm & Hald 1940; Glob 1974). Since the 1980s there has been a substantial body of work on Bronze Age burial mounds and their construction and location in the landscape (Asingh 1987; Boysen & Andersen 1983; Breuning-Madsen & Goldhahn 2008; Haack Olsen 1990; Holst 1998; Holst, Breuning-Madsen, & Rasmussen 2001; Holst & Rasmussen 2012; Johansen 1985; Lewis 2008). Certain features of the mounds and burial rites have also been interpreted as rituals based in the ideological beliefs of the period, possibly revolving around the importance of the sun (Kristiansen & Larsson 2005, 242–45; Randsborg & Nybo 1984).

The Burial Mounds of Southern Scandinavia through a Wrapping Analysis

The wrapping analysis presented in this section first describes the formal layers of wrapping materials surrounding the dead bodies in the Bronze Age barrows; then it considers these in the context of the period. Although there are many barrow burials, only a handful have well preserved organic materials including textile, leather, and wood (major studies: Bender Jørgensen 1986; Bergerbrant 2007; Broholm & Hald 1940; Glob 1974; Randsborg 2011). Others have benefitted from modern excavation techniques and the analyses used to investigate the turf mound or barrow (for example, Asingh 1987; Holst, Breuning-Madsen, & Rasmussen 2001; Holst & Rasmussen 2012). Because no single mound burial provides information for all these layers, examples are cited according to the quality of the information available.

Textiles, Leather, and Grave Goods

This description of textiles, leather, and grave goods deals with a man's burial that was excavated in 1883 from a long barrow at Muldbjerg, Ringkjøbing Amt, Denmark (Boye 1986/1896, 30; Broholm & Hald 1940, 13). The dendrochronology date of the coffin is 1365 cal. B.C. (felling date of tree) (Christensen 1998, 113).

The man buried at Muldbjerg wears what is described as a wrap-around (Bergerbrant 2007, 50–51) (Figure 6.1). The wrap-around is a roughly rectangular garment, stitched together from nine pieces of textile with extended upper corners that fastened around the neck (Broholm & Hald 1940, 19–22; Stæmose Nielsen 1989, 40–42). It was worn with a broad leather belt around the waist and fastened with a horn double button at the back (Bergerbrant 2007, 50–51; Broholm & Hald 1940, 19–22). Worn in this way, the wrap-around covered the upper chest to the knees (Bergerbrant 2007, 50).

Figure 6.1 The two layers of textile clothing worn by the Muldbjerg man. On the left, the wrap-around and cap were worn on the body; the cloak shown on the right was laid over the man's body in the coffin (after Boye 1896, pl. IV)

On the wrap-around lay two small bronze discs (Glob 1974, 78). As recorded in the original excavation drawings, a sword in a well-preserved wooden sheath with pelt lining lay on the chest of the man, seemingly partly covered and partly resting on the wrap-around (Boye 1986/1896, pl. III; Broholm & Hald 1940, 26; Glob 1974, 78–79). Two strips of textile were wrapped around the feet like socks (Broholm & Hald 1940, 22), and some leather remains indicate the presence of shoes (Glob 1974, 80). On his head he wore a dome-shaped cap (Broholm & Hald 1940, 18–19). The cap was made from several layers of textiles, its surface covered with thousands of short stitched threads creating a furry effect (*pile*), and its inside embroidered with rows of buttonhole stitches (Broholm & Hald 1940, 18–19).

All the textiles were made of dark pigmented sheep's wool (Broholm & Hald 1940, 13). Similar wrap-around garments are known from other male burials—for example, at Trindhøj in central Jutland (Broholm & Hald 1940, 33–35). The two men buried at Borum Eshøj wear kilts tied at the waist, rather than a wrap-around (Broholm & Hald 1940, 55–57). Domed hats, with or without pile, are known from other burials; there are currently eight known preserved examples (Bender Jørgensen 1986, 289; Broholm & Hald 1940, 30–31, 40, 48; Tidow 1992, 31). The textile cloak seems to be common to all the well-preserved men's burials; at Trindhøj, coarse wool threads are embroidered over the surface of the cloak (*pile*) (Broholm & Hald 1940, 27–29; Stæmose Nielsen 1989, 37), producing a fleecy effect akin to the Muldbjerg hat mentioned previously. Fragments of similar fleecy textile are also known from a woman's grave at Melhøj (Bender Jørgensen, Munksgaard, & Stærmose Neilsen 1982, 34, figs. 14 & 15; Stæmose Nielsen 1989, 45).

The garments found in women's graves were a different shape but made of the same type of dark wool textiles (Bergerbrant 2007, 50–60; Broholm & Hald 1940, 13–103). There has been some debate as to how they were worn (Randsborg 2011, 43). As materials, it seems likely that these textiles were items of wealth and value, as has been suggested by Klavs Randsborg's comparison with Aegean and Near Eastern written records of a similar date (Randsborg 2011, 34).

It is apparent from the best-preserved graves that the clothing is the first layer of wrapping around the inhumations. As these wool textiles are soft to the touch and warm to wear, they would have been very suitable for clothing. The role of clothing style to express social identity has been used to investigate gender in the southern Scandinavian Bronze Age burials (Bender Jørgensen 1986; Bergerbrant 2007, 44–91; Randsborg 2011; Sørensen 1997, 98). According to Sophie Bergerbrant's study, the combination of garments in the men's outfits suggests three different outfits (Bergerbrant 2007, 52). The women's costume is more difficult to reconstruct. The preserved clothing seems to share a similar style of blouse, but there are at least two skirt types (Bergerbrant 2007, 54–59). The different women's costumes have led to various interpretations, such as being indicative of a married or unmarried status or of a priestess's outfit (summarised in Bergerbrant 2007, 59–60). There is also a debate as to whether, and how, the clothing in the graves was worn in life (for example, Bergerbrant 2007, 56–58; Randsborg 2011, 41–45; Sørensen 1997, 101–02). In terms of this wrapping analysis, however, the significance of these garments is that they were worn by the dead. Whether these garments were intended to make people look like their living selves, to dress their bodies appropriately for death, or to protect the dead person in another way cannot be established from the evidence available.

In addition to clothing, the burials contain a rich array of grave goods. Although not layers of wrapping in the sense of layering materials, they are important to mention here since they have been used as the basis for the interpretation of the role, status, and gender of the dead. The presence of swords in many of the southern Scandinavian graves, and indeed throughout Europe, is not only an achievement of metal-working skill but also indicative of the central role of the warrior in these societies (Jensen 1999, 93). Other grave goods may represent ritual roles; the women's round belt ornaments in gold or bronze, for example, may represent the sun disk and signify the role of women in these rituals (Kristiansen & Larsson 2005, 298). Heavy bronze swords, palstaves, folding chairs, staves with bronze mounts, and certain dress ornaments are believed to represent symbols of political power (Jensen 1993, 134). Grave goods also seem to be differentiated according to gender. Male burials, like

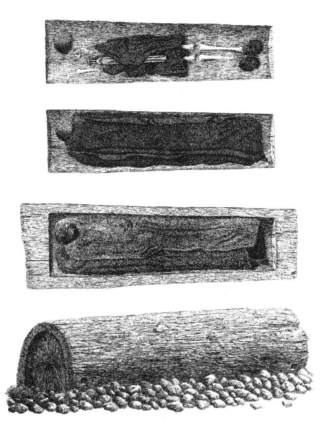

Figure 6.2 Four views of Muldbjerg man's grave: at the top, the clothed body with grave goods; below, the textile covers followed by the cow-skin wrapping in the wooden coffin; at the bottom, the covered wooden coffin and stone platform (after Boye 1896, pl. III)

that of Muldbjerg, already outlined, were accompanied by swords, axes, socketed axes, belt hoods, razors, tweezers, flint strike-a-lights, and slate pendants. Female burials are accompanied by belt plates, neck rings, neck collars, and bronze tubes (that adorned short skirts). Daggers, awls, arm rings, finger rings, pins, fibulae, and double buttons are associated with both male and female burials and burial assemblages and can therefore be described as 'unisex' (Bergerbrant 2007, 8). The man's clothed body from Muldbjerg was placed lying on his back, on a large cow skin (Broholm & Hald 1940, 13) (Figure 6.2).

A rectangular textile measuring 211 × 131 cm was laid lengthways on top of the clothed body (Broholm & Hald 1940, 22–26). Over this rectangular textile lay a kidney-shaped textile folded lengthways, maximum dimensions of 231 × 118 cm, with two, two-piece fibulae pinned on one edge (Broholm &

Hald 1940, 13–18). This textile is interpreted as a cloak because of its shape, the fibulae, and the damaged holes made in the textile owing to the pin fastening (Broholm & Hald 1940, 17–18). Folded lengthways over the clothed body and rectangular textile, it covered the body from the cap to the feet (Broholm & Hald 1940, 13). The clothing and folded layers suggest that the body was covered by four or five layers of textiles in total. The cow skin on which the body was resting was then wrapped over the body with its hair side uppermost, covering the cloak layer (Broholm & Hald 1940, 13; Glob 1974, 77). These layers were large and flexible enough to wrap around the whole body, covering the face, head, hands, and costume, and grave goods were concealed beneath the layers or laid above it. The cow skin has been interpreted as the remains of a communal meal (Glob 1974, 40). That it was freshly flayed (rather than cured) is supported by the presence of maggot skins on the cow-skin wrapping at another site, Borum Eshøj (Glob 1974, 40). Kristiansen and Larsson suggest that the cow skins used to wrap the dead were the remains of an ox sacrifice, pointing to the description of similar rituals in the Odyssey (Kristiansen & Larsson 2005, 245).

On the basis that metal was a valuable material that had to be imported into Scandinavia, its presence in graves is seen as an indicator of power, status, and wealth. Using a quantitative analysis of metal grave goods, researchers have suggested that there was a significant degree of variation in the wealth and social status of individuals in the Early Bronze Age, with men possessing more metal valuables than women (Jensen 1993, 134; Randsborg 1974, 60). If, however, the textiles are also considered as valuable grave goods, then the balance of status between men and women becomes more equal (Randsborg 2011, 36). This argument shows the importance of considering the organic wrappings in Bronze Age burials.

Wood Coffin and Stone Features

Wrapped in the cow skin, the man's body at Muldbjerg was laid inside a coffin made from a split hollowed oak trunk that had been stripped of its bark (Glob 1974, 77). The oak coffin was then covered by a second massive oak trunk—split lengthways and hollowed out like a trough—that enveloped it and served as a huge lid (Glob 1974, 77). Some coffins were fastened with stakes at either end, as, for example, the smaller coffins at Guldhøj and Trindhøj; in some instances, they were provided with carrying handles (Boye 1986/1896, pl. XIII and XVIII; Broholm & Hald 1940, 10). All wooden coffins, whether from hollowed trunks or planks of wood, are hard, confining layers. Whether such layers acted to keep something inside or to prevent access to the inside is uncertain. In some cases, the direction in which the coffin pointed toward the sunrise or sunset has been used to suggest the importance of solar cosmology in the funerary rituals (Randsborg & Nybo 1984). In a few cases, holes measuring a few centimetres square were cut in the base of the coffin (Boye

1986/1896, 47), as at Egtved, where there is a cut hole directly below the textile bundle containing the cremated remains of a child (Randsborg 2011, 89). The holes suggest that a provision was made to let something pass between the coffin and ground, or out of the coffin.

As was practised in other Bronze Age barrow burials, the Muldbjerg coffin rested on, and was surrounded by, a bed of stones (Glob 1974, 77). In other instances, the burial or barrow may have been surrounded by a circle of kerbstones (Boysen & Andersen 1983, 118; Haack Olsen 1990, 137) or other stone features. Near Trustrup in Djursland, northeastern Denmark, an Early Bronze Age inhumation burial was cut into a stone cairn before being covered by a heap of stones and covered by turf (Asingh 1987, 132–35, 141–42).

The stone platforms and cairns may be seen as additional wrapping for the wooden coffin. The circular pattern of kerbstones and segmented patterns created beneath some burial mounds are reminiscent of the symbol of the wheel-cross or sun (Kristiansen & Larsson 2005, 242–44). The Muldbjerg coffin and the stone platform on which it rested were buried beneath a round mound (Boye 1986/1896, 31; Glob 1974, 77). Owing to the waterlogged preservation, the Muldbjerg man's burial is an excellent example of the layer of textiles, leather, and wood that wrapped and covered the body. How the mound was constructed, however, can be better understood by studying mounds that have been excavated using more modern techniques.

Turf Mound

Skelhøj is a large mound, located near Ribe in southwestern Jutland and excavated between 2002 and 2004 (Holst & Rasmussen 2012, 263). The centre of Skelhøj was dug into and robbed twice, once probably soon after it was built and again in the nineteenth century (Thomsen et al. 2008, 1293). For this reason, no coffin remains, but its position is clear from the disturbed centre. The following description of the barrow is taken from Holst and Rasmussen's summary of the mound construction (Holst & Rasmussen 2012, 263–70) (Figure 6.3).

The barrow has been radiocarbon dated to the fifteenth century B.C.E. It originally had a diameter of 30 m and an approximate height of 7 m and at the time of excavation stood 5 m high (Holst & Rasmussen 2012, 263). Before the coffin was placed in the mound, the circular-plan barrow site was divided into segments (Holst & Rasmussen 2012, 263). The coffin was then placed on the east-west axis of this segmentary division. This alignment is the predominant one found in other Early Bronze Age barrow burials and is also believed to be associated with the cosmology and sun-symbolism (Holst & Rasmussen 2012, 263). Furthermore, the spoke-wheel shape of the segments within the circular plan is believed to reflect other Bronze Age iconography, suggesting a metaphorical link between burial architecture, cosmology, and the journey of the sun (summarised in Holst & Rasmussen 2012, 263).

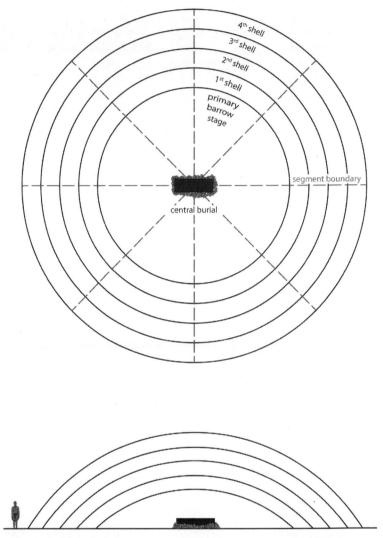

Figure 6.3 Schematic representation of the construction of Skelhøj burial mound showing the position of the central burial, the separately worked segments, primary turf, and four turf shells (graphic by Mads Holst reproduced with permission; in Holst & Rasmussen 2012, 266, fig. 7)

The individual pieces of turf (or sods) used to build the barrow can be seen in the cross section of the barrow excavation, and these allowed the excavators to reconstruct the building phases (Holst & Rasmussen 2012, 258, fig. 2, 265, fig. 6). Pieces of turf were first laid horizontally in layers, with the vegetation surface downward; they measured 25 × 35 cm and 10–15 cm thick (Holst &

Rasmussen 2012, 267). The first phase of mound construction was to build the primary barrow over the central burial. This phase was planned before the coffin was put in place, because the circular plan was marked into radial segment using a boundary row of turf (Holst & Rasmussen 2012, 267). The inside area of each segment was then filled with rows of turf and the process repeated in subsequent layers. The radial segments were worked separately. This approach led to irregularities in the maintenance of geometrical order owing to the unevenness of the turf. These issues were rectified by smoothing, correcting the shape, and supporting the base to prevent erosion. In the second phase of building, four additional shells were added over the primary barrow to increase the size of the mound to its final diameter of 30 m and height of 7 m (Holst & Rasmussen 2012, 265). This second stage probably occurred immediately or shortly after the first. The excavator suggests that the segments were worked on by separate groups of people. Given the narrowness of the segments, he estimates that between 100 and several hundred people were working on the mound at any one time (Holst & Rasmussen 2012, 267).

The horizontal pieces of turf and multiphased construction of barrows is known elsewhere, though with some variations. At the large barrow excavated near Trustrup in Djursland, the central coffin was covered by a heap of stones and layered by turf to form a flat disc barrow (Asingh 1987, 132–35). Again, the turf, described as rich in humus, was laid horizontally in layers with the vegetation surface downward and roots pointing up; it measured 15–20 cm long by 10–20 cm thick and was used to build the initial flat disc barrow (Asingh 1987, 132–35). In a later phase the mound was expanded into a large, dome-shaped barrow 22–26 m in diameter and over 3.5 m high (Asingh 1987, 130). At Muldbjerg the round mound described earlier stood beside a second round mound. Postdating them, a third burial was placed in the space between these two round mounds, and the entirety was covered by a long figure-eight mound (Boye 1986/1896, 31; Glob 1974, 77) (Figure 6.4). It has been suggested that this grouping represents a chieftain and his two wives (Glob 1974, 81).

The turf barrows constructed over the coffins represent an extraordinary amount of effort on the part of the mound builders. Estimates suggest that an average mound of approximately 200 cubic metres would have taken around 200 working days to complete (Goldhahn 2008, 65). The total number of mounds built in Period II and III suggests that every day, in Denmark alone, approximately 100 people must have been occupied in mound building (Goldhahn 2008, 65). Although only estimates, figures such as these provides a useful insight into the scale of human effort and social organisation invested in barrow building. Construction features of a barrow such as Skelhøj suggest that it was built by several teams of workers (Holst & Rasmussen 2012, 268–70). The size and manner of barrow construction, involving both the allocation of land for the removal of turf and the input of labour, suggest that many people were involved in their construction (see also Karg 2008).

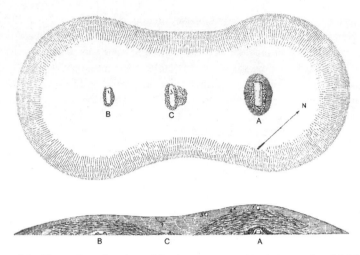

Figure 6.4 Plan and section view of the three graves and burial mounds at Muldbjerg. At the top, the plan shows the position of the man's coffin (A) illustrated in Figures 6.1 and 6.2. Below, the cross section of the barrow shows the two central coffins A and B covered with separate turf mounds and later joined together by the extension of the mound over both barrows (after Boye 1896, 31)

From another perspective, Kristiansen and Larsson suggest that the use of turf may have held ritual significance, pointing to a Hittite royal burial ritual involving the sacrifice of turf (Kristiansen & Larsson 2005, 242). Within the barrows some burials are enclosed by an iron pan (a chemically produced crust) in the soil of the mound. Its formation shortly after the burial provided the anaerobic, waterlogged conditions necessary for the preservation of the organic materials. Whether the formation of this iron pan was deliberate or a naturally occurring phenomenon is open to debate. The experimental construction of a barrow at the Land of Legends, Centre for Historical-Archaeological Research and Communication, Lejre, shows that an iron pan will form if the pieces of turf are packed together very densely and then wetted (Breuning-Madsen & Holst 1998, 1106–09).

The burial mounds not only are visually imposing and monumental but also provide an additional layer of containment over the contents within. The turf itself is heavy and difficult to move, with the iron pan preserving the coffin contents. However, since their construction, the barrows have drawn the attention of grave robbers apparently interested in the gold and bronze grave goods. A survey of Early Bronze Age oak coffin graves demonstrates frequent grave plundering both shortly after burial and later (Randsborg 1998, 115–58). As mentioned earlier, Skelhøj was robbed twice (Thomsen et al. 2008, 1293). Coffins at Guldhøj and Storehøj (central Jutland) have holes cut in their lids where they were entered by robbers; discarded hooked sticks were evidently used to pull out the bronze and gold items (Glob 1974, 94–96). The formation of an iron pan over the robbed Guldhøj coffin is taken to prove that the theft happened shortly after burial (Glob 1974, 96). The construction of these prominent visual mounds in the landscape changed the appearance of the landscape and probably had a devastating effect on the landscape (Kristiansen 2012, 388–89). Ard marks, visible in the subsoil surface of excavated barrow land surfaces such as around Diverhøj barrow, show that the ard was driven around the mound following its construction (Asingh 1987, 144, fig. 17).

Discussion

The ultimate purposes of this wrapping activity was, arguably, to bury the dead. What, then, is the reason for the many layers of wrapping—and how can archaeologists investigate this process in order to understand more about southern Scandinavian societies in the Bronze Age?

First, the multiple layers of wrappings change the appearance of the burial at each stage and create a permanent modification of the dead person. The face and areas of skin are visible only in the first layer (clothing) and are lost behind the textile blankets and cow skin. The shape of the body is hidden inside the coffin. The wooden coffin is hidden beneath mounds of stones and earth. What did this visual transformation represent? Is the deceased buried within the mound and hidden away, or does the mound and the manner of burial make the person more potent and visible? Either option, or indeed another, is possible. Like tattooing in Polynesia (Gell 1993), these layers permanently transform the person. By so doing, not only is the individual highlighted; so, too, are some essential aspects of politics, trade, production, and religion.

Second, the wrappings represent a series of transformations. The bodies are dressed in clothing that demonstrates the social identity of the individuals as men and women, their status, achievements, role, and wealth. The grave goods accompanying them add additional layers of meaning to their social identity, adding ideas of actions as warriors, ritual keepers, political leaders, or healers. The valuable nature of these goods—gold, bronze, textiles, land, and symbols of rank such as swords, folding stools, and elaborate ornaments—also suggest a world of privilege and the sacrifice of such precious resources by those still living. The textile and cow-skin coffin covering that enclose the living persona as it lies in the coffin represent not only additional manufactured goods but also, perhaps, the remains of a funeral feast. The heavy thick layers of wood that are sometimes additionally fastened with stakes act as a protective barrier. The turf layers protect the burials within and create a permanent feature in the landscape. The depth and strength of the material layers suggest that the builders were also attempting to protect the precious grave goods within, although sometimes without success. Some researchers have interpreted certain burial features as symbolically associated with a sun cult: the circular metal ornaments worn by women, the shiny metals, the patterns of stones, the sunrise orientation of the coffin—and the domed shape of the barrows themselves. In its final form the monumental scale of the barrows is a permanent presence in a landscape dominated by many other barrows constructed in the landscape at that time. The wrappings therefore represent a transformation from the individual, with his or her specific social identity, to the dead body transformed by cosmological beliefs, to its enduring visual and physical presences in the occupied landscape.

Third, the wrappings can be interpreted as a material expression of the maintenance of social order at death. Although grave contents and burial mounds may differ slightly, they all follow predictable patterns. Given this predictability, one can suggest that these repeated practices express a way of ordering the world or of acting appropriately. Furthermore, it is suggested that the deceased was believed to need these layers of possessions and elements in death. It is all the more striking to consider what intrinsic value, if any, the layers (metals, textiles, turf) might have held. All these layers not only required effort to produce but all could have been reused or recirculated had they not been 'used up' in this manner. The theory and practice of wrapping presented at the start of this chapter, however, suggest an alternative perspective. These wrapping layers may have been integral to the creation of the very personhood of that individual to the extent that his or her presence could not be denied in death. The presence of these layers may have influenced a person's continued existence in death. If this is so, and these wrappings were important not only as an expression of the self but also as a means of preserving the existence of the self, they would add to our understanding of the significance of artefacts to the creation of social order in the Bronze Age. It may be suggested that the ownership of high-quality manufactured goods was important not only in life but also as a means to the correct transition to death. It would have been the living who chose to provide these items for the burial, and the possible funeral feast and the provision of the stone and turf suggest that groups of people were investing significant time and effort in working toward this aim. It was clearly important for these (sometimes valuable) wrappings to go with the dead body into the grave. These wrappings were deposited without any intention of retrieving them. This act of deposition is repeated throughout hundreds of excavated graves. The wrappings present the correct treatment of the individual in death, and as such they represent the prevailing social order.

The wrapping of these burials was a significant act to the people of the Bronze Age. The depth and strength of the wrapping layers demonstrate that these layers were intended to remain in place; in this they were largely successful until fairly recently. The perspective of wrapping—that is, adding layers to a central content—is quite different from the perspective of unwrapping or taking off layers. The methods of archaeological research are generally much more concerned with unwrapping. The process of excavation is one of removing layers. Excavation reports reflect this process: the layers at

Diverhøj, for example, have been written up from the most recent phase to the earliest (Asingh 1987). By focusing, instead, on wrapping, attention is drawn to the original intentions of the barrow builders and away from the excavation of the contents by archaeologists.

Conclusion

In the southern Scandinavian mound burials, the finished artefact was the result of a process of wrapping. The burials lie at the heart of a deliberate accumulation of many layers of different materials (textile, animal skins, wood, stone, turf), representing many hours of effort to acquire and produce. These layers also add the potential that these physical, visual transformations have not only to enrich the possessions but also to alter significantly the contents within. Unwrapping is a process of seeking the centre. But in this case, the central core (the body) was not meant to be unwrapped. It is suggested, therefore, that the intention here was to gain something definitive from the very act of wrapping. After the death of one of their kin, relatives used the layers of the burial mounds to transform the corpse and reorder their world. Layer by layer, the end of a life was transformed into permanence; grief was transformed into monumentality, and the symbolism of each layer permeated the proceedings. The existing social order was maintained by the deposition of valuable materials in each layer and by the effort expended in mound building.

As a concluding note: archaeologists too often dwell on what might be called an *unwrapping view*, interpreting social order through the deposition of the grave goods belonging to the individuals whom they excavate. By taking a *wrapping view*, as this chapter does, social order is, instead, interpreted through recognising the significance of the accumulation of multiple layers of materials, as in these burials.

Acknowledgements

I would like to thank Marie Louise Stig Sørensen, Sue Hamilton, and Colin Richards for their useful suggestions following the presentation of this research at the conference Wrapping and Unwrapping the Body: Archaeological and Anthropological Perspectives at UCL in May 2010. Thanks to Sophie Bergerbrant, Sarah Byrne, and an anonymous reviewer for helpful comments on an earlier draft of this chapter. I am grateful to Susanne Küchler, Ruth Whitehouse, Irene Skals, and Margarita Gleba for their interesting discussions of wrapping; Pippa White and Jon White for proofreading; and Mads Kähler Holst for his permission to use Figure 6.3. I am indebted to Susanne Klingenberg and Flemming Kaul at the National Museum of Denmark for their permission to study the textiles and leather from the Bronze Age burials. And thank you to all those colleagues and friends who have over the years accompanied me on visits to Bronze Age barrows. The research for this chapter was made possible through the financial support of the British Academy and my host institution, the Institute of Archaeology, UCL.

References

Asingh, P. 1987. Diverhøj: A Complex Burial Mound and a Neolithic Settlement. *Journal of Danish Archaeology* 6, pp. 130–54.

Barnes, R., & Eicher, J. B. 1993. Introduction. In R. Barnes & J. B. Eicher, eds., *Dress and Gender: Making and Meaning in Cultural Contexts*, Vol. 2. Oxford: Berg Providence, pp. 1–7.

Bender Jørgensen, L. 1986. *Forhistoriske textiler i Skandinavien: Prehistoric Scandinavian textiles*. København: Kongelige Nordiske Oldskriftselskab.

———. 1992. *North European Textiles until AD 1000*. Aarhus: Aarhus University Press.

Bender Jørgensen, L., Munksgaard, E., & Stærmose Neilsen, K.-H. 1982. Melhøj-fundet. En hidtil upåagtet parallel til Skrydstrup-fundet/English Summary: Melhøj—an Unheeded Parallel to the Skrydstrup Find. *Aarbøger for Nordisk Oldkyndighed og Historie*, pp. 19–75.

Bergerbrant, S. 2007. *Bronze Age Identities: Costume, Conflict and Contact in Northern Europe 1600–1300 BC*. Lindome: Bricoleur Press.

Boye, V. 1896. *Fund af Egekister fra Bronzealderen i Danmark: et monografisk Bidrag til Belysning af Bronzealderens Kultur,* Vol. 2. Copenhagen: Høst.

———. 1986. *Fund af egekister fra bronzealderen i Danmark. Illustreret af A. P. Madsen. Med efterskrift af Mogens Ørsnes*. First published 1896, reprinted by the publishers. Aarhus: Wormianum.

Boysen, A., & Andersen, S. W. 1983. Barrow and House from the Early Bronze Age. *Journal of Danish Archaeology* 2, pp. 118–26.

Breuning-Madsen, H., & Holst, M. K. 1998. Recent Studies on the Formation of Iron Pans around the Oaken Log Coffins of the Bronze Age Burial Mounds of Denmark. *Journal of Archaeological Science* 25, pp. 1103–10.

Broholm, H. C., & Hald, M. 1940. *Costumes of the Bronze Age in Denmark: Contributions to the Archaeology and Textile History of the Bronze Age*. Copenhagen, NYT Nordisk Forlag: Arnold Busck.

Burgopak Ltd. 2009. Creative Packaging Solution for Sony's EyePet. Packaging Suppliers & News, www.packaging-int.com/article/creative-packaging-solution-sony-eyepet.html, accessed on October 11, 2010.

Caplow, T. 1982. Christmas Gifts and Kin Networks. *American Sociological Review* 47(3), pp. 383–92.

———. 1984. Rule Enforcement without Visible Means: Christmas Gift Giving in Middleton. *American Journal of Sociology* 89(6), pp. 1306–23.

Carrier, J. G. 1993. The Rituals of Christmas Giving. In D. Miller, ed., *Unwrapping Christmas*. Oxford: Clarendon Press, pp. 55–74.

Christensen, K. 1998. Tree-Ring Dating of Bronze Age Oak Coffins from Denmark. In K. Demakopoulou, C. Eluère, J. Jensen, A. Jockenhövel, & J.-P. Mohren, eds., *Gods and Heroes of the European Bronze Age*, London: Thames and Hudson, pp. 110–13.

Díaz-Andreu, M., & Lucy, S. 2005. Introduction. In M. Díaz-Andreu, S. Lucy, S. Babić, & D. N. Edwards, eds., *The Archaeology of Identity: Approaches to Gender, Age, Status, Ethnicity and Religion*. London: Routledge, pp. 1–12.

Eicher, J. B. 1995. Introduction: Dress as Expression of Ethnic Identity. In J. B. Eicher, *Dress and Ethnicity: Change across Space and Time.* Oxford: Berg, pp. 1–6.

Gell, A. 1993. *Wrapping in Images: Tattooing in Polynesia.* Oxford: Clarendon Press.

Gleba, M. 2008. You Are What you Wear: Scythian Costume as Identity. In M. Gleba, C. Munkholt, & M.-L. B. Nosch, eds., *Dressing the Past: Costume through 21st Century Eyes,* Ancient Textile Series 3. Oxford: Oxbow, pp. 13–28.

Glob, P. V. 1974. *The Mound People: Danish Bronze Age Man Preserved*; translated from the Danish by Joan Bulman. London: Faber and Faber.

Goldhahn, J. 2008. From Monuments in Landscape to Landscapes in Mounments: Monuments, Death and Landscape in Early Bronze Age Scandinavia. In A. Jones, ed., *Prehistoric Europe: Theory and Practice.* Malden, MA: Blackwell, pp. 56–85.

Grasseni, C. 2003. Packaging Skills: Calibrating Cheese to the Global Market. In S. Strasser, ed., *Commodifying Everything: Relationships of the Market.* New York: Routledge, pp. 259–88.

Haack Olsen, A.-L. 1990. A Bronze Age Barrow with Early Urn Graves from Thy. *Journal of Danish Archaeology* 9, pp. 133–52.

Harding, A. F. 2000. *European Societies in the Bronze Age.* Cambridge: Cambridge University Press.

Hendry, J. 1990. Humidity, Hygiene, Ritual Care: Some Thoughts on Wrapping as a Social Phenomenon. In E. Ben-Ari, B. Moeran, & J. Valentine, eds., *Unwrapping Japa: Society and Culture in Anthropological Perspective.* Manchester: Manchester University Press, pp. 18–35.

———. 1993. *Wrapping Culture: Politeness, Presentation and Power in Japan and Other Societies.* Oxford: Clarendon Press.

Henshall, A. S. 1950. Textiles and Weaving Appliances in Prehistoric Britain. *Proceedings of the Prehistoric Society* XVI, pp. 130–62.

Holst, M. K., Breuning-Madsen, H., & Rasmussen, M. 2001. The South Scandinavian Barrows with Well-Preserved Oak-Log Coffins. *Antiquity* 75, 126–36.

Holst, M. K., & Rasmussen, M. 2012. Combined Efforts: The Cooperation and Coordination of Barrow-Building in the Bronze Age. In N. Johannsen, M. D. Jessen, & H. J. Jensen, eds., *Excavating the Mind: Cross-Sections through Culture, Cognition and Materiality.* Aarhus: Aarhus University Press in collaboration with the Jutland Archaeological Society, pp. 255–79.

Jensen, J. 1982. *The Prehistory of Denmark.* London: Methuen.

———. 1993. The Bronze Age. In S. Hvass & B. Storgaard, eds., *Digging into the Past: 25 Years of Archaeology in Denmark,* translated by John Hines. Aarhus: Royal Society of Northern Antiquaries, Aarhus Universitetsforlag, Jutland Archaeological Society, pp. 132–35.

———. 1999. The Heroes: Life and Death. In K. Demakopoulou et al., eds., *Gods and Heroes of the European Bronze Age.* London: Thames and Hudson, pp. 88–97.

———. 2002. *Danmarks Oldtid: Bronzealder 2000–500 f Kr.* Copenhagen: Gyldendal.

Johansen, E. 1985. A Burial Mound with Cultural Layers from the Early Bronze Age Near Torslev, Northern Jutland. *Journal of Danish Archaeology* 4, pp. 115–20.

Jordan, P. W. 2000. *Designing Pleasurable Products: An Introduction to the New Human Factors.* London: Taylor & Francis.

Karg, S. 2008. Direct Evidence of Heathland Management in the Early Bronze Age (14th Century B.C.) from the Grave-Mound Skelhøj in Western Denmark. *Vegetation History and Archaeobotany* 17, pp. 41–49.

Kristiansen, K. 2012. Bronze Age Dialectics: Ritual Economies and the Consolidation of Social Divisions. In T. L. Kienlin & A. Zimmermann, eds., *Beyond Elites: Alternatives to Hierarchical Systems in Modelling Social Formations.* Teil 2. Bonn: Habelt, pp. 381–92.

Kristiansen, K., & Larsson, T. 2005. *The Rise of Bronze Age Society: Travels, Transmissions and Transformations.* Cambridge: Cambridge University Press.

Lewis, H. 2008. The Pleasant Land of Counterpane: Linking Site-Specific Archaeological Land Use to the Landscape of Prehistoric Field Systems. In A. M. Chadwick, ed., *Recent Approaches to the Archaeology of Land Allotment.* Oxford: Archaeopress, pp. 239–50.

Randsborg, K. 1974. Social Stratification in Early Bronze Age Denmark. *Praehistorische Zeitschrift* 49, pp. 38–61.

———. 1998. Plundered Bronze Age Graves: Archaeological and Social Implications. *Acta Archaeologica* 69, pp. 113–38.

———. 2011. *Bronze Age Textiles: Men, Women and Wealth.* London: Bristol Classical Press.

Randsborg, K., & Nybo, C. 1984. The Coffin and the Sun: Demography and Ideology in Scandinavian Prehistory. *Acta Archaeologica* 55, pp. 161–84.

Rasmussen, M., & Adamsen, C. 1993. Settlement. In S. Hvass & B. Storgaard, eds., *Digging into the Past: 25 Years of Archaeology in Denmark*, translated by John Hines. Aarhus: Royal Society of Northern Antiquaries, Aarhus Universitetsforlag, Jutland Archaeological Society, pp. 136–44.

Sørensen, M. L. 1997. Reading Dress: The Construction of Social Categories and Identities in Bronze Age Europe. *Journal of European Archaeology* 5(1), pp. 93–114.

Stæmose Nielsen, K.-H. 1989. Bronzealderdragterne som blev en messe værd. *Fynske Minder*, pp. 31–66.

Taçon, P. S. C., & Chippindale, C. 1998. An Archaeology of Rock-Art through Informed Methods and Formal Methods. In C. Chippindale & P. S. C. Taçon, eds., *The Archaeology of Rock-Art.* Cambridge, NY: Cambridge University Press, pp. 1–10.

Thomsen, I. K., Kruse, T., Bruun, S., Kristiansen, S. M., Knicker, H., Petersen, S. O., Jensen, L. S., Holst, M. K., & Christensen, B. T. 2008. Characteristics of Soil Carbon Buried for 3300 Years in a Bronze Age Burial Mound. *SSSAJ* 72(5), pp. 1292–98.

Tidow, K. 1992. Wollengewebe aus dem Bronzezeitlichen Baumsargfund von Harrislee bei Flensburg. In L. Bender Jørgensen & E. Munksgaard, eds., *Textiles in European Archaeology: Report from the 4th NESAT Symposium*, May 1–5, 1990, in Copenhagen, Vol. 5. Copenhagen: Konservatorskolen Det Kongelige Danske Kunstakademi, pp. 31–36.

Vandkilde, H. 1996. *From Stone to Bronze: The Metalwork of the Late Neolithic and Earliest Bronze Age in Denmark, with a Contribution by Peter Northover.* Moesgard, Aarhus, Jutland: Archaeological Society.

Wels-Weyrauch, U. 1989. Mittelbronzezeitliche Frauentrachten in Süddeutschland. In *Dynamique du Bronze Moyen en Europe Occidentale.* Strasbourg: Actes du 113e, Congres national des Sociétés savantes, pp. 117–34.

Wobst, H. M. 1977. Stylistic Behaviour and Information Exchange. In C. E. Cleland, ed., *For the Director: Research Essays in Honor of James B. Griffin*, 61, Vol. 61. Michigan: Ann Arbor, pp. 317–42.

Zotefoams plc. 2009. Foam Packaging Has Aesthetic Appeal, http://www.packaging-int.com/article/innovative-packaging-technology.html, accessed March 2, 2014.

7   Wrapped Up for Safe Keeping: 'Wrapping' Customs in Early Iron Age Europe

Margarita Gleba

During the Early Iron Age (first half of the first millennium B.C.E.), central and southern Europe saw the development of stratified societies, manifested among other things in sumptuous burials of the elite members of society. These so-called princely burials provide important information regarding ancient funerary rituals and beliefs in afterlife (for example, see Bartoloni 2000; Riva 2010). One of the curious phenomena documented in these assemblages is the practice of wrapping in textiles and/or skins not only the body of the deceased, whether inhumed or cremated, but also various burial goods. The finds indicate that various 'wrapping' practices existed throughout Italy, Greece, France, and the Alpine area, suggesting that wrapping as part of the funerary rite had a wide, pan-European significance. This chapter presents some preliminary observations on the different categories of wrapping and their possible meanings.

Although ancient textiles surviving in their original organic form are relatively rare in southern Europe, a vast amount of textile fragments has been preserved in association with metal objects and survive in the form of often minute traces on metal surfaces. While in many cases they are found on fibulae and other personal objects directly associated with clothing, numerous textile traces have also been noted in circumstances where contact of an object with a garment is unlikely or even impossible. This evidence suggests that, frequently, in addition to being used for clothing, textiles in burials were utilised for wrapping either human remains or objects placed together with human

Wrapping and Unwrapping Material Culture: Archaeological and Anthropological Perspectives by Susanna Harris & Laurence Douny, 135–146 © 2014 Left Coast Press, Inc. All rights reserved.

remains as burial gifts. These cases can be summarised as fitting into the following broad categories:

- Wrapping or covering of the body with a funerary shroud
- Wrapping of the cremated remains placed in the urn
- Wrapping of the urn containing cremated remains
- Wrapping of both the cremated remains placed inside the urn and the urn itself
- Wrapping of specific burial goods
- Wrapping of all objects in the burial

The following overview considers each of these cases drawing largely on the evidence from Italian archaeological contexts.

Wrapping or Covering of the Body in Funerary Shroud

The most obvious nongarment use of textiles in burials is as funerary shrouds in inhumation graves, although despite the frequent interpretation of surviving fragments as such, there is little direct evidence. What is known is that at least sometimes funerary shrouds were made for the purpose, the most famous example being the funerary shroud that Penelope was weaving for her father-in-law Laertes in the Homeric *Odyssey* (on Homeric use of shrouds see Stampolidis 1996, 113).

Traces of an actual shroud have been noted in the ninth century B.C.E. Tomb 3 at Osteria dell'Osa in Latium (Figure 7.1), thanks to the rectangle of small bronze rings and buttons that were probably originally sewn onto the edge of the cloth (Bietti Sestieri 1992, fig. 3a, 391). In Tomb 47 of the same cemetery a double line of bronze rings suggests that the body may have been laid on a shroud, which was folded over it (Bietti Sestieri 1992, 755, no. 6, fig. 3a, 403). A shroud with a border consisting of small bronze rings has also been hypothesised for an Early Iron Age female inhumation in Tarquinia (Trucco 2006, 100). These finds suggest that the bodies were interred covered or wrapped in a large piece of textile that was not a garment and likely had a distinct function in the funerary ritual.

Wrapping of the Cremated Remains Placed in the Urn: 'Homeric Ritual'

More intriguing evidence comes from the cremation burials. In the Mediterranean region, cremated remains of notable individuals are frequently found wrapped in cloth and deposited in a special kind of bronze urn or vessel. Many scholars connect this practice to a ritual described by Homer for the burials of Hector and Patroklos, who died in the Trojan War, generally

Figure 7.1 Traces of a rectangular shroud were indicated by the position of inorganic material thought to be attached to the edge of the cloth, Tomb 3 at Osteria dell'Osa, ninth century B.C.E. Here is an artist's idea of the cloth position (drawing by Jasmine Parker, adapted from Bietti Sestieri 1992, fig. 3a, 391)

placed in the Late Bronze Age, although the Homeric poems are believed to be later in date, and the rituals described in them are more likely to reflect the situation in the Early Iron Age (*Illiad* 34.796 and 23.254; Stampolidis 1996, 96). Hector's bones were wrapped in soft purple robes and placed in a gold ash-chest (*larnax*). The remains of Patroklos were wrapped in or covered with a thin veil and placed in a shallow bowl (*phiale*) to be united with Achilles' remains at some later stage. Thus, in both cases, after cremation the ashes were wrapped in a shroud, and the bundle was then laid inside an urn, which was buried under a burial mound.

Perhaps the earliest evidence for the 'Homeric' burial custom was discovered at Lefkandi, on the Greek island of Eubea, where a tenth-century B.C.E.

tomb of an important male individual yielded a bronze amphora inside of which was packed a folded 'robe of ankle length, made of two sheets of linen sewn up the sides' (Popham, Touloupa, & Sackett 1982, 173) and some decorated bands (Barber 1991, 197). Additional evidence for this practice has been suggested in the case of a Late Geometric funeral pyre excavated at Orthi Petra (ancient Eleutherna) on Crete. Here, a bronze phiale that covered an amphora containing the cremated remains had thin cloth traces around the rim (Stampolidis 1996, 142, fig.192). In a Late Geometric Tomb 6 at Eretria, a bronze cauldron contained cremated remains that were apparently wrapped in linen cloth (Bérard 1970, 13; Bloesch & Mühletaler 1967; Kurtz & Boardman 1971, 53). The textiles from Korfu, dated to the end of the seventh century B.C.E., were also used to contain the cremated bones of the deceased placed in bronze urns, inside of which they are still visible as mineralised traces (Metallinou, Moulhérat, & Spantidaki 2009). The same practice is documented in the fifth–fourth century B.C.E. burials of Attica, although probably no longer connected to warrior cult (Andrianou 2012; Spantidaki & Moulherat 2012). One of the later and arguably most spectacular manifestations of this ritual was discovered in 1977, in the so-called royal Tomb of Philipp II at Vergina, dated to the second half of the fourth century B.C.E. (Andrianou 2012, 46; Andronikos 1984). The gold and purple tapestry found inside the golden larnax placed in the antechamber of Tomb 2 of the Great Tumulus contained the cremated remains of a woman.

From Greece the practice is assumed to have been adopted by the elites throughout the Mediterranean and beyond during the Iron Age (Bérard 1970, 28; d'Agostino 1977, 59–60). In Italy, the rite was probably adopted by the native populations from Greek, specifically Euboean, colonists. The earliest evidence of this practice in Italy comes from Cuma and Pontecagnano sites, which were the first to come into contact with Euboeans (d'Agostino 1977). This 'Homeric' ritual then spread quickly among the Etruscan elites, as attested by the textile finds from seventh-century B.C.E. Etruscan burials. A bronze cinerary urn in Tomb A at Casale Marittimo, near Volterra, contained textile remains that probably served as wrapping for cremated bones (Esposito 1999). In some cases the custom was modified for local needs, and bronze containers were substituted for the local type of clay urns as, for example, at Este (Figure 7.2) (Bianchin Citton, Gambacurta, & Ruta Serafini 1998, 92).

In Tomba del Duce at Vetulonia, a linen cloth was found inside a bronze and silver *larnax*, which contained cremated bones (Camporeale 1967, 141; Falchi 1887, 506; Torelli 2000, 582, no. 130; von Duhn 1924, 239)—and this custom of including a cloth survived into later times. Travertine urns in the second–first century B.C.E. Strozzacapponi cemetery of Perugia contained mineralised textile remains in which cremated remains were wrapped (Cenciaioli 2004, 8). Even when textiles are not preserved, fibulae that bear no traces of cremation

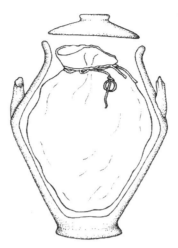

Figure 7.2 Reconstruction of the deposition of cremated remains wrapped in cloth inside the burial urn (drawing by Jasmine Parker, adapted from Bianchin Citton, Gambacurta, & Ruta Serafini 1998, 92, fig. 39)

but are found inside burial vases may indicate that the remains were wrapped in a textile and closed before being deposited in the urn (Boiardi 2006b, 17).

Wrapping of the Urn Containing Cremated Remains

At the time of the Greek colonists, however, Italy had a well-developed 'wrapping' custom of its own, as attested by the grave finds from central and northern Italy dated as early as the ninth century B.C.E. The cinerary urns at Este (Bianchin Citton, Gambacurta, & Ruta Serafini 1998, 92, fig. 39; Chieco Bianchi 1987, fig. 59), Bologna (von Eles 2002, 22; 2006, 73) and, in particular, the ossuaries in the burials of Verucchio were wrapped in textiles that were then fastened with fibulae and decorated with other accessories, as if wearing a garment (Boiardi 2006a, 15; von Eles 2006, 73). In the latter case, it has been established that both male and female ossuaries were dressed (von Eles 2006, 74).

While textiles often do not survive, the position of various small decorative objects such as beads and fibulae around the urn may indicate the presence of a cloth that was decorated or fastened with them. Such, for example, is the case of several ninth-century B.C.E. cinerary urns at Tarquinia (Figure 7.3 and Figure 7.4) (Iaia 1999, 114; Trucco 2006, 98–99) or a seventh-century Tomb 18 of Saletto necropolis at Este; the custom of wrapping the burial urn continued into later periods. Thus, a ceramic cinerary urn from the Tuscania-Tarquinia area of central Italy, dated to the second–first century B.C.E., had

Figure 7.3   Reconstruction of the burial urn wrapped in cloth, based on the position of artefacts on its exterior (drawing by Jasmine Parker adapted from Trucco 2005, 97, fig. 1B)

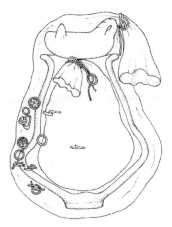

Figure 7.4   Reconstruction of the cremation burial with cremated remains and burial urn wrapped in cloth (drawing by Jasmine Parker adapted from Trucco 2005, 97, fig. 1B)

patches of white mineralized traces on its exterior and around the rim, indicating that a textile had been wrapped around it (Gleba & Turfa 2007, 38–39).

These textiles have been interpreted as clothing for the urns and thus as representations of the deceased (Bonfante 1975, 106, note 3). It has also been suggested that biconical urns—containers of cremated remains typical for the Villanovan period in Central Italy and frequently covered with bronze or ceramic helmets—represent the deceased and that their incised geometric patterns, similar to woven motifs, are intended to represent a garment (Delpino 1977; Iaia 1999, 29, 114; Toms 1996; Tuck 1994, 626). The Archaic 'canopic' urns from the Chiusi area, so called because they often had plastically rendered arms and were covered with lids shaped like heads, strongly support this theory. Furthermore, the single fibulae often found in association with these 'canopic' ossuaries are believed to have held together the textile 'mantles' in which they were wrapped.

In the seventh-century B.C.E. Tomba del Carro di Bronzo, at the Osteria cemetery of Vulci, textile traces were noted on the wrist of one bronze hand that supposedly made up the effigy of the deceased (or an ancestor) placed inside the tomb (Cristofani 1985, 288, no. 108; Ricciardi 1989, 43, note 64). These examples indicate that the phenomenon of the anthropomorphisation of burial urns in Early Iron Age Italy also included dressing them.

Recently, Demitra Andrianou (2012) also collected evidence for textiles found on the outside of the funerary urns in Classical Greece. Although less frequent than instances of textiles found on the inside, these cases document the existence of an urn-wrapping tradition in the Balkan Peninsula. Unlike the Italian custom of 'dressing' the urn, however, Andrianou interpreted this phenomenon in terms similar to the painting of textile ribbons (*tainiai*) on tombstones—that is, imbued with 'a more decorative connotation' (Andrianou 2012, 48).

Wrapping Both the Cremated Remains Placed Inside the Urn and the Urn Itself

Occasionally, finds indicate a combination of wrapping the cremated remains with 'dressing' the ossuary. Thus, in the Orientalising princely Morelli tumulus at Chianciano Terme, an anthropomorphic cinerary urn found in the southern cella of the tomb was wrapped with a textile that was fixed around the neck of the urn with a fibula (Paolucci 2006, 14; Rastrelli 2006, 17, 20). The iron fibula preserved the mineralised traces of the textile. Inside the ossuary, traces were identified of another fabric, which was likely to have contained the cremated remains (Rastrelli 2006, 17, 20).

Wrapping of Specific Burial Goods

Surviving textile traces indicate that, apart from cinerary containers, certain metal objects came into close contact with textiles, because they were intentionally wrapped or enclosed in fabric. Knives, weapons, strygils, spits, and mirrors are among the most common objects to bear textile traces. At both seventh-century B.C.E. Cales in South Italy (Chiesa 1993, 73, 41, nos. 37, 39, 40, 43, 50; Gleba 2008, 57, no. 64) and fifth-century B.C.E. Vassallaggi in Sicily (Gleba 2008, 62, no. 89), for example, most of the knives found in burials were subjected to this procedure.

In some cases, the traces are clear enough to reconstruct the direction of a cloth band wrapping a particular object. The deposition of thus 'enclothed'

Figure 7.5 Sword wrapped in a textile band from a cremation grave in Hallstatt (© Natural History Museum Vienna)

objects in urns excludes the possibility of accidental contact with textiles. It is unclear whether this phenomenon has a ritual significance in funerary context or represents a regular practice of safekeeping of precious metal objects.

In Central Europe, there existed a widely spread phenomenon of wrapping swords (Figure 7.5). It first appears in the ninth century and disappears during early La Tène period (Grömer 2010, 273). The geographical distribution of the swords containing fabric traces matches relatively closely the distribution of the western and central groups of Hallstatt culture, that is, an area covering the North-West Alps and the Main/Rhine confluence (Central and Eastern Gaul, South Germany, Austria, and the Czech Republic) (pers. comm. Christophe Moulhérat 2008). From the seventh century B.C.E. onward, the practice of wrapping a narrow band of fabric approximately 5–10 cm wide around the sword blade came into usage. The well-preserved examples clearly show that the fabric has been used as intentional wrapping—and the sword was not exposed to incidental contact with clothing or a funerary shroud.

It has been suggested that iron swords were wrapped with oil-soaked bands to protect them from rust (Kern 2005, 8). Although it is difficult to distinguish between ritual wrapping and simply protecting the weapon, what is certain is that this was a widespread practice and one that formed an integral part of funeral rites for the aristocracy in the Iron Age Europe.

The wrapping of mirrors and other utilitarian metal objects may be related to the ritual 'killing' of objects placed in graves as documented in Etruscan area. Here, particularly during the fourth and third centuries B.C.E., mirrors and other objects were mutilated by gouging or hammering or were inscribed with a special word, reflecting a need to alter an object for use in the afterlife (de Grummond 2009). It may be that by wrapping an object the same objective was achieved. A recent investigation of Egyptian mirrors wrapped or covered in textiles indicates that mirrors were purposefully covered probably for more than pragmatic reasons and that textiles aided the controlling of their supernatural power within funerary contexts (Price & Gleba 2012).

Wrapping of All Objects in the Burial

The ultimate expression of the European Iron Age wrapping phenomenon is exemplified by the particularly rich burials where the body of the deceased and every object were subjected to wrapping. They are known throughout Central Europe, but the best preserved and studied is the princely burial at Eberdingen-Hochdorf, in Germany, where the deceased and all his rich furnishings were wrapped in a coarse fabric (Banck-Burgess 1999 and in this volume). Even parts of the wagon show clear traces of several layers of wrappings. The deceased was dressed in sumptuous garments and decorated with gold jewellery before being wrapped in an undyed wool fabric (Banck-Burgess 1999, 18–32).

The Eberdingen-Hochdorf burial is not unique. The famous princely burial excavated at Vix in France may have been subjected to a similar ritual. During the excavation, the presence of fabric on the chariot wheels and various bronze appliqués was noted. During recent reexamination of the burial textile finds, researchers concluded that these fabrics were certainly used as wrapping but that they may also have played a functional role in the lubrication of the chariot wheels (Moulherat & Rolley 2003). In another chariot burial found in France, at Apremont, a bronze cauldron, an iron sword, an iron razor, and all the iron parts of a chariot had textile traces (Masurel 1990; Perron 1880, 354–55). The extent of and the systematic nature of wrapping in these three cases seem to indicate a formal funeral rite.

Conclusions

The categories of wrapping I have outlined had different purposes and intentions, and while providing protection they most likely carried other, deeper significance in the context of Early Iron Age European burial rituals. There is a clear distinction between items that were made invisible by wrapping and urns that were made more visible by being dressed like the dead person or tied with ribbons.

Wrapping practices whereby the deceased and/or the objects that accompanied him or her were made invisible, thereby possibly making them lose their power, may be connected to a broader phenomenon. A similar practice may be observed in the use of bier-cloths, canopies, parasols, and curtains in Greek, Etruscan, and Roman funerals. These items feature prominently in funerary portrayals and probably symbolize the need for caution during the liminal phase between death and burial. Thus, in the *prothesis* (laying out of the body) and *ekphora* (funerary procession) scenes on Greek geometric pottery, an important element is a rectangular chequered area, thought to represent a funerary cloth, suspended above the bier or held above the body of the deceased by attendants (Ahlberg-Cornell 1971; Stampolidis 1996, 113, 118). The cloth served as a roof of an impromptu pavilion. The clay model of a funeral cart carrying a bier covered with what looks like an ornamented cloth, found at Vari (Kurtz & Boardman 1971, 78 & pl. 16), seems to support this suggestion. Numerous Etruscan painted tomb ceilings are decorated with ornamental motifs that are unquestionably textile patterns, the entire tombs representing tents or pavilions with roofs made of cloth (Holloway 1965; Naso 1996, 349–52; Stopponi 1968, 1983, 39, 41; Tonini 1970). Greek and Roman literary and legal sources also imply that a body should not be exposed before the burial. The Digest (Paulus *Opinions* 21.2–5) designates as sacrilege the exposure of a body 'entrusted to permanent burial or left for a short period of time in some place' (Shelton 1988, 97, no. 113; additional references in Turfa 1999, note 32).

Investigation of the use of textiles for various wrapping in funerary contexts throughout ancient Italy, Greece, and other areas offers new insights into the complex funerary rituals of past societies and underlines the importance of textiles in these social practices. More attention to textile traces preserved on metal items found in burials may help in understanding these rituals and the intentions behind the practice of wrapping.

References

Ahlberg-Cornell, G. 1971. *Prothesis and Ekphora in Greek Geometric Art*. Studies in Mediterranean Archaeology Vol. XXXII. Göteborg: Paul Åströms Förlag.

Andrianou, D. 2012. Eternal Comfort: Funerary Textiles in Late Classical and Hellenistic Greece. In M. Carroll & J. P. Wild (eds.), *Dressing the Dead in Classical Antiquity*. Stroud: Amberley Publishing, pp. 42–61.

Andronikos, M. 1984. *Vergina: The Royal Graves*. Athens: Ekdotike Athenon.

Banck-Burgess, J. 1999. *Hochdorf IV, Die Textilfunde aus dem späthallstattischen Fürstengrab von Eberdingen-Hochdorf (Kreis Ludwigsburg) und weitere Grabtextilien aus Hallstatt- und Latenezeitlichen Kulturgruppen*. Stuttgart: Theiss.

Barber, E. J. W. 1991. *Prehistoric Textiles: The Development of Cloth in the Neolithic and Bronze Age with Special Reference to the Aegean*. Princeton, NJ: Princeton University Press.

Bartoloni, G. (ed.) 2000. *Principi Etruschi tra Mediterraneo ed Europa*. Venezia: Marsilio.

Bérard, C. 1970. *L'hérôon à la Porte de l'ouest. Eretria III*. Berne: Éditions Francke Beme.

Bianchin Citton, E., Gambacurta, G., & Ruta Serafini, A. (eds.) 1998. *'Presso l'Adige ridente . . .' Recenti rinvenimenti archeologici da Este a Montagnana*. Padova: Adle Edizioni.

Bietti Sestieri, A. M. 1992. *La necropoli Laziale di Osteria dell'Osa*. Roma: Quasar.

Bloesch, H., & Mühletaler, B. 1967. Stoffreste aut Spätgeometrischen Gräbern südlich des Westtores von Eretria. *Antike Kunst* 10, pp. 130–32.

Boiardi, A. 2006a. Il Costume. In *Il Potere e la morte: Aristocrazia guerrieri e simboli*. Verucchio: Pazzini, pp.15–16.

———. 2006b. Gli oggetti di ornamento. In *Il Potere e la morte: Aristocrazia, guerrieri e simboli*. Verucchio: Pazzini, pp.17–18.

Bonfante, L. 1975/2003. *Etruscan Dress*. Baltimore: The Johns Hopkins University Press.

Camporeale, G. 1967. *La Tomba del Duce a Vetulonia*. Firenze: Leo S. Olschki.

Cenciaioli, L. (ed.) 2004. *Il piacere della seduzione: Materiali dalle necropoli perugine*. Perugia: Futura.

Chieco Bianchi, A. M. 1987. Dati preliminari su nuove tombe di III secolo da Este. In D. Vitali, ed., *Celti ed Etruschi nell'Italia centro-settentrionale dal V sec. a.C. alla Romanizzazione*. Bologna: University Press Bologna, pp. 191–236.

Chiesa, F. 1993. *Aspetti dell'Orientalizzante recente in Campania. La Tomba 1 di Cales*. Milano: Cisalpina.

Cristofani, M. 1985. *I bronzi degli Etruschi*. Novara: Istituto Geografico De Agostini.

d'Agostino, B. 1977. *Tombe 'Principesche' da Pontecagnano. Monumenti Antichi Serie Miscellanea* 2:1. Roma: Academia Nazionale dei Lincei.

de Grummond, N. T. 2009. Rituals of Breakage and Mutilation in Etruscan Religion. In M. Gleba & H. W. Becker, eds., *Votives, Places and Rituals in Etruscan Religion: Studies in Honour of Jean MacIntosh Turfa*. Leiden: Brill, pp. 171–82.

Delpino, F. 1977. Elementi antropomorfi in corredi villanoviani. In *La civiltà arcaica di Vulci e la sua espansione, Atti X Convegno Studi Etruschi Italici (Grosseto—Roselle—Vulci 1975)*. Firenze: Istituto Nazionale di Studi Etruschi ed Italici, pp. 173–82.

Esposito, A. M. 1999. *I principi guerrieri: La necropolis etrusca di Casale Marittimo*. Milano: Electa.

Falchi, I. 1887. Nuovi Scavi della necropoli di Vetulonia. *Notizie degli Scavi* 3, 472–530.

Gleba, M. 2008. *Textile Production in Pre-Roman Italy*. Oxford: Oxbow Books.

Gleba, M., & Turfa, J. M. 2007. Digging for Archaeological Textiles in Museums: 'New' Finds in the University of Pennsylvania Museum of Archaeology and Anthropology. In A. Rast-Eicher & R. Windler, eds., *Archäologische Textilfunde—Archaeological Textiles, NESAT IX—Braunwald 18.–21. Mai 2005*. Ennenda, pp. 35–40.

Grömer, K. 2010. *Prähistorische Textilkunst in Mitteleuropa: Geschichte des Handwerkes und der Kleidung vor den Römern*. Vienna: Naturhistorisches Museum Wien.

Holloway, R. R. 1965. Conventions of Etruscan Painting in the Tomb of Hunting and Fishing at Tarquinii. *American Journal of Archaeology* 69, pp. 341–47.

Iaia, C. 1999. *Simbolismo funerario e ideologia alle origini di una civiltà urbana: Forme rituali nelle sepolture 'villanoviane' a Tarquinia e Vulci, e nel loro entroterra*. Grandi contesti e problemi della protostoria italiana, 3. Firenze: all'Insegna del Giglio.

Kern, A. 2005. Hallstatt—eine Einleitung zu einem sehr bemerkenswerten Ort. In P. Bichler, K. Grömer, R. Hofmann-de Keijzer, A. Kern, & H. Reschreiter, eds., *Hallstatt Textiles: Technical Analysis, Scientific Investigation and Experiment on Iron Age Textiles*, BAR-IS 1351. Oxford: Archaeopress, pp. 1–10.

Kurtz, D. C., & Boardman, J. 1971. *Greek Burial Customs*. London: Thames & Hudson.

Masurel, H. 1990. Tissus et Tisserands du Premier âge du Fer. *Antiquités Nationales*, mémoire 1.

Metallinou, G., Moulhérat, C., & Spantidaki, G. 2009. Archaeological Textiles from Kerkyra. *Arachne* 3, pp. 30–51.

Moulherat, C., & Rolley, C. 2003. L'organisation de la tombe de Vix. In C. Rolley, ed., *La tombe princière de Vix*. Paris: Picard, pp. 24–28.

Naso, A. 1996. *Architetture dipinte: Decorazioni parietali non figurate nelle tombe a camera dell'Etruria meridionale (VII–V sec. a. C.)*. Roma: l'Erma di Bretschneider.

Paolucci, G. 2006. Il tumuli in località Morelli, la tomba 'principesca'. In G. Paolucci & A. Rastelli, eds., *La tomba 'principesca' di Chainaciano Terme*. Chianciano: Pacini Editore, pp. 11–15.

Perron, E. 1880. La Motte d'Apremont (Haute-Saône). *Matériaux pour l'histoire primitive et naturelle de l'homme*, XVIe année, 2e série, T. XV, pp. 337–59.

Popham, M. R., Touloupa, E., & Sackett, L. H. 1982. The Hero of Lefkandi. *Antiquity* 56, pp.169–74.

Price, K. & Gleba, M. 2012. Textiles on Egyptian Mirrors: Pragmatics or Religion? *Archaeological Textiles Review* 54, pp. 2–13.

Rastrelli, A. 2006. Camera sinistra: il corredo. In G. Paolucci & A. Rastelli, eds., *La tomba 'principesca' di Chainaciano Terme*. Chianciano: Pacini Editore, pp. 17–38.

Ricciardi, L. 1989. La necropoli settentrionale di Vulci: Resoconto di un'indagine bibliografica e d'archivio. *Bollettino d'Archeologia* 58, pp. 27–52.

Riva, C. 2010. *The Urbanisation of Etruria: Funerary Practices and Social Change, 700–600 BC*. Cambridge: Cambridge University Press.

Shelton, J. 1988. *As The Romans Did: A Sourcebook in Roman Social History*. London: Oxford University Press.

Spantidaki, Y., & Moulherat, C. 2012. Greece. In M. Gleba & U. Mannering, eds., *Textiles and Textile Production in Europe from Prehistory to AD 400*. Oxford: Oxbow Books, pp. 185–200.

Stampolidis, N. 1996. *'Reprisals': Contributions to the Study of Customs of the Geometric-Archaic Period*. Rethymno: Publications of the University of Crete.

Stopponi, S. 1968. Παραπετασματα Etruschi. *Bollettino d'Arte* 53, pp. 60–62.

———. 1983. *La Tomba della 'Scrofa Nera'*. Materiali del Museo Archeologico Nazionale di Tarquinia, VIII. Roma: Bretschneider.

Toms, J. 1996. Symbolic Expression in Iron Age Tarquinia: The Case of the Biconical Urn. In R. F. Docter & C. Briese, eds., *Die Akten des Internationalen Kolloquiums —Interactions in the Iron Age: Phoenicians, Greeks and the Indigenous Peoples of the Western Mediterranean*, Amsterdam, 26–27. März 1992. Mainz: von Zabern, pp. 139–61.

Tonini, A. 1970. La Tomba Tarquiniese del Cacciatore. *Studi Etruschi* 38, pp. 45–65.

Torelli, M. (ed.) 2000. *Gli Etruschi*. Milano: Bompiani.

Trucco, F. 2006. Considerazioni sul rituale funerario in Etruria meridionale all'inizio dell'età del Ferro alla luce delle nuove ricerche a Tarquinia. In P. von Eles, ed., *La ritualità funeraria tra età del Ferro e Orientalizzante in Italia, Atti del convegno, Verucchio, 26–27 giugno 2002*. Pisa and Roma: Fabrizio Serra Editore, pp. 95–102.

Tuck, A. S. 1994. The Etruscan Seated Banquet: Villanovan Ritual and Etruscan Iconography. *American Journal of Archaeology* 98, pp. 617–28.

Turfa, J. M. 1999. Parasols in Etruscan Art. *Source Notes in the History of Art* 18.2, pp. 15–24.

von Duhn, F. K. 1924. *Italische Gräberkunde*. Heidelberg: C. Winter.

von Eles, P. 2002. *Guerriero e sacerdote: Autorità e comunità nell'età del ferro a Verucchio—La Tomba del Trono*. Firenze: All'Insegna del Giglio.

———. 2006. Il rituale funerario nel Villanoviano dell'Emilia Romagna: considerazioni alla luce di nuovi scavi e studi. In P. von Eles, ed., *La ritualità funeraria tra età del Ferro e Orientalizzante in Italia, Atti del convegno, Verucchio, 26–27 giugno 2002*. Pisa and Roma: Fabrizio Serra Editore, pp. 67, 78.

8 Wrapping as an Element of Early Celtic Burial Customs: The Princely Grave from Hochdorf and Its Cultural Context

Johanna Banck-Burgess

Ideas about wrapping and unwrapping the body can enhance our understanding of the burial mound from Eberdingen-Hochdorf, which belongs to the early Celtic people of southwest Germany. This grave constitutes part of an early Iron Age princely burial set within a cultural context identified specifically as the western group of the late Hallstatt period (620–470 B.C.E.). During the onset of the late Hallstatt period (HaD), that is, the last quarter of the seventh century B.C.E., there is evidence for the rise of specific centres of power in Southern Germany, Eastern France, and Switzerland.

The rise of such centres is marked by the appearance of burial mounds with remarkably rich burials that are often closely associated with hill-top settlements. These are marked as centres of authority by the construction features and defences placed on or near their distinctive elevations. At the lower reaches of the Danube, the Heuneburg, with its widespread suburb (Kimmig 1983b; Kurz 2005) is a prime example of the settlement structures with urban characteristics that are found especially toward the end of the seventh century and the first half of the sixth century B.C.E. The oft-cited mud brick wall excavated by Egon Gersbach in the 1950s illustrates the vibrant contact between the early Celts and the advanced civilisations of the Mediterranean. The numerous Greek colonies founded on the west Mediterranean coast between 750 and 450 B.C.E. significantly influenced the development of the early Celtic Hallstatt period (Kimmig 1983a). Discussions about the emergence of this

Wrapping and Unwrapping Material Culture: Archaeological and Anthropological Perspectives by Susanna Harris & Laurence Douny, 147–156 © 2014 Left Coast Press, Inc. All rights reserved.

early Celtic society and how it was structured continue and have recently been well summarised by Martin Kuckenburg (Kuckenburg 2010, 47–58).

Wolfgang Kimmig (1969) set out the criteria for late-Hallstatt-period aristocratic residences. These criteria, still valid although criticised by Eggert (1991), among others, include the presence of specific items, fortifications, and imports from the Mediterranean and also of other richly endowed burials close by.

The Hochdorf Burial and the Archaeological Textile Analyses

The remains of the burial mound from Hochdorf first came to light in 1977, when stones were ploughed up that belonged to the original outer layer of the burial chamber. The chamber itself was excavated over a two-year period from 1978 to 1979. The undisturbed burial chamber was that of an approximately 40-year-old man and had been sealed circa 540 B.C.E. It was equipped with a decorated bronze couch, a huge bronze cauldron of Greek origin with a capacity of 1,000 litres, a four-wheeled wagon, a food and drinking set, gorgeous drapings for the dead and for the chamber walls, rich gold jewellery, and individual belongings such as hunting gear. These items all demonstrate the high status of the deceased individual.

The degree of preservation within the burial was highly unusual. The chamber itself must have collapsed shortly after the internment of the body, thus creating compact and almost airtight conditions. The burial had never been looted and had not been disturbed by modern-day ploughing techniques. The well-preserved furnishings and the richness of the chamber thus allow us to draw wide reaching conclusions about the life of the early Celtic people (Biel 1995; Verger 2006).

Many of the items discovered in the chamber, such as the bronze couch and the cauldron, were removed in blocks and brought to the archaeological restoration laboratory at the Landesmuseum in Stuttgart, where they were meticulously documented, conserved, and restored. To date, seven monographs have been published; this literature demonstrates the wealth of information found in the Eberdingen-Hochdorf burial (Bieg 2002; Koch 2006; Krausse 1996; Küster & Körber-Grohne 1985; Schatz & Stika 2009; Verger 2006). Even so, these publications together barely touch the surface of all that there is to be learned from this unique burial.

A textile archaeologist in central Europe typically deals with fragments. Pieces that are often only a few centimetres in size, often much smaller, are usually preserved because of their close contact with materials that more easily survive, such as metal artefacts. Compared to the other archaeological finds of iron, bronze, gold, and ceramic, archaeological textiles are usually unsightly pieces that make no sense on first appearance, although a clearer picture can begin to develop after careful analysis (Figures 8.1, 8.2, 8.3). Their undistinguished appearance is certainly one of the main reasons why textiles in archaeology do not receive the attention that they deserve. But there are other reasons, too. There is still a strong tradition in archaeology, especially in Germany, of creating typologies. Some typologies are based on selecting distinguishing marks that take account only of the information relating to the finds themselves. The contextual information from the deposition process is often poorly researched and unsoundly published.

Nowadays, the analysis of archaeological textiles tends to be carried out to the same standards as any other type of find and/or features, meaning that the description of a grave has become much more precise and individualised.

Figure 8.1   The original fabric (scale: 1 cm) from the early Celtic burial of Eberdingen-Hochdorf (image by Johanna Banck-Burgess; Landesamt für Denkmalpflege, Esslingen)

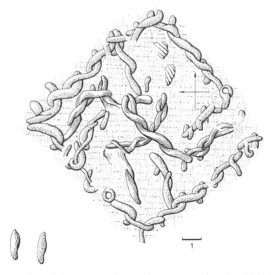

Figure 8.2   Drawing of the pattern element in Soumak; details of fabric from the early Celtic burial of Eberdingen-Hochdorf (image by Johanna Banck-Burgess; Landesamt für Denkmalpflege, Esslingen).

Figure 8.3 Experimental archaeology to demonstrate the production of fabric from the early Celtic burial of Eberdingen-Hochdorf (image by Yvonne Mühleis, Landesamt für Denkmalpflege, Esslingen)

Comparing more modern grave descriptions with those in older publications is therefore difficult to do because of the information that is missing in the latter.

It was the archaeologist Hans-Jürgen Hundt who first began the work of analysing the textiles from Hochdorf, and he eventually passed this project on to me. I then worked intensively on analysing and examining the material over a four-year period. It was no easy task, because the majority of the finds were mostly fingernail-size fragments that were nothing more than compact packets of organic substance with a thickness of just a few millimetres. Some slightly larger fragments survived, consisting of the fragments that were origi-nally draped over the bronze couch and the cauldron. Detailed analyses made it possible to reconstruct the position of the textiles within the chamber (Banck-Burgess 1999). The splendour of the textiles has been reconstructed and reveals distinctive blue and red colours, thanks to the results of the analyses undertaken by Penelope Walton Rogers (Walton Rogers 1999). It has also been possible to piece together the fragments so as to reconstruct the textiles that were once dis-played within the chamber. Piecing together our knowledge like this has allowed us to bridge a gap in our limited information about the textiles inside this burial chamber and about their context and cultural significance (Figure 8.4).

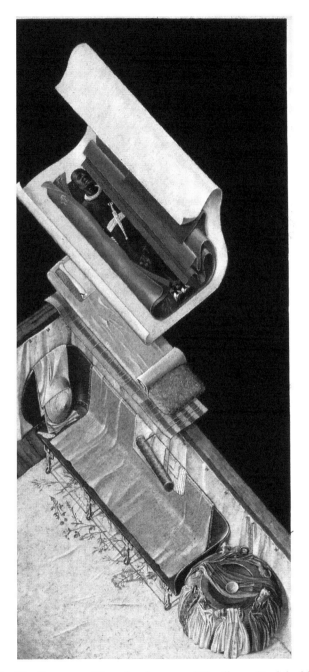

Figure 8.4 The discovery of the princely grave of Eberdingen-Hochdorf for the first time revealed the elaborate and precious textile equipment of early Celtic princely burials (image by Clark Urbans, Landesamt für Denkmalpflege, Freiburg)

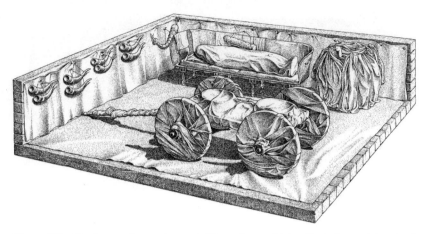

Figure 8.5 The impressive equipment of the prince, which reflects the social rank of the deceased, was completely covered with fabric and therefore deprived of its visual effect (image by Clark Urbans, Landesamt für Denkmalpflege, Freiburg)

The textiles in the chamber were used as coverings and hangings to decorate the burial chamber. The body was laid on a couch constructed from bronze, which included a lavish mattress that was layered with precious textiles. Among these textiles was one very luxurious red-coloured textile, dyed using the insect known as *Kermes vermilio*. The cauldron alone was covered with no less than four exquisite textiles, all with differing weave-structures and colours. Analyses of the fibre showed that the majority of the textiles were made of wool, but other unusual materials, such as the under wool from a badger's fur, have also been identified. The poor condition of some of the plant fibres has meant that only fabrics made of hemp have survived; linen could be identified only in very tiny proportions.

All these objects, however, were altered when they were wrapped (Figure 8.5). The deceased, with his rich textile furnishings, was wrapped in a coarse piece of fabric. And it was not only the deceased who was wrapped; there is clear evidence to show that parts of the wagon were also wrapped with several layers of wrappings, similar to the practice already seen in different Late Hallstatt graves in Germany and France, especially in Apremont (Joffroy 1958, 43; Masurel 1988, 49f.). All the precious burial goods were also covered, and thus made invisible, at the entrance into the otherworld. The textile fragments found at Hochdorf demonstrate how important it is to observe the finds *in situ* if one is to understand the context of such textiles.

The reconstruction of the wrappings is based on a sequence of analyses that were carried out in the laboratory of the Landesmuseum in Stuttgart. The bronze couch with the mattress, the body, and different organic layers were brought into the laboratory, and it took almost a year to remove the layers. The process of documenting the finds was an even more complex task and, as already mentioned, took four years to accomplish. One of the main problems was the different states of preservation of the organic material, which made distinguishing the textiles extremely difficult, with similar textile fragments looking very different even though found just a few millimetres apart.

The final evidence for the wrapping of the body was revealed by microstratigraphy. This is indeed an excavation where clarification followed layer by layer; it was carried out on a scale different from most other excavations', with much of the researchers' time spent looking through a microscope.

The woven cloth used to wrap the body, including the feet and the head, was a simple undyed weave of wool that was manufactured differently than was the fine and coloured cloth that lay beneath the deceased. The cloth underneath the deceased had a fine texture and differing colours with richly decorated borders that, together with the gold jewellery, would have made a splendid impression. However, the wrappings gave the opposite impression. Likewise, the other objects in the chamber that were wrapped in the same simple cloth, such as the wagon, were removed from visibility by this act of wrapping. But it is important to note that one must be careful about how one interprets this simple cloth in an archaeological context. Production methods and appearance were dependent on the purpose and expectations of the makers. And it is known that wrapping the burial gifts was a common practice from the prehistoric to the early medieval period.

Interpreting the quality of the fabric in the light of the burial makes sense only when one understands the purpose of the cloth. Ethnology reveals that the production of cloth intended for a special use is quite often run through specific production methods and can take months to complete. Thus the purpose of the cloth is not always easy to deduce and can be misinterpreted if the context is not understood. Distribution maps of so-called textile types make sense only when the function of the cloth is taken into account.

Wrapping as an Act for the Living and the Deceased

In the case of the man from Hochdorf, the complete wrapping seems to have obscured all the objects and the arrangements that marked his wealth. Any immediate perception of the splendour and the powerful social status of the deceased has been preempted; the golden jewellery—for example, the necklace, a sign of power, and the three exquisite cloths, which not only are of an impressive quality but which would also have demonstrated a strong and close relationship to the Mediterranean world—are not immediately apparent. Wrapping the body immediately removes their status.

But the wrapping in this burial was not confined to the body in the way that is evident in the Egyptian method of wrapping mummies. In ancient Egypt, the wrapping of the body was part of a transformation process of the deceased. In Hochdorf, by contrast, the wrapping itself is part of the visible and invisible signs of power and status.

Before one can begin to interpret the wrapping of the deceased one has to ask what sort of activities accompanied the burial ceremony. When did the wrapping occur? Immediately before the chamber was closed? Or did it happen earlier, to be put on display as part of a ceremony? This question is important, because the early Celtic princely burials, especially the burial at Hochdorf, are mostly interpreted as being symbols/signs of power. Jörg Biel, who was the supervisor of the excavation, recently suggested that the Hochdorf burial was a presentation of power intended to take possession of the man of power (Biel 2009). For those who would have been watching this process of change, it would have signified a transition from the imposing to the unimposing. Does the effect of the wrapped body belong to the dead person or to the bereaved? Or both? These questions cannot yet be fully answered. There is room, too, for further interpretations, as becomes clear when one considers the many terms used to describe the act of wrapping. Such terms include *to cover, preserve, conserve*; *to veil, camouflage, transform*; *to hide, conceal*; *to mask, disguise*; and *to reveal, highlight, exhibit*. The intention of the wrapping in Hochdorf seems to belong mostly to the last group—that is, to reveal, highlight, and exhibit.

At Hochdorf, artefacts such as the wrappings of the burial gifts and of the deceased seem to suggest, given their context, not only the end of a life but also the end of an era. The extent of the production and effort involved in the burial would likewise suggest a purposeful process in the preparation, revelation, demonstration, exhibition, and communication of its content. If you take as a starting point the view that the wrapping of the corpse was both a crucial part of and an act or demonstration during a burial ceremony, then the wrapping could have meant different things at different times during the enactment of that ceremony. It could have signalled not only the recognition that earthly values do have not the same significance in the kingdom of death but also that the deceased will submit to that kingdom. Maybe it reveals how these early Celtic people thought about earthly wealth, meaning that they differentiated between the status quo during life and the person himself: a dead person is just a human being, irrespective of who he may have been during his lifetime.

Independently of how one explains the wrappings of the dead, the burial at Hochdorf demonstrates rather impressively that a burial and the burial process were not static events. The burial and the chamber with all its contents was a window into a unique and complex world, a world that also demonstrated the thinking of these early Celts in central Europe. It is not only the wrapping of the burial gifts and the deceased that yield information about the context of the artefacts; the chamber itself seems to have been closed up unexpectedly and very quickly—there is evidence that heavy iron hooks were simply hammered through the textiles that hung on the chamber walls. The carpet found on the burial chamber floor was also pulled out of shape, suggesting that the burial gifts were brought into the chamber in a hurry.

Experience and modern research techniques enable us to interpret the information found inside the Hochdorf chamber. Textiles in this burial chamber yield valuable insights into ancient beliefs. And we are only just beginning to understand these beliefs within their archaeological context.

References

Banck-Burgess, J. 1999. Hochdorf IV: Die Textilfunde aus dem späthallstattzeitlichen Fürstengrab von Eberdingen-Hochdorf (Kreis Ludwigsburg) und weitere Grabtextilien aus hallstatt- und latènezeitlichen Kulturgruppen. Mit Beiträgen von Lise Raeder Knudsen, Karlheinz Mann, Penelope Walton Rogers, Werner Hübner. *Forschungen und Berichte zur Vor- und Frühgeschichte in Baden-Württemberg*, Band 70. Stuttgart: Konrad-Theiss Verlag, pp. 18–28, 91–132.

Bieg, G. 2002. Hochdorf V: Der Bronzekessel aus dem späthallstattzeitlichen Fürstengrab von Eberdingen-Hochdorf (Kreis Ludwigsburg). Griechische Stabdreifüße und Bronzekessel der archaischen Zeit mit figürlichem Schmuck. Mit Beiträgen von Peter Eichhorn, Werner Gauer. *Forschungen und Berichte zur Vor- und Frühgeschichte in Baden-Württemberg*, Band 83. Stuttgart: Konrad-Theiss Verlag.

Biel, J. 1995. *Der Keltenfürst von Hochdorf*. Stuttgart: Konrad-Theiss Verlag.

———. 2009. Das frühkeltische Fürstengrab von Eberdingen-Hochdorf: Eine Inszenierung. In J. Biel et al., eds., Landesarchäologie, Festschrift für Dieter Planck zum 65. Geburtstag. *Forschungen und Berichte zur Vor- und Frühgeschichte in Baden-Württemberg,* Band 100. Stuttgart: Konrad-Theiss Verlag, pp. 163–74.

Eggert, M. K. H. 1991. Prestigegüter und Sozialstruktur in der Späthallstattzeit: Eine kulturanthropologische Perspektive. *Saeculum Jahrbuch für Universalgeschichte* 42, Freiburg/München: Karl-Alber Verlag, pp. 1–28.

Gersbach, E. 1982. *Die Heuneburg bei Hundersingen: Aus der Geschichte einer bedeutenden Wehranlage*, 2. Hundersingen: Heuneburg-Museumsverein.

Joffroy, R. 1958. *Les sépultures à char du premier âge du fer en France*. Paris: A. & J. Picard.

Kimmig, W., 1969. Zum Problem späthallstättischer Adelssitze. In K.-H. Otto & J. Hermann, eds., Siedlung, Burg und Stadt-Studien zu den Anfängen (*Festschrift Paul Grimm*). Berlin: Akademie-Verlag, pp. 95–113.

———. 1983a. Die griechische Kolonisation im westlichen Mittelmeergebiet und ihre Wirkung auf die Landschaften des westlichen Mitteleuropa. *Jahrbuch des Römisch-Germanischen Zentralmuseums Mainz 30*, pp. 5–78.

———. 1983b. *Die Heuneburg an der oberen Donau*, 2. Stuttgart: Konrad Theiss Verlag.

Koch, J. K. 2006. Hochdorf VI: Der Wagen und das Pferdegeschirr aus dem späthallstattzeitlichen Fürstengrab von Eberdingen-Hochdorf (Kr. Ludwigsburg). *Forschungen und Berichte zur Vor- und Frühgeschichte in Baden-Württemberg*, Band 89. Stuttgart: Konrad-Theiss Verlag.

Krausse, D. 1996. Hochdorf III: Das Trink- und Speiseservice aus dem späthall-stattzeitlichen Fürstengrab von Eberdingen-Hochdorf (Kr. Ludwigsburg). Mit Beiträgen von Gerhard Längerer. *Forschungen und Berichte zur Vor- und Frühgeschichte in Baden-Württemberg*, Band 64. Stuttgart: Konrad-Theiss Verlag.

Kuckenburg, M. 2010. *Das Zeitalter der Keltenfürsten: Eine europäische Hochkultur.* Stuttgart: Klett-Cotta Verlag.

Kurz, S. 2005. *Zentralort und Umland: Untersuchungen zur Struktur der Heuneburg-Außensiedlung und zum Verhältnis der Heuneburg zu den umgebenden Höhensiedlungen.* http://tobias-lib.uni-tuebingen.de/volltexte/2005/2076/, accessed December 14, 2010.

Küster, H., & Körber-Grohne, U. 1985. Hochdorf I: Neolithische Pflanzenreste aus Hochdorf, Gemeinde Eberdingen (Kreis Ludwigsburg). Die biologischen Reste aus dem hallstattzeitlichen Fürstengrab von Hochdorf, Gemeinde Eberdingen (Kreis Ludwigsburg). Mit Beiträgen von Jörg Biel, Klaus Haas, Günther Vorwohl, Roland Wurster. *Forschungen und Berichte zur Vor- und Frühgeschichte in Baden-Württemberg*, Band 19. Stuttgart: Konrad Theiss Verlag, pp. 87–164.

Masurel, H. 1988. Vorlegung eines Indexes für zwei Gewebefragmente. In L. Bender Jørgensen, B. Magnus, & E. Munksgaard, 2nd ed., *Archaeological Textiles. Report from the 2th NESAT symposium 1.–4.5.1984.* Copenhagen: Arkaeologisk Institut, Københavns Universitet, pp. 39–52.

Schatz, K., & Stika, H.-P. 2009. Hochdorf VII: Archäobiologische Untersuchungen zur frühen Eisenzeit im mittleren Neckarraum. *Forschungen und Berichte zur Vor- und Frühgeschichte in Baden-Württemberg*, Band 107.

Verger, S. 2006. La grande tombe de Hochdorf, mise en scène funéraire d'un cursus honorum tribal hors pair. *Siris,* Studi e ricerche della Scuola di specializzazione in archeologia di Matera, 7, pp. 5–44.

Walton Rogers, P. 1999. Dyes in the Hochdorf. In J. Banck-Burgess, Hochdorf IV: Die Textilfunde aus dem späthallstattzeitlichen Fürstengrab von Eberdingen-Hochdorf (Kreis Ludwigsburg) und weitere Grabtextilien aus hallstatt- und latènezeitlichen Kulturgruppen. *Forschungen und Berichte zur Vor- und Frühgeschichte*, Band 70. Stuttgart: Konrad-Theiss Verlag, pp. 240–45.

9 Wrapping the Wrapped: The Development of Minimal Conservation of Ancient Human Wrapped Mummies from the Region of the Nile

Barbara Wills

This chapter aims to show the benefits of wrapping as a conservation treatment for ancient mummies. These benefits are explored using case studies from the British Museum and are discussed in the context of other contemporary and historical practices used to conserve mummies. Wrapping involves encapsulating the original covered body in a fine reticulated net fabric to keep textile bindings in position. The treatment is minimal, avoids invasive treatment, and the net is easily removable. The fabric is also stable with little need for adhesives or stitching through into the original textiles; gentle tension alone is used to keep them in place. The curator's responsibilities and knowledge are here taken into account in the decision-making process.

Wrapping provides an appropriate means of display in line with a museum's aim to present sensitive finds to the public in a clear, ethical, and scientific manner. Aesthetically, wrapping is advantageous; the mummy is seen clearly, while the conservation netting remains largely invisible to the museum visitor unless closely scrutinised. The treatments use methods developed primarily from textile conservation practise that also incorporate skills from other disciplines, with the intention of promoting an understanding of the body as a composite whole.

Conservators seek to preserve the past for the future using a variety of techniques, having first acquired and assimilated the necessary knowledge. The principal aim of conservation treatment is to extend the life of the artefact by slowing down the rate of decay. Thus the information that is intrinsic—the story of the object—remains available over an extended period of time. Conservation intervention relies on a foundation of scientific, historical, technical, and cultural knowledge, applied using developed craft/art skills. The conservator may discover, in the process of conservation, information that adds to scholarship in conservation and in other disciplines.

Mummies are bodily remains that include the preservation of soft tissues along with the skeletal remains. Thus mummified material retains significant supplementary information held within the soft tissues and accompanying wrappings (Leslie & Levell 2006). The stabilisation treatments applied to mummies have developed over recent decades, moving from what are now considered crude methods (although often the best available, given time and place) to current less-invasive techniques. How have conservators responded to the challenges of preserving mummies, and, more specifically, how have developing techniques been applied in the latter part of the twentieth and early twenty-first centuries? This chapter describes and considers the benefits of wrapping (also termed *encapsulation*) as a conservation method using two case studies of ancient Egyptian mummies and one of a Sudanese naturally mummified body.

Although often treated as primarily a textile conservation problem, mummies are of course composite, made from a range of materials in addition to the human remains. For ancient Egyptian mummies, that range includes textiles (generally linen, sometimes dyed or painted), various resins (for example, bitumen and those used in rituals), cartonnage casings (consisting of adhered layers of linen or papyrus covered with painted and gesso) and amulets of various materials, such as ceramic, glass, and metal, either in or on the wrappings. The concept of wrapping, therefore, covers not only the conservation of the linen textiles but also the composite whole.

In summary, a conservator needs to understand:

- the materials present
- the stability of the body within
- the methods used to make and conserve the non-body components
- the present condition and how this has come to be
- the types of decay and the rates of deterioration
- any past conservation/restoration interventions
- institutional, national, and international policies regarding the care of human remains (the rights of the dead and of the living)
- current professional ideas regarding treatments and condition recommendations
- present and future curatorial, study, and housing needs

- the range of scientific analytical processes presently used in the interpretation of the remains as well as the anticipation of those most likely to be significant in the future
- the end use, such as loan, display, study, or storage

A Brief Conservation History in Relation to the Care of Mummified Material

Early textile treatments derive from traditional household methods. When textiles were first collected by museums in the nineteenth century, they were cleaned and restored often by laundering followed by stitched repair. Aesthetic value was considered important, and cosmetic repairs were often undertaken. With archaeological material, Flinders Petrie (1853–1942) devoted a chapter of his seminal work *Methods and Aims in Archaeology* to artefact conservation, clearly stating that the responsibility for preserving excavated finds lies with the excavator: 'The preservation of the objects that are found is a necessary duty of the finder. To disclose things only to destroy them, when a more skilful or patient worker might have added them to the world's treasures, is a hideous fault' (Petrie 1904).

Early restoration treatments of human tissue were robust and intrusive. Those seeking to market ancient bodies would make good any losses or disjointed areas using locally available repair materials such as animal glue and plaster of Paris, sometimes in combination with textile bindings and/or reinforcing strips. In the restoration of a mummy and coffin ensemble (which includes a broad range of original components) one might find any of the following: beeswax, paraffin wax, flour paste, cardboard, wood, shellac and variants, natural gums and resins, and a wide range of fillers. These were combined in various ways often designed to obscure the fact of the item's restoration (Oddy 1992).

In the 1920s, the first Director of the Museum Schnütgen in Cologne, Dr. Fritz Witte, in his essay *A Serious Word about Restoration*, called for change: 'Under no circumstances should restoration go further than preserving and stabilising the damaged part' (Witte 1920, 57). This seemingly obvious premise is now intrinsic to conservation. From the 1960s, in conservation as elsewhere, there was an enthusiasm to use and apply some of the newly synthesised plastic materials into the treatment of objects. One example of this practice was the use of heat-reactive (thermoplastic) adhesives to support vulnerable textiles. Modern materials with their unusual and advantageous properties could perform specific and previously unthought-of functions (Landi 1985, 4). Experimenting with new materials was a challenge to some traditionalists, who preferred natural fibres and stitching techniques for supporting and stabilising textiles.

Much later the conservation profession realised that the thoughtful treatment of ancient Egyptian material, including mummified remains, required special focus. Submissions were offered to two conferences on the subject of the conservation of ancient Egyptian materials in the late twentieth century. Two Predynastic ancient bodies were investigated and stabilised by exploring the use of more modern synthetic resins (Johnson & Wills 1988). Techniques developed further, and materials deriving from the specialism of paper conservation began to be included (Johnson et al. 1995), especially in the repair and support of fragile linen textiles. Present treatments derive from an amalgam of adhesive and stitching approaches, informed and developed by contact with other disciplines. Adhesion of a textile to a stable substrate remains a favoured technique in some studios (Abdel-Kareem et al. 2008). The key factors remain: the ability to undo treatments in the future if needed; minimal intervention; clarity; and accessibility of information.

Within the British Museum, work carried out on mummies is overseen by a physical anthropologist or specialist curator. The Department of Culture, Media, and Sport Guidance for the care of Human Remains in Museums document (DCMS 2005) clearly states that the conservation of skeletal human remains should be carried out by an accredited conservator who is trained and experienced in caring for biological materials and that such work should also be overseen by an osteologist.

Conservation and the Wrapped Mummified Human Body

A mummified body is a composite single object though generally visible primarily as an assemblage of textiles. Treatments have therefore often been undertaken by those trained in textile conservation. It is seen as necessary to supplement textile-related knowledge not only by researching and applying techniques found in other relevant conservation disciplines but also by understanding the nature and needs of human remains.

Physical unwrapping is no longer necessary, since internal structures may be viewed using other techniques that have often been derived from medical investigation, such as CT (computer-aided tomography) scanning, which makes visible subtle interior forms (Parkes & Watkinson 2010). Conservation treatment is thus intended to keep the whole as intact as possible, with each element kept in relation to its adjacent part. The following case studies demonstrate that a subtle outer conservation wrapping can work effectively to keep the mummy in one piece. It is also easy to undo the process if necessary. The minimal nature of the intervention, in that most treatments do not adhere to or penetrate the original surfaces, is a great advantage, because it lessens the chance of contamination. The range of information inherent in the body remains, therefore, extant and available to future investigation. The aesthetic aspect is also of value because, even though detail is visible on close examination, the wrapped mummies appear reasonably intact.

In treating the following mummies, all stages of the conservation process were carried out in consultation with the curator, discussing further when necessary any supplementary questions that might arise as part of the process.

Case Study 1: The Late Roman Shroud of a Youth

The conservation of the painted shroud (EA 6709) was necessary as part of the refurbishment of the Roxie Walker (Upper Egyptian) Galleries at the British Museum (rooms 62–63). The aim was to strengthen the shroud so that it might safely go on long-term display wrapped around its mummy. Part of this treatment involved reversing an earlier intervention whereby a net had been stitched and stuck to the shroud. This conservation thus contrasts the techniques of the 1960s and 1970s with later, more successful developments. It also illustrates a flat treatment made three-dimensional, unlike the following two case studies, which retain the three-dimensionality at all stages.

Condition   Large holes present in the shroud had presumably led to the earlier remedial treatment of covering the surface with an adhesive net (documentation was absent). One can surmise, based on written accounts of similar treatments, that the shroud had been removed from the wrapped body and flattened. A piece of nylon net would have been dyed to blend with the average colour of the painted shroud and a thermoplastic adhesive painted on as an emulsion to one side. When dry, the net would have been attached to the painted surface using a hot iron. To ensure that the attachment was secure, lines of stitching were added. When examined in 1995, the net was poorly stuck to the shroud and becoming detached in areas, so it was not performing its original function. The stitching appeared unsightly and unnecessary in areas, and it obscured the vibrant image of the boy. The painted surface was at risk of detaching where the net had been stuck on. Some creases in the shroud appeared not to be original. This was deduced by examining earlier photographic images to gain an understanding of what most likely went where and thus to comprehend the way the shroud would have most effectively wrapped the body.

Treatment   The shroud was taken off the wrapped body and laid flat. To facilitate the removal of the adhered and stitched nylon net, the lines of stitching were first cut and gently pulled out. Where it had already begun to come off, the adhesive net was gently prised from the original surface by sliding in a broad spatula. A range of solvents and adhesive-removal treatments were tested on a small representative area to find out how best to reverse the adhesion. Only one was found to be successful: where the net was strongly stuck a small amount of industrial methylated spirits (IMS) on a cotton wool swab was held close to the surface. This softened the adhesive so that the net could then be safely eased away. The non-original creases in the shroud were relaxed by exposing those areas to controlled, raised humidity and flattened using padded glass weights until the shroud was dry (Figure 9.1).

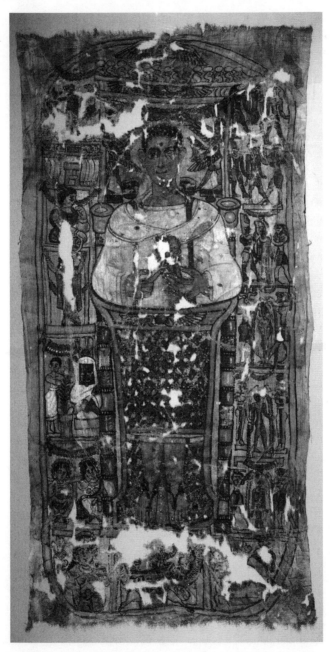

Figure 9.1   The mummy of a youth, early third century, after the 1995 treatment; British Museum Accession Number EA 6709 (© The Trustees of the British Museum. All rights reserved.)

A new support was made by dyeing two fabrics, one for backing and one for covering the surface. A fine plain-woven fabric (cotton lawn) was dyed to match the colour of the underside of the shroud using Ciba Geigy Solophenyl cellulose dyes. A very fine nylon net dyed to a neutral shade (Lanaset protein dyes) was prepared to cover the front. The shroud was then sandwiched between the cotton fabric, which went beneath, and the netting, which covered the painted surface. A thin (monofilament) strand of silk was used to stitch around the holes in the shroud avoiding piercing the original textile. Some areas required additional lines of stitching for strength, laid in where possible without disrupting the pigment layer. The backing and net were trimmed to give a 2 cm edge, which was then turned back and secured with herringbone stitch (using polyester thread Gütermann no. 120). The shroud was then placed back in position, following the original folds. The edges of the shroud on the underside of the body were joined using cotton tape in a zig-zag pattern to accommodate the variations in tension in the net shroud sandwich.

Evaluation   The 1995 conservation wrapping worked much better than the earlier wrapping in that the paint surface was secure and protected; the original folds were recovered to some degree; and the whole wrapped body was sufficiently secure for long-term exhibition. The aesthetic effect is good; the covering net is almost invisible. It is interesting to consider the use of the modern nylon net in contrast to the old; one obscures and threatens the stability of the painted surface, the other protects it. When this chapter was written, visitors to the British Museum could see the effect of treatment: EA 6709 is on display in room 63 (Figure 9.2).

How successful was the earlier adhesive net treatment? It had been applied to a textile in need of some support, and it evidently fulfilled its function for a period of time. Had this not been done, the shroud might have not survived as well as it did. It allowed retreatment, although a careful approach was required to do this well.

Case Study 2: The Mummy of an Elderly Woman of Thebes

The aim of conservation treatment was to stabilise the mummy of Bekrenes (EA 15654, Twenty-fifth–Twenty-sixth Dynasty) for loan in 2001. It was destined for three British venues as part of the exhibition Egypt Revealed: Life and Death in Ancient Egypt. The conservation treatments were designed to accommodate the controlled stresses of road travel and display, as well as CT scanning and a move to a new store. It was important to care for, and make some sense of, the original wrappings as far as possible. This was best done, however, by removing some of the wrappings in order to expose and maintain the visible binding pattern of the rest beneath. The conservation encapsulation

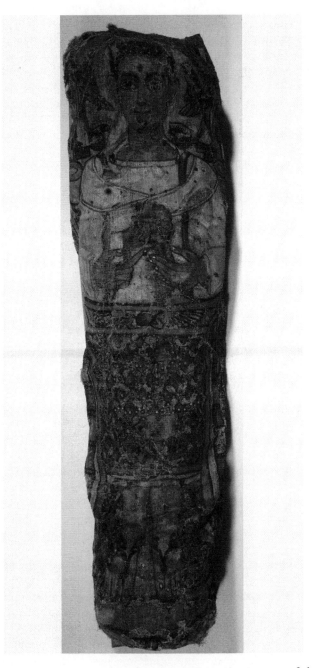

Figure 9.2 The wrapped mummy after treatment (© The Trustees of the British Museum.)

in netting could then be successfully applied to keep the remaining wrappings and, by extension, the mummy within, in good order.

The conservation process illustrates some of the complex curatorial decisions that need to be made, including what to keep on the body and what to store separately. It also shows the progress of wrapping and stitching treatments in the 1990s and early part of this century. Covering a flat textile with net using a stitching technique, as with the painted shroud discussed earlier, is relatively straightforward though requiring sensitivity to carry out (Singer & Wylie 1995). A similar method applied to a three-dimensional shape requires more complex thinking, involving the inherent elasticity of the netting and the use of sewn tailoring darts. The reason for using this technique is the need to accommodate the varying tensions encountered over the changes in shape, which involves constant adjustment of the stitching as the work progresses.

The use of adhesives to support very fragile textiles has also developed from the earlier heat-reactivated net technique (Keyserlingk 1990). Treatments influenced by paper conservation techniques (Cruickshank & Morgan 1993, 1995; Kite & Webber 1995; Peacock 1995; Wills 1995) were applied in this case.

Condition   When received for conservation, the mummy was draped in bundles of detached and disordered linen bindings that spilled out over the edge of the handling tray (Figure 9.3). Their condition varied from good and flexible, notably in the foot area, to extremely brittle. Linen bindings near the head and on the underside were stained dark brown and so fragile that they crumbled if handled. Staining by body fluids or original libations may have led to this differential deterioration. The surface was very dusty, with accumulations in the folds of the linen. Around the neck were deposits of a white saltlike material, and additional white patches were seen around the hole where the nose of the mummy had been. Analysis showed this to be palmitic acid, a breakdown product of beeswax and other fats and oils; this was considered to be original, a remnant of ritual practice. Signs of movement around the hips and neck indicated that the mummy may have been broken in these places.

The abdominal area had been damaged by robbers, perhaps in search of amulets, before collection. The nose was missing, leaving a hole in the centre of the face so that the cranial cavity was visible. The feet had also been damaged, and toes were missing.

Treatment   The surface dust and dirt on the mummy were removed using a soft brush to sweep them toward a vacuum cleaner nozzle on low suction. To protect the linen bindings from further damage it was decided to wrap the whole mummy in fine nylon net. However, many of the bindings had been loosely draped over the body, providing no clue as to their original positions. If these were wrapped with the rest, that would give a misleading impression. Consultation with the curator determined that some of the loose bandages be removed to reveal original layers in place beneath. Where bindings could be replaced convincingly into position, this was done. The loose bindings were treated and stored separately from the body, packaged in a hinged Melinex (clear polyester sheet) folder that was kept in Melinex pockets and stored flat in acid-free boxes. Long linen bindings were gently folded, and silk textile (Habutai) pillows enclosing polyester wadding were placed in the folds to support them. These were laid on shaped trays made from acid-free card covered in cotton lawn and contained in a Correx (polypropylene) corrugated sheet box.

The very brittle textiles required additional support before encapsulation. Patches of Japanese *kozo* (a very stable paper made of the inner bark of the paper mulberry tree *Broussonetia papyrifera* were coloured to match using acrylic paints and stuck to the undersides to bring joins together. Klucel G (hydroxypropyl cellulose) was used as a tack adhesive, so that it bonded to a surface but did not penetrate.

Nylon net was also dyed to match the linen. The net was dyed a paler colour for the body and a darker colour for the head. The entire mummy was wrapped in the net, which was tailored by creating dressmakers' darts where needed, stitching with silk thread. Although every attempt was made to avoid stitching into the wrapping of the mummy, such stitching was occasionally necessary to secure the wrapping in position (Figure 9.4).

Evaluation On her return from loan, the mummy of Bekrenes was examined by conservators, and the success of the wrapping treatment was evident. No damage had occurred. The treatment by wrapping in fine net had allowed the mummy to be more clearly seen and understood. Any future removal would be straightforward and without damage.

Conclusion

The advantages of wrapping mummies in fine netting are clear: the treatment is minimally invasive, with little or no alteration to the object covered and with appropriate strength in holding fragile textiles in place. It is visually acceptable and easy to disassemble in the future. There are also some disadvantages: it is difficult sometimes to find the appropriate colour if the object beneath varies in hue and intensity, and it takes tailoring skills to ensure that the right degree of tension is maintained over a variable three-dimensional shape. The surface, too, is partially obscured. Older methods and other contemporary methods involve the use of an adhesive applied to a fragile textile surface or stitching through the fragile weave to attach another layer of textile as support. Both techniques have significant disadvantages: adhesive inevitably contaminates a surface to some degree, and adhesion is only to a small surface area of a fragile fabric, thus opening up the possibility of further damage. Stitching

Figure 9.3 The mummy of an elderly woman, Twenty-fifth–Twenty-sixth Dynasties, EA 15654, before conservation (© The Trustees of the British Museum. All rights reserved.)

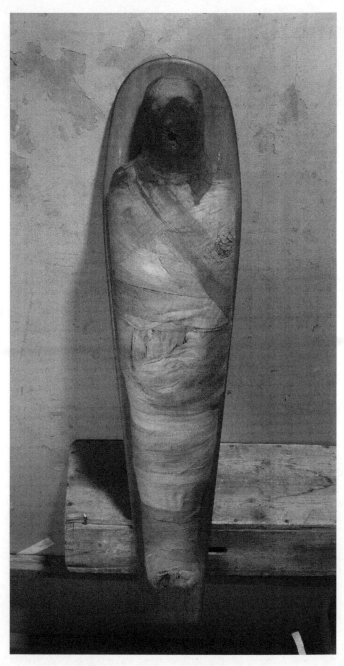

Figure 9.4 EA 15654 after conservation (© The Trustees of the British Museum. All rights reserved.)

can work very well if one is able to stitch through the holes in the original textile to reduce any potential damage to the threads and to distribute tensions evenly. However, wrapping is often chosen when treating mummies at the British Museum because of the ease of application and the satisfactory result.

As conservators, we constantly reevaluate our decisions and look out for new developments. What works for us now may not be suitable in the future (Curtis 2003). Conservation methods mature and change as a result of both ethical perceptions and the practical demands coming from the profession (ECCO 2002) and from elsewhere, whether from curators, bio-anthropologists, scientists, or museum visitors. The sensitivity that is brought to the treatment of objects translates well into caring for human remains. Indeed, to a conservator an inanimate object can almost take on life. Conservators are therefore generally comfortable in following protocols such as the requirements to treat with respect and the need for specific storage conditions to ensure long-term preservation. Certainly the development of the current benign, non-intrusive conservation wrapping methods accords well with the demands and sensitivities of most stakeholders.

References

Abdel-Kareem, O., Zidan, Y., Lokma, N., & Ahmed, H. 2008. Conservation of a Rare Painted Ancient Egyptian Textile Object from the Egyptian Museum in Cairo, http://www.morana-rtd.com/e-preservationscience/2008/Abdel-Kareem-24-03-2008.pdf, accessed August 16, 2013.

British Museum Policy on Human Remains, 2006, http://www.britishmuseum.org/PDF/Human%20Remains%206%20Oct%202006.pdf, accessed February 4, 2011.

Cruickshank, P., & Morgan, H. 1993. Lining a Banana-Fibre Belt—A Cool Vacuum Table Technique. *Scottish Society for Conservation and Restoration Journal* 4, pp. 10–14.

Curtis, N. 2003. Human Remains: The Sacred, Museums and Archaeology. *Public Archaeology* 3, pp. 21–32.

Department of Culture, Media and Sport (DCMS) 2005. *Guidance for the Care of Human Remains in Museums*, http://webarchive.nationalarchives.gov.uk/+/http://www.culture.gov.uk/images/publications/GuidanceHumanRemains11Oct.pdf, accessed January 20, 2011.

European Confederation of Conservator-Restorers' Organisations (ECCO) Ethical Code 2002. http://www.ecco-eu.org/about-e.c.c.o./professional-guidelines.html, accessed January 20, 2011.

Johnson, C., & Wills, B. 1988. The Conservation of Two Pre-Dynastic Egyptian Bodies. In S. C. Watkins & C. E. Brown (eds.), *Conservation of Ancient Egyptian Materials*. London: United Kingdom Institute for Conservation, pp. 79–84.

Johnson, C., Wills, B., Peacock, T., & Bott, G. 1995. The Conservation of an Egyptian Mummy, Cartonnage Cover and Mask. In C. E. Brown, F. Macalister, & M. M. Wright (eds.), *Conservation in Ancient Egyptian Collections Conference*, United Kingdom Institute for Conservation of Historic and Artistic Works. Archaeology Section, London: Archetype, pp. 47–56.

Keyserlingk, M. A. 1990. The Use of Adhesives in Textile Conservation. *Preprints of the 9th Triennial Meeting of the ICOM Committee for Conservation, Dresden*, Los Angeles: ICOM, pp. 307–12.

Kite, M., & Webber, P. 1995. The Conservation of an English Embroidered Picture Using an Oriental Paper Method: A Joint Approach. *The Conservator* 19, pp. 29–35.

Landi, S. 1985. *The Textile Conservator's Manual*. London: Butterworths.

Leslie, K., & Levell, N. 2006. Cutaneous Findings in Mummies from the British Museum. *International Journal of Dermatology* 45, pp. 618–21.

Oddy, A. 1992. *The Art of the Conservator*. London: Published for the Trustees of the British Museum by British Museum Press.

Parkes, P., & Watkinson, D. 2010. *Computed Tomography and X-Radiography of a 21st/22nd Dynasty Coffin*. In J. Dawson, C. Rozeik, & M. Wright, eds., Decorated Surfaces on Egyptian Objects: Technology, Deterioration and Conservation. Proceedings of a conference held in Cambridge UK, September 7–8, 2007. London: Archetype, pp. 58–66.

Peacock, T. 1995. The Repair of Textiles Using Starch and Cellulose-Based Adhesives. In P. Cruickshank & Z. Tinker, eds., *Starch Paste and Other Carbohydrate Adhesives for Use in Textile Conservation*, London: United Kingdom Institute for Conservation of Historic & Artistic Works, pp. 41–43.

Petrie, W. M. 1904. *Methods and Aims in Archaeology*. London: Macmillan.

Singer, P., & Wylie, A. 1995. The Conservation of a Fourth-Century AD Painted Egyptian Mummy Shroud. *The Conservator* 19(1), pp. 58–64.

Wills, B. 1995. The Preparation and Use of Two Starch Pastes. In P. Cruickshank & Z. Tinker, eds., *Starch Paste and Other Carbohydrate Adhesives for Use in Textile Conservation*. London: United Kingdom Institute for Conservation of Historic & Artistic Works, pp. 20–22.

Witte, F. 1920. Ein ernstes Wort über das Restaurieren. In *Zeitschrift für Christliche Kunst* 4, pp. 57–60.

Part IV: The Materiality of Wrapping:
Materials, Places, and Objects

10   Wild Silk Textiles of the Dogon People of Mali: Wrapping and Unwrapping Material Identities

Laurence Douny

West African woven wrappers, or wrap-arounds, are large rectangular pieces of fabric, woven by hand or industrially, that women wrap around their body either from under their armpits or from their waist down. In Mali, these prominent and easy-to-wear garments are commonly known as *pagne* ('loincloth') and are worn with a matching headscarf wrapped and tied around the head. Two layers of wrappers are meant to conceal the body, but a single layer of cloth can reveal its shape. An astoundingly diverse variety of eye-catching textiles are abundant in market stalls and in tailors' shops in the towns, highlighting the presence of style-conscious customers.

There, the bright colours and sheen of pre-dye cotton damask fabrics are naturally heightened by the sunlight while their stiff textures create a paper-like sound with every body movement. New fashions are constantly springing up alongside the traditional textiles, with the latter becoming increasingly less popular in some places. In rural areas, however, wrappers with regional characteristics—and therefore the designs and motives associated with particular ethnic communities that materialise their cultural identities—are much more visible.

This chapter explores aspects of the Dogon *Tengu* and *Tommon* collective, individual and 'shared' material identities (Sofaer 2007). Here, I suggest that Dogon cultural identities materialise in their wild silk indigo cloths of prestige called *tombe toun* throughout the making process and social usages of this flamboyant woven fabric. I highlight the cultural significance implicit in the

Wrapping and Unwrapping Material Culture: Archaeological and Anthropological Perspectives by Susanna Harris & Laurence Douny, 173–192

forms of the *tombe toun* wrappers, first through an examination of the material practices involved in production and in the use of wild silk as a wrapping material and, second, by discussing Dogon wrapping techniques in relation to wild silk indigo textiles. From this perspective, I envisage 'wrapping' as a cultural and technical process of materialising identities (Gosselain 2000; Tilley 2011).

Tombe Toun Wild Silk Indigo Wrappers as a Material Identity

In the Dogon region of Mali, the most popular traditional indigo wrappers are plain and/or decorated wrappers that are known as *gara. Gara* cloth may, for example, display colourful embroidery similar to that seen on the *souna* marriage shawls; or tight-dyed *gara* wrappers can reveal successions of discrete white geometric patterns that rise up from a plain indigo base (Brett-Smith 1990, 164). *Gara* wrappers are fashionable every-day and ceremonial outfits worn by Dogon women across the Dogon region and, in particular, in the *Toro so* and *Dono so* areas, where their popularity and production increased considerably from the 1990s as tourism advanced. It is noteworthy that the use of indigo cloth in that part of Mali and West Africa is a long-standing tradition, as the fragments of indigo dyed textiles identified as Tellem demonstrate. Such fragments were recovered from burials in the caves of the Bandiagara escarpment by Dutch archaeologist Rogier Bedaux and his team, who have dated them back to the eleventh and/or twelfth century C.E. (Bedaux 1988; Bolland 1991).

This chapter[1] is concerned with a different kind of indigo woven wrapper, that is, the indigo textile tradition called a *tombe toun* (Figure 10.1), a wrapper that is worn by the Dogon women of the *Tommon* and *Tengu* areas situated in the southeast cliffs area and in the Seno plain (the Bankass Cercle). These wrappers are decorated with horizontal white and blue indigo woven stripes and are made from dyed indigo hand-spun cotton and wild silk yarns. According to oral tradition,[2] these wild silk indigo textiles originate in a Marka-Dafing craft that dates to around the sixteenth century. Dogon women have been producing them for over 200 years. However, despite their mention in Gardi's work (2009, 9), these wild silk textiles of the Dogon have never been subjected to in-depth research in the Mali region.

Wild silk indigo cloth is found in both the Dogon and Marka-Dafing communities of Mali and of Burkina Faso (Hill-Thomas 2012; Roy 2010, 225), where it is considered to be a luxury cloth praised for its durability and its sheen. It is seen as a women's concern, because it is women who both manage its entire production and generally wear the material. Its high price stems primarily from the rarity of wild silk as well as from the complex techniques required to transform the raw material. In addition, its manufacture involves many costs at each stage of the production sequence. Cheaper alternatives to

Figure 10.1 *Tombe toun* wrapper of the Dogon of Mali (photo by Salif Sawadogo)

wild silk wrappers, bearing the same design and made of substitute materials that pass for wild silk, are widely produced but do not enjoy the *tombe toun*'s high quality reputation. For these reasons, *tombe toun* wrappers remain a 'must have' among the Dogon *Tengu* and *Tommon* speaking and Marka-Dafing rural communities of Mali because they are essentially a way for women both to display their wealth and social status and to enhance their personal worth and well-being. Finally, this prestigious cloth is not only a key component of the bride-wealth but is also used as a woman's shroud in that part of the Dogon region, whereas plain cotton woven cloth is used elsewhere across the Dogon region (Gardi 2003; Lane 2008).

In this chapter I examine some of the ways whereby the *tombe toun* materialise not only the Dogon women's individual identity but also the collective identities of the *Tengu* and the *Tommon*, together with a Mande heritage that Dogon are said to share with Marka-Dafing, a neighbouring community. It is worth emphasising that a Dogon's Mande origin remains highly debated[3] by scholars (notably, see Mayor 2011; Robion-Brunner 2010). I do not intend to discuss here the Dogon's ethnicity and origins but more simply to show some aspects of a Dogon's shared material identity as expressed by the *Tengu* and the *Tommo kan* Dogon people today and as acknowledged by the Marka-Dafing people with whom the Dogon coexist. I suggest that an examination of the production and use of *tombe toun* wrappers as a shared material practice enables us to emphasise the nature of the Dogon and Marka-Dafing's interethnic relationships. I am, therefore, proposing that the production and use of the wild silk indigo wrappers enables us to highlight those external cultural influences that make up and exemplify the collective identity of the *Tengu* and the *Tommo kan* Dogon. In other words, I am concerned here with the role that wild silk indigo textiles play in the formation and expression of a Dogon cultural identity that I see as complex and in-the-making.

Dogon and Marka-Dafing Identity and a Shared Mande Heritage

The Dogon and Marka-Dafing people live in neighbouring territories and on both sides of the Malian and Burkinabe political border. The Marka-Dafing communities live in the northwest of Mali and of Burkina Faso, in the Mouhoun and the Sourou province. The *Tommon* and *Tengu* Dogon of Mali occupy the southern part of the Bandiagara cliffs, the Koro and the Bankass Cercle in the plain, where they coexist with the Marka-Dafing in both Dogon and Marka-Dafing villages. The Dogon and the Marka-Dafing explain that their communities once left the Mande (Manden) together and migrated to the cliffs, where they then separated. As Mayor and associates suggest: 'Historically, the first Dogon settlement of the cliff zone can be placed within a range of two centuries, between 1230 and 1430 AD' (Mayor et al. 2005, 31).

Various versions of the history of the Mande tell of many events—wars, jihads, slavery, and recurrent episodes of drought—that would have forced people to move to safer places. The Dogon settlements would have arisen through multiple waves of migration spreading over centuries during which people would have intermingled and dispersed (Dieterlen 1941; Niane 1974). The *Tommon* and *Tengu* Dogon and the Marka-Dafing communities trace their common shared origins to the Mande, a 'vast and coherent ideological system' (Mayor et al. 2005, 31), which extended over a large area that includes the western part of Mali proper and Guinea Conakry, the heart of the Mali Empire (thirteenth–fifteenth century C.E.). This shared Mande identity, which includes other Malian and West African communities such as the Bambara, the Senoufo, and the Soninke, brings to them a sense of unity. It can also be seen as a political statement that affirms and symbolically displays the peaceful relationships that exist between the Dogon and the Marka-Dafing as they coexist in the same villages and cultivate their adjacent lands. In both Dogon (*Tommon/Tengu*) and Marka-Dafing regions, the interviewees recalled that the Mande was a country made of several provinces in which people, who are today called the Dogon and the Marka-Dafing, were living together in the province of Mande Kaba, in the village of Dogoro. They would have left the Mande and migrated to the Bandiagara cliffs together.[4]

While the etymology of the names 'Marka-Dafing' and 'Dogon' may reveal the particular characteristics that are assigned to them, these names also carry meanings about social relationships and their articulation among these groups in specific historical contexts. The Marka-Dafing interviewees of Burkina Faso and Mali suggested that the term 'Marka' (also pronounced 'Mareka', 'Maraka', or 'Meka') is a distortion of the original term 'Maninka' or 'Mandeka', meaning 'Mande' and commonly used to designate a group of people who practice an animism religion. The name 'Dafing', associated with a group of Marka who converted to Islam, is said to be a contraction of the Djoula appellation *Daba fing tigui*. It designates a group of people 'who possess black ink' and who count among themselves powerful marabouts (Muslim scholars) who practice a black magic that combines Arabic calligraphy with traditional animist black magic.[5] The 'Marka-Dafing' people, as they are named in Mali, are regarded as economically powerful communities who practice long-distance trade. It is noteworthy that the Marka-Dafing of Mali designate themselves the *Maninka*, whereas the Dogon called them *Banou*, meaning 'those who are undecided'.

The Dogon of the Seno plain are very often described as *kaado*, a Fulbe term that sometimes translates as 'people who easily lose their temper when provoked' or as 'sharp and brave', a reference to their hard-working nature as cultivators. Nevertheless, they are called *dogoni*, meaning 'young brother', by the Marka-Dafing. In this context, the term refers to their brotherhood relationships that are expressed as *dein oundjan* ('big brothers'/'young brothers') in the *Tengu* and *Tommon* areas (especially in the *Tommon*), where the Dogon population is greatly intermixed with the Marka-Dafing through their co-existence and the intermarriages in which the *tombe toun* plays an essential role in the bride-wealth. This factor might explain the diffusion of *tombe toun* fashion in the Dogon *Tengu* and *Tommon* areas. It is also interesting to note the role of Dogon women in setting fashions and in producing these shared Dogon and Marka-Dafing material identities. Here, the Dogon women's appropriation of Marka-Dafing's production techniques for the wild silk indigo wrappers is legitimised by the fact that both communities claim a common Mande origin, one that is grounded in their long, shared history and their enduring social and economic relationships. While inquiring about the cultural significance of wild silk indigo wrappers, my Dogon and Marka-Dafing interviewees unanimously explained that 'this [wild silk indigo wrapper] is the wrapper[6] of the Mande people, you will see it anywhere you find Malinke/Maninka people and their descendants in Africa and worldwide'.

While *tombe toun* wrappers signal a Mande heritage and identity, they also reveal a Dogon *Tommon* and *Tengu* textile tradition that has been perpetuated over centuries by Dogon women.

Unwrapping the *Tombe Toun*-Making Process:
Shared Material Practice and Interethnic Collaboration

Before colonial times, wild silk could be found in the luscious wooded regions of Mali, such as Baye, Kolokani, and Sikasso, as well as in some of the caves of the southern part of the Bandiagara cliffs. However, climate change and long-term human exploitation of timber resources have destroyed the caterpillars that produce wild silk. As a result, Marka-Dafing traders have extended their search for these precious cocoons further south, that is, into the remote bush and forest areas of the Ivory Coast, Guinea Conakry, and Ghana as well as into Nigeria and Northern Cameroon. In Mali, Marka-Dafing traders have long enjoyed a reputation for the high quality and the plentiful supplies of their cocoons, a broad range of wild silk indigo wrapper designs, and stocks of cheaper alternatives. As a result, the Marka-Dafing village of Massakana in Mali has been for centuries an important trade centre for wild silk. The large quantities of cocoons collected by the traders are divided among the Marka-Dafing itinerant merchants of Burkina and Mali, who sell the goods on to markets in the Dafing and Dogon regions.

Wild Silk: Varieties and Material Properties

In the Dogon *Tengu* and *Tommon* areas, the type of wild silk most readily available comes from the *goro ba* ('thick skin'), a large whitish cocoon found in Nigeria[7] and Guinea Conakry (Figure 10.2). It contains a lot of fibre, and it grows on the tamarind tree (*Tamarindus indica*). Another variety is the *goro dialen* ('very hard skin'), which is harvested from the kola tree in the Ivory Coast and the Republic of Guinea and which can also be bought on the Dogon markets. A small red cocoon called *tuntun bleni*, of a light reddish

Figure 10.2 Cocoon from Nigeria *Epanaphe Moloneyi* (*Druce*) (photo by Laurence Douny)

Figure 10.3 Degummed and dried wild silk showing a coarse texture (photo by Laurence Douny)

colour ('red caterpillar') and the *tuntun de* ('creamy colour') are more rarely imported from Ghana. In the past, a tiny white cocoon the size of the palm of a hand, called *tome*, was collected in the caves of the Bandiagara cliffs. In addition, vegetal fibres[8] that are much more readily available and affordable than wild silk are used as an alternative. They consist of the fibre extracted from the dried pods of two varieties of kapok and an indigenous variety of cotton called *kouni kagadji*, which has a relatively hard texture.

Although wild silk has a coarse and lumpy texture (Figure 10.3) compared to cotton, it has three noteworthy material qualities: sheen, a remarkable strength; and durability (Douny 2013, 65). Furthermore, the living larvae that can be found in the cocoons are consumed for their medicinal properties— they are believed to cure diabetes (*cikoro nouran*) and tetanus (*nin*, 'the incurable wound') and to reduce high blood pressure. Last, wild silk, perceived as a magical material secreted by insects, is used in magic practices such as the making of amulets (Douny 2013, 68). Overall, wild silk is seen by the Dogon as a living and proactive material owing to the magical and healing properties ascribed both to the insect and to the substance that it secretes.

Processing Cocoons, Dyeing and Weaving Yarns

The production[9] of wild silk yarns is a long and costly task that demands both a high level of skill and knowledge about technical and chemical processes and the properties of raw materials—all skills that the Dogon women have acquired through long experience. In the first stage of silk production, cocoons are boiled in an alkaline water solution (potash) in order to free the threads from the silk gum (sericin) that binds them together. This task is exclusively performed by old women who are highly skilled, since it is believed that clumsy

Figure 10.4   Carding techniques (photo by Laurence Douny)

young women could injure themselves and spoil the product. Furthermore, it is believed that cooking cocoons still containing living caterpillars will trigger the birth of infants with deformities or stillborn babies. This fear is based on the belief that there is a symbolic connection between gestation into a woman's womb and the metamorphosis of a larva into a moth inside the cocoon. The second step consists of softening the fibre through repeated washing, drying, beating, and carding, so as to untangle (Figure 10.4) it before spinning it into the single yarn, which is continuously drawn out from a lump of carded silk.

Together with pre-indigo cotton threads, wild silk yarns are woven on a horizontal double-heddle loom into narrow bands by *sourougan* (Figure 10.5), who are Dogon and Marka-Dafing men weavers. Finally, the women sew

Figure 10.5   Weaving wild silk and indigo cotton yarns on a horizontal loom (photo by Laurence Douny)

together the strips to form a 2 m–1 m wrapper that is then dyed indigo either by the caste of *gwara* dyers (women) or, more usually, by the Marka-Dafing dyers of Massakana (mostly men/non-caste), whose dyeing work is said to be of a much higher quality because their recipe uses a mixture of natural and chemical indigo. However, the Dogon's wrappers are said to last longer than the Marka-Dafing's since the Dogon cook their cocoons with ashes and natural potash, which do not weaken the yarns in the way that chemical potash does. Finally, while the majority of the Dogon wrappers bear one or more aphorisms that have certain meanings in the Marka/Dafing (Malinke) language, some are named in the Dogon *Tengu* and *Tommon* language or are simply renamed something else.

Some Dogon women develop lucrative businesses involving the sale of wrappers made of wild silk or alternative fibres, bobbins, and rolls of woven bands. The Marka-Dafing, however, remain the biggest producers of *tombe toun*, and overall the wrappers made of alternative materials are far more affordable and sell very well at the Dogon markets of Dialassagou, Tori, Koro, and Bankass (Figure 10.6). The production of *tombe toun* wrappers involves knowing how to apply a complex set of techniques that the Dogon women initially acquired from the Marka-Dafing and have since developed over time. They have developed this knowledge in accordance with their perceptions,

Figure 10.6   Marka-Dafing sellers' stall on Dogon market (photo by Laurence Douny)

beliefs, and understanding of the properties of this prestigious insect material and alongside their long-standing experimentation and experience with wild silk. For the *Tengu* and *Tommon* Dogon, therefore, the production of wild silk wrappers represents a Dogon tradition that has become a part of their heritage, as I shall now explain.

A Dogon *Tommon* and *Tengu* Identity and Heritage

As I have shown, the production of wild silk wrappers represents a long-standing craft that requires expertise and signifies a Dogon *Tengu* and *Tommon* identity through the act of 'making'. From this perspective, Dogon material identities are still 'in-the-making'—that is, they are still being shaped and reshaped over time both by Dogon and Marka-Dafing cultural and economic relationships and by the Dogon women's complex methods of producing the wild silk.

The Dogon people produce a Marka-Dafing textile that, over the course of more than 200 years, has become a material identity for the *Tengu* and *Tommon* communities of the region. How and why this has happened can be explained not only by the Dogon's shared Mande origin, their interethnic cooperation at the level of craft production, fashions, and trade, but also by interethnic marriages. In other words, this Dogon tradition results from their legitimate appropriation of Marka-Dafing techniques, design, and materials on the basis of, first, a feeling of brotherhood that is grounded in their shared Mande origin and history and, second, the Dogon's ancestral heritage within their own *Tengu* and *Tommon* communities.

Tombe toun wrappers are expressed in terms of Dogon tradition and heritage as *atemu* (*atem/atiembe*): 'what we (Dogon) "found" with our ancestors'. The term refers to the customs and practices that the Dogon people have inherited from their ancestors and that constitute their identity as Dogon. Picton has described the Ebira's (of Nigeria) woven cloth tradition as found in the proverb '*Um'okuku um'oboba—iruvo pit'acit*', which

> summarises notions of time and tradition, making use of cloth as both artifact and metaphor in order to provide an understanding of ancestral precedent. The present is an inheritance. Current practice is legitimated by placing its inception in the past. It was established by others, and they have handed it on to us. (Picton 2009, 298)

Similarly, in a Dogon context, making and wearing wild silk indigo wrappers are legitimate acts because of their continuity with the past. These wrappers have become a specialised craft over the long term through everyday practices to do with processing silk, weaving, indigo dyeing, and through their routine and ceremonial uses. In other words, all these material practices bring together people, ideas, techniques, knowledge, beliefs, usages, and customs, transporting them into the same cultural and temporal continuity that is represented in the materiality of the wild silk wrappers.

Tombe toun wrappers also reveal regional collective identities through the way women display themselves at national festivals: Women's Day (March 8th); the Biennale des Arts in Bamako, a celebration of Mali's cultural diversities through art; and Ginna Dogon, a biennial event celebrated throughout the Dogon region. The head and founder of a cultural NGO explains:

> Ginna Dogon that was founded in 1991 aims to show the specificities of Dogon cultures through multiple performances and to highlight cultural influences brought by all ethnic communities that coexist with Dogon people. It celebrates and strengthens interethnic relationships. So, it gives a sense of unity, as you know that our country Mali has a great cultural diversity but underlying tensions exist between these communities.[10]

Every Ginna Dogon festival, therefore, celebrates within its name not only the 'Dogon mother or family house' but also the history of the Mande and the Dogon migration from the Mande—that is to say, the very essence of their belief in their claimed ancestral affiliation. Herein lies Ginna Dogon's hidden political agenda, to legitimise the economic practices of the Dogon elite and to underline a constructed Dogon culture (Bouju 1995, 95–117). Yet, from a Dogon's point of view, knowing one's family origin and the meaning of one's family name, and knowing that they are embedded in history, is vital for the Dogon. As they say: '*borodouman yaa goyema, in kouna aayema, ko djougasse emeni dianko*', meaning 'it is vital to know where we come from in order to know who we are'.

At the most recent Ginna Dogon event, when various masquerades, processions, and craft demonstrations took place from all over the Dogon country, a dozen women from the *Tengu* and *Tommon* areas performed traditional dances in *tombe toun* garments (Figure 10.7). Their performance, and the display of *tombe toun* wrappers on sale in the stalls, reaffirmed Marka-Dafing and Dogon relationships. And the *Tengu* and *Tommon* performers proudly represented their own Dogon community and demonstrated their respect toward their Dogon ancestors, from whom they had inherited this unique textile tradition. They were, in other words, wearing *tombe toun* 'to feel beautiful and to honour one's community', as one performer emphasised.[11] By wearing these *tombe toun* wrappers, the Dogon women were flaunting both their collective and their individual identities as producers of this expensive and prestigious cloth. I now explain how this cloth enhances Dogon women's worth and social status.

Figure 10.7 Dogon women of the *Tommon* area wearing wild silk wrappers and performing at Ginna Dogon celebration in Bandiagara (February 25, 2011) (photo by Laurence Douny)

Dressing Up the Body: The Social Significance
of Wild Silk Indigo Wrappers

In the Seno plain, a married Dogon woman traditionally wears two layers of wrappers (*borotoun*). These layers of cloth produce a thick outfit that conceals her body shape and serves as a means of dressing modestly, respectfully, and in a way that avoids attracting men's looks. A first small wrapper called a *yapooran toun dagi* is wrapped around the waist and fastened on its upper edge. It reaches to the knees. The second layer of cloth, worn on top of the first, is called a *yapooran-toun*, meaning 'a complete woman' (an expression that refers to a married woman), and fully covers her legs. Traditionally, a woman's status (married/unmarried) can therefore be seen by the length of the wrapper that she wears. In addition, the wrapper may be partly covered with a *boubou*, a long and ample shirt that forms a sort of third layer. Wrappers are fixed, or as they say 'attached' (*borotoun paga*), in such a way that the cloth's left side edge remains visible; this is considered to be the proper way of dressing. Finally, there is the 'meta-language' at play: *tombe toun* wrappers are implicit and effective ways of expressing moral statements, criticisms, and insults that the wearer is unable to verbalise. Similarly, the Yoruba's indigo resist-dyed *adire* cloth (Aronson 1995) or the Bamana's mud cloth, the *Bogolanfini* (Brett-Smith 1984), are famous examples of African textiles that carry within them visual, nonverbal messages. Here, the *tombe toun* displays one or more aphorisms embedded in a design that consists of contiguous and horizontal indigo and white silk strips, with gradations of blue and white lines of various widths. Thus they create a 'syntax of cloth' destined to send, with impunity, messages to a husband, an enemy, or a rival, such as a co-wife.

The *Tombe Toun* as an Expression of Social Status through Self-Display

Wild silk indigo wrappers are described by the Dogon women as being their most coveted piece of clothing. This fashion emerged in the Dogon rural areas of Dogon just at a time when clothing opportunities were limited to plain white cotton or indigo cloth. Hence, the *tombe toun* became a means whereby Dogon women could distinguish themselves socially from others by wearing wrappers decorated in a novel, original, costly, and beautiful manner. Over time, the social value of this wrapper has grown as the textile emerged as an *atemu*—a well-respected long-established ancestral tradition. The *tombe toun*'s visual aesthetic manifests itself through the sheen that is a physical property of a wild silk that has been extracted from the raw material using specific techniques. It is said to 'attract people's eyes on the wearer', as Salimata[12] explains. The same interviewee[13] goes on to say that Dogon women enjoy competing through fashion at ceremonies and at the market, where they outshine their rivals by dressing up conspicuously. In this way, the *tombe toun* wrapper and matching head scarf are worn with an embroidered shirt (*bou-bou*), some jewellery, a strong yet sweet perfume, and a body cream that brings a natural glow to the skin. Added to this is some make-up that overemphasises the contours of the eyes and, particularly, the eyebrows, which are redrawn and dramatically extended with a thick black eyeliner. Such performances on the part of the women inevitably spark jealousy and comments from observers—who may at the same time be the subject of criticism and insults sent via the *tombe toun* implicit woven messages. These Dogon wild silk indigo wrappers are therefore visually compelling not only because of their beauty but also because their ability to create a charismatic envelope around the wearers, ensuring that those wearers stand out in a crowd of men and women dressed up in western clothes, in cotton-made waxed or in plain indigo garments. In fact, as Lere[14] explains:

> *Tombe toun* is a very visual thing because of its sheen. If you want to be looked at, but also want to be heard, then you just have to wrap it around to become straight away the target of *griots*[15] who eagerly and loudly compliment you. So, they don't stop raving about your outfit, your beauty and elegance through songs and by declaiming your family's history. You are glorified, it shores you up because it makes you visible.

As described, *tombe toun* wrappers not only bestow beauty and honour on women; they also serve as an effective display of social visibility as the weaver's wealth and respectfulness toward her family and her tradition is, at the same time, publically proclaimed by the *griot* in all his splendour. Unlike the *tombe toun*, wrappers made of kapok and the like, instead of wild silk, do not enjoy such a prestigious status and are immediately spotted as 'counterfeit'. It is noteworthy, however, that these counterfeits also serve to increase their wearers' visibility because of their vibrant, almost fluorescent, permanent blue colour; they are cheaper and most often worn by teenage girls and young women. Finally, as I learned from Dogon women across the region, the social significance of wild silk textiles also lies in the fact that it can mark significant events in a woman's life cycle—for example, a woman's marriage, childbirths, and funeral. These are expressed by the *tombe toun*'s indigo and white colours: the colour white, called *pe*, is widely associated with baptism or marriage; and indigo, perceived as black, symbolises not only death but also moistness and fertility (Brett-Smith 1990, 164–65).

Wrapping the Living: The Role of Wild Silk Indigo Wrappers in Dogon Marriage

'Marrying' in the *Tengu* and *Tommon* regions translates as *fourou paga*. The term signifies to 'attach or bind a man and woman together'. In Dogon tradition, several *tombe toun* wrappers crown the dowry given to the bride by her parents-in-law on behalf of her future husband. Various gifts and money are offered at different stages of a marriage process that can spread over three years. From a Dogon perspective, wild silk wrappers ensure the success of a marriage whereas, as is often said, 'a marriage without a *tombe toun* wrapper is a failed marriage', because shame is said to fall on the groom and his parents. As a result, the marriage may even be called off. The presence of one or more *tombe toun* wrappers in a marriage arrangement sparks positive comments from the young woman's community, and the woman immediately gains social recognition from these symbols of social prestige, wealth, and the respect that a stepfamily feels toward their future daughter-in-law. In some ways, the wrapper seals their son's engagement and his responsibility toward her once she has moved with him into his parents' compound after the wedding ceremonies.

The bride traditionally wears her *tombe toun* garments while being introduced for the first time by her husband to his extended family and friends and to the elders of his village and neighbourhood, as well as to the local religious authorities from whom the young couple receive their blessings. By wearing this wrapper, the bride shows in return her full commitment and respect toward her husband and his community. Her newly acquired married status is marked through her wearing the wrapper as the *yakana*, 'the new woman'.

Hence, *tombe toun* wrappers serve both as the material and visual means by which social status and values, such as commitment and respect, are expressed and as the way that social relationships can by sealed and legitimised. In addition, *tombe toun* wrappers feature among both the various cooking utensils and personal effects that the bride brings to her marriage and the gifts that she receives from the women of her family, particularly her mother. Dogon mothers produce one or more wrappers that they offer to their daughters at their weddings as a reminder to them that their mothers can always be counted on. Consequently, the *tombe toun* is a highly praised and traditional wrapper that brings to the bride not only marital social status but also the social significance of appearing to be well married. In other words, wild silk wrappers strengthen relationships within and between families as much as they demonstrate and legitimise an individual's social identity.

Wrapping the Dead: Ending Life 'on a High Note'

As it can be seen in many other parts of West Africa (see Picton 2009, 304), the death of a married woman in the Dogon *Tengu* and *Tommon* regions is signalled by hanging one of her *tombe toun* wrappers on the façade of her compound. For the family of the deceased, this practice constitutes a way of inviting relatives, friends, and local dignitaries to pay tribute to the deceased and to grieve her loss. Her dead body is first dressed in her clothes and then wrapped in a plain white cotton *gaamba* cloth. Then, the *tombe toun* wrapper is taken down from the façade and used to cover her body as a shroud as her corpse is taken to burial. Before the dead woman is placed in her grave, the *tombe toun* shroud is removed and given to her daughters or nieces, who may reuse the wrapper as a shroud for their own funerals.

In the Dogon view, displaying the dead covered with a *tombe toun* constitutes a way to remember both the identity and the social status of the deceased as well as her personal worth. As the producers of wild silk wrappers explained, it is not easy for the great majority of Dogon women to obtain this sort of wrapper, because of the cost of producing both the cloth and the finished garment. In rural areas, Dogon women derive their income mainly from the sale of small goods and foodstuffs, and this income is rapidly spent on cooking utensils, spices, and vegetables, not to mention their children's clothing, healthcare, and, sometimes, schooling. Hence, it is a matter of great pride for Dogon women to own one or more *tombe toun* wrappers at the end of their life; owning one or more of these wrappers celebrates their importance, their usefulness, and their personal achievement as women, mothers, and wives. Old women store such precious wrappers in their bedrooms, folded and preserved in a *carabara* (Figure 10.8) (a decorated calabash fitted with a lid), until the day of their death. The *tombe toun* shroud is known as *andayeii*, the 'eternal voyage', as Yassan[16] explains when showing her shroud:

> When we, Dogon women, have to travel in another village or in town, to visit relatives, to give our condolences, or to attend a marriage, we wear our most beautiful wrapper that we call *andayeii* . . . A dead woman wears her most beautiful wrapper called *andayeii* to show that this is her 'final travel', and she ends her life in beauty.

Although this funerary practice is still very much alive across the Dogon region, many Dogon women have raised concerns about the disappearance of this tradition in places where Islam and, notably, Wahhabi Islam is practiced, because these faiths forbid the covering up of the dead with colourful cloth. Traditionally, the *tombe toun* shroud is displayed as a means both to appease the soul of the dead and to mark, as well as to alleviate, the sadness of the deceased's family and friends by celebrating her dignity and worth for one last time. Consequently, the draping, wrapping, and unwrapping of the dead with a wild silk indigo cloth is the way that Dogon women acknowledge, in public, both their own individual identity and the end of their life cycles.

Conclusion

In this ethnography of wrapping, I have examined Dogon *Tengu* and *Tommon* material practices to do with wrapping and unwrapping the body in relation to the *tombe toun* wild silk indigo wrappers, which are perceived to be a form

Figure 10.8 Dogon *tombe toun* shroud in a *carabara*; private collection (photo by Laurence Douny)

of heritage. Through an analysis of Dogon material practices involving both techniques and materials, I have highlighted the implicit social significance of wild silk indigo wrappers. I have suggested that these prestigious cloths give substance to the collective and individual Dogon identities through their manufacture and display. I have suggested, too, that Dogon material identities 'in-the-making' are created and shaped over time through, initially, the interethnic collaborative production of the cloth and, subsequently, through its use in various social contexts to dress and cover the body. The *tombe toun* wrappers made of wild silk, perceived by the Dogon as a living and proactive substance of power, constitute the shared Mande material identity and practice of the Dogon and Marka-Dafing. As we have seen, these wrappers are the products of the knowledge and techniques initially developed by the Marka-Dafing people and later transferred to the Dogon through interethnic marriages, collaboration, and trading networks. Through their long-standing practices, the Dogon women of the *Tengu* and *Tommon* areas specialised in the production of these textiles, leading to their becoming the community's symbol of identity at national and regional events. In this respect, the *tombe toun* forms a Dogon tradition, a heritage legitimised through its beginnings in time immemorial. The *tombe toun* serves a very practical use in the context of the marriage and the funeral. At these events, the wild silk wrapper and the shroud have come to symbolise a Dogon woman's life cycle, her social significance and her personal worth.

Notes

1. The data included in this paper are taken from the ongoing research on wild silk indigo textiles in West Africa that was sponsored by The Leverhulme Trust (2009–2012). This research was made possible thanks to Dr. Claude Ardouin (1950–2011) and Salif Sawadogo. I am also thankful to Julie Hudson and Anthony Griffiths at The British Museum, Dogon and Marka-Dafing of Mali and Burkina Faso who participated in this research, Point Sud and the CNRST in Bamako, and Paul Lane for his feedback on an earlier draft.
2. These dates are only approximate; they are based on oral history and on calculations derived from the genealogies of producers. Information was collected between 2009 and 2012.
3. Over sixty-five interviewees so far (March 2012) have claimed a Mande origin for the Dogon. However, as Mayor and associates rightly point out, other places of origin must also be considered (2005: 31).
4. March 13, 2011: Bankass (interview); January 15, 2011: Massakana (interview); January 22, 2011: Baye (interview).
5. Roberts identifies *Maraka fin*, 'black Maraka', and also *Maraka jalon*, 'dyed or coloured Maraka', which, according to the author, 'has come to refer to recently converted Muslims' (Roberts 1987, 7).
6. The wrapper is called *tun-tun* in the Dafing tongue.
7. It was identified as *Epanaphe Moloneyi (Druce)* (Ene 1964).
8. From 5,000 cfa (£6.50) as opposed to 12,000 (£17) up to 30,000 cfa (£36) for a wild silk wrapper.
9. As I gather from observations and interviews, although the manufacturing process of the wrapper remains the same, notable differences exist between the Dogon and the Marka-Dafing communities in relation to beliefs; and perceptions of the raw materials and their transformation and social uses. For instance, Islam and modernism affect the production and consumption of the wrappers in both groups in different ways.
10. January 7, 2011: Bamako (interview with Amadou Togo).
11. February 26, 2011: Bandiagara (interview).
12. March 30, 2011: Sama (interview).
13. Idem.
14. March 28, 2011: Segue (interview).

15. In Mande tradition, *griot*s called *jeli* are poets, musicians, and story-tellers—historians and keepers of people's genealogies.
16. February 17, 2011: Dialassagou (interview).

References

Aronson, L. 1995. Threads of Thought: African Cloth as Language. In M. W. Coy & L. Plotnicov, eds., *African and African-American Sensibility*. Pittsburgh: University of Pittsburgh Press, pp. 67–90.

Bedaux, R. M. A. 1988. Tellem and Dogon Material Culture. *African Arts* 21(4), pp. 38–45, 91.

Bolland, R. 1991. *Tellem Textiles: Archaeological Finds from Burial Caves in Mali's Bandiagara Cliff*. Amsterdam: Tropenmuseum/Royal Tropical Institute.

Bouju, J. 1995. Tradition et identité: La tradition dogon entre traditionnalisme rural et néo-traditionnalisme urbain. *Enquête* 2, pp. 95–117.

Brett-Smith, S. 1984. Speech Made Visible: The Irregular as a System of Meaning. *Empirical Studies of the Arts* 2, pp.127–47.

———. 1990–1991. Empty Space: The Architecture of Dogon Cloth. *RES Anthropology & Aesthetics* 19:20, pp. 162–77.

Dieterlen, G. 1941. *Les âmes des Dogon*. Paris: Institut d'Ethnologie.

Douny, L. 2013. Wild Silk Textiles of the Dogon of Mali: The Production, Material Efficacy and Cultural Significance of Sheen. *Textiles: The Journal of Cloth and Culture* 11(3), pp. 58–77.

Ene, C. J. 1964. Indigenous Silk-Weaving. *Nigeria Magazine*, June, pp. 127–36.

Gardi, B. 2003. Textiles Dogon. In R. M. A. Bedaux & D. Van der Waals, eds., *Regards sur les Dogon du Mali*. Leiden: Rijksmuseum voor Volkenkunde & Gand: Editions Snoeck, pp. 176–81.

———. (ed.) 2009. *Woven Beauty: The Art of West African Textiles*. Basel: Christoph Merian Verlag.

Gosselain, O. P. 2000. Materializing Identities: An African Perspective. *Journal of Archaeological Method and Theory* 7(3), pp.187–217.

Hill-Thomas, G. 2012. Silk in the Sahel: Tuntun and Marka Faso Dan Fani in Northwestern Burkina Faso. *African Arts* 45(2), pp. 58–69.

Lane, P. 2008. The Social Production and Symbolism of Cloth and Clothing among the Dogon of Mali. *Anthropos* 103, pp. 77–98.

Mayor, A. 2011. *Traditions céramiques dans la boucle du Niger. Ethnoarchéologie et histoire du peuplement au temps des empires précoloniaux (Journal of African Archaeology. Monograph Series Volume 7)*. Frankfurt: Africa Magna Verlag.

Mayor, A., Huysecoma, E., Gallay, A., Rasse, M., & Ballouche, A. 2005. Population Dynamics and Paleoclimate over the Past 3,000 Years in the Dogon Country, Mali. *Journal of Anthropological Archaeology* 24(1), pp. 25–61.

Niane, T. D. 1974. Histoire et tradition historique du Manding. *Présence africaine* 89, pp. 59, 74.

Picton, J. 2009. Cloth and the Corpse in Ebira. *Textile: The Journal of Cloth & Culture* 7(3), pp. 296–313.

Roberts, R. L. 1987. *Warriors, Merchants and Slaves: The State and the Economy in the Middle Niger Valley 1700–1914*. Stanford: Stanford University Press.

Robion-Brunner, C. 2010. *Forgerons et sidérurgie en pays dogon: vers une histoire de la production du fer sur le plateau de Bandiagara (Mali) durant les empires précoloniaux. (Journal of African Archaeology. Monograph Series Volume 3[1]).* Frankfurt: Africa Magna Verlag.

Roy, C. 2010. Burkina Faso. In J. B. Eicher, ed., *Berg Encyclopedia of World Dress and Fashion*, Vol.1. Oxford: Berg, pp. 220–27.

Sofaer, S. 2007. *Material Identities*. Malden, MA: Blackwell.

Tilley, C. 2011. Materializing Identities: An Introduction. *The Journal of Material Culture* 16(3), pp. 347–57.

11 Unveiling Clay and Metal: The Context and Use of Mesopotamian Textile Wrappings

Agnès Garcia-Ventura and Mireia López-Bertran

Traditionally, textiles have received less attention from researchers than have other archaeological remains—partly because they have often been used as wrappings for corpses or for goods, and research prioritised the study of the contents rather than the containers. These 'containers'—that is to say, the textiles—are the focus of this chapter. It explores the practice of using textiles to wrap two interesting Mesopotamian objects, cuneiform tablets and foundation figurines. The concept of wrapping is used to show how these objects are transformed from figurines and clay tablets into artefacts that protect public buildings, such as temples or palaces. Beginning with these examples, we then reflect on the relationship between content and container; the practice of wrapping and its symbolic meanings; and the perception of materials as perishable objects. The first two sections present the materials within their geographical and chronological framework. The last two sections discuss some ideas about the relationship between contents and containers and about the possible meanings underpinning the act of wrapping foundation deposit objects with a perishable material such as a textile. The conclusion offers some reflections about the relationship between power, memories, and the wrapping of objects.

Geographical and Chronological Framework

The materials examined in this chapter are from some Mesopotamian settlements dating from the very end of the third millennium B.C.E. (ca. 2100–2000 B.C.E.). At this time, Tello (ancient Girsu), Umma, Ur, and Nippur were among the most important cities in the territory, all located in the south of modern Iraq. Traditionally, it has been thought that this area saw the birth of the first cities, in areas that now respond to modern-day Syria and Iraq. In these places, cities were adapted to suit different climatic and orographic conditions. The cities just mentioned were close to the sea (the Gulf) and clearly dependent on rivers. They had a motley layout; their streets and canals marked a clear separation between houses, palaces, and temples, with the last structures being the most imposing. This chapter concentrates on two settlements in this area, Tello and Nippur.

Although the materials presented here were contemporary, scholars of ancient Mesopotamian history do not attribute them all to the same political period (see the discussion in Van de Mieroop 2004, 62–84). Whereas the figurines from Tello date to Gudea's reign, the figurines and tablets from Nippur—and also the tablets from Tello—date to the Third Dynasty of Ur, also known as the Ur III Period (for a discussion of the chronology of Gudea's Reign, see Suter 2000, 15–17; for the Ur III Period, see Sallaberger 2004). The main difference between these two political periods is that, under Gudea's reign, the south was formed by different city-states while during the so-called Ur III period, power was again centralised. This centralisation led to a high degree of bureaucratisation, and for this reason a large number of administrative documents have been recovered from Ur III.

Most of the administrative tablets preserved as a product of this great bureaucracy deal with the textile industry, which was one of the flourishing industries at that time; large workshops are known to have depended on institutions such as the temples and palaces. It is also known, thanks to the texts, that southern Mesopotamia produced valuable and fine textiles that were exported to the north of the territory and to other areas (see Waetzoldt 1972 for the most comprehensive study of textile industry during Ur III period). The use of textiles as wrappings for some goods appears to be worthy of attention, given the importance of textiles to the second-millennium B.C.E. economy.

In many areas of the world, moreover, textiles were produced by women, and the ancient Near East is no exception in this respect. Increasing the visibility of the textiles that are the result of this production process could be a way to recover and reappraise the value of women's work.

Materials

Cuneiform Tablets

The remains of two kinds of materials used to wrap cuneiform tablets have been found: clay and textiles. Cuneiform tablets originally consisted of small clay pieces inside clay balls (*bullae*) that acted as containers. The contents were three-dimensional pieces called *tokens*, the oldest of which date from 5000 B.C.E. Within a few centuries, these tokens had evolved into two-dimensional signs on the outside of the *bullae* (Postgate 1994, 53–60; Schmandt-Besserat 1981), becoming the first known written documents.

Some of these texts were literary, lexical, or mathematical, but the vast majority, dating between 2100 and 2000 B.C.E., were economic and administrative: accounts and lists of goods, products, cattle, and workers. The tablets were usually stored by the institutions for which they were written (temples and palaces), but they were sometimes transported from one place to another to record the kind of products or raw materials being delivered. For both these purposes, for storage and transport, they might be wrapped with clay or with textiles. Clay envelopes were commonly used for letters and other official documents. Many of them have fortunately been preserved (for reflections on the uses and the first evidence of clay envelopes, see Postgate 1994, 60–62). Wrapping with clay was a safety measure taken to preserve the information contained within the text and to certify its authenticity; and of course it was necessary to break this envelope in order to read its contents. Examples of Nippur tablets with clay envelopes are HS 1230 and HS 1231 + HS 1234, both preserved at the University of Jena; an example from Tello, preserved at the Oriental Institute (Chicago), is OIM A02517 (see Table 11.1 for the

Table 11.1 Table with cuneiform tablets quoted, classified as bearers of textile impressions as possible textile wrappings remains or clay envelopes or wrappings

Museum Number	Museum	Provenance	Clay Wrapping (Envelope)	Textile Wrapping (Imprint)	CDLI Number
HS 1230	University of Jena	Nippur	X		P134541
HS 1231 + HS 1234	University of Jena	Nippur	X		P134542
OIM A02517	Oriental Institute Museum	Tello	X		P123230
CFC 114	Collège de France	Tello		X	P100162
CFC 125	Collège de France	Tello		X	P100155
CFC 126	Collège de France	Tello		X	P100146
CBS 03380	University of Pennsylvania	Nippur		X	P105704
CBS 08115	University of Pennsylvania	Nippur		X	P120737
Cornell 106	Cornell University Library	Nippur		X	P118430

corresponding CDLI catalogue numbers and the locations where good-quality images of the tablets and clay envelopes can be found).

Ancient Mesopotamian textile wrappings have rarely survived. However, their imprints or negatives can still be found in the impressions left on some of the wet clay tablets; of course, these imprints are subject to different possible interpretation, as will be seen. We begin with some examples that are thought to be the remains of textile wrappings because of (mainly administrative) documentation: from Tello, CFC 114, CFC 125, and CFC 126 in the collection of the Collège de France (Paris); and from Nippur, CBS 03380 and CBS 08115 (Figure 11.1), now at the University Museum of the University of Pennsylvania (Philadelphia), and Cornell 106 in the Cornell University Library (Ithaca, New York).

Figure 11.1   Ur III cuneiform tablet with possible textile impressions on the surface (probably traces of a textile envelope). Tablet from Nippur, now in the collection of the University Museum of the University of Pennsylvania, catalogue number CBS 08115 (CDLI number P120737) (image courtesy of the University Museum of the University of Pennsylvania).

Figure 11.2   Kneeling god foundation figurine commissioned by Gudea, excavation number TG 16 (after de Genouillac 1936, pl. 87, 2)

The examples included in this study are part of a widespread phenomenon, and they have been selected mainly because good-quality images of them are available at the Cuneiform Digital Library Initiative (CDLI website) (see table 11.1 for the CDLI corresponding catalogue numbers). Some of the imprinted tablets have seals on them, suggesting that they were valuable, since tablets were sealed only to identify their owner or the institution producing them.

Note that textile impressions on clay tablets do not necessarily mean evidence of textile wrapping. They may, instead, be hem imprints; sometimes parties to a legal document would use the imprint of the hem of their robes instead of a seal (v. *sissiktu* in *Akkadisches Handwörterbuch* and *Assyrian Dictionary of the Oriental Institute of the University of Chicago*, Vol. 15). Textile impressions can also, at first glance, be easily confused with fingerprints. It is therefore necessary to be cautious in equating clay tablet impressions with textile wrappings. Further analyses are needed before their presence can be confirmed; and, in recent years, microscopic analyses on some samples of tablets from the British Museum have revealed traces of flax fibres on two Ur III *bullae* (BM 108546 and BM 108547; see Cartwright & Taylor 2011, 68–69).

Foundation Figurines

Many of the Mesopotamian rituals were associated with the construction of temples and other public buildings (Ambos 2004; Ellis 1968, 2001; Suter 2000, 92–96). During these rituals, various objects were buried in the foundations, usually in a box containing at least one cuneiform tablet and a figurine. These objects not only provide us with information about the rituals themselves, the political situation, and images of power; they are also extremely valuable as artistic or epigraphic sources. Some foundation figurines deposited in these boxes still bear fragments of textile wrappings; others have only textile impressions rather than the remains of textiles themselves. Ancient textile remains only very rarely survive, and most of the textiles that have survived have done so because they were mineralised by being in contact with metals such as copper, iron, silver, and lead (Chen, Jakes, & Foreman 1998, 1015–16). This is the case with the remains described next.

The Tello figurines were found mainly during the excavations directed by Ernest de Sarzec (1877–1900), Gaston Cros (1903–1909), and Henri de Genouillac (1929–1931). These figurines were found in a variety of locations all over the site (see Parrot 1948, 203–04 for a description of some of them). Three kinds of figurine were found: those representing a kneeling god; those representing the king carrying a basket on his head, as, for example, the Nippur figurines; and figures of animals (Ellis 1968, 61). All the figurines are peg-shaped. Evidence of textile remains or impressions for the first two types is confirmed not only in the early reports and publications (Cros 1910, 66, 282; de Genouillac 1936, 89–90, pl. 87, fig. 11.3; de Sarzec & Heuzey 1884–1912, 241–43, pl. 28) but also in some of the later catalogues and comprehensive studies (Parrot 1948, 202–04; Rashid 1983, 20–21, in which figs. 82, 84, 97, and 112 bear textiles).

The biggest group consists of the thirty-three kneeling god figurines commissioned by Gudea, the ruler of Lagaš, to commemorate the construction of the Eninnu Temple devoted to Ningirsu (see Hruška 1999 on the building rituals for this temple). At least ten of these foundation figurines had textile remains still adhering to them when they were recovered (Garcia-Ventura 2012, 238). In spite of the difficulty of matching the ten figurines quoted in the first reports to the ones quoted in later publications (see Suter 2000, 313–19 for a catalogue of all the figurines), it is interesting to see that some of them were still described as bearing textiles in the later literature (Ellis 1968, 62).

In particular, in Rashid's catalogue (1983), textile remains are mentioned in the descriptions of both EŞEM 1572 and EŞEM 1721 (Archaeological Museum, Istanbul) and MNB 1384 (Louvre Museum, Paris) (Rashid 1983, figs. 82, 84, 97). Finally, a pair of figurines now in the Louvre Museum (AO 76 and AO 77) were also described as bearing textile remains in the catalogue of an exhibition on the foundation of ancient cities that was held in Barcelona (Spain) in 2000 (Azara et al. 2000, 183). Moreover, textile remains on one of these two Louvre Museum figurines (AO 76) have been analysed recently as part of a planned restoration (Thomas 2012, 151).

Of the Nippur figurines, eleven foundation boxes were probably recovered from the Inanna and the Ekur temples (there is some doubt about the final number) (Garcia-Ventura 2012, 240, footnote 10). The first deposit was found during the expeditions organised by the University of Pennsylvania between 1888 and 1900 and the other ten by the archaeological team of the University of Chicago during the fifth and sixth excavation seasons at Nippur (1955–1956 and 1957–1958). In all, seven deposits were found at the Inanna Temple and four at the Ekur. The Ekur figurines represented Ur-Namma, one of the kings of the Third Dynasty of Ur, and the seven from the Inanna Temple represented Ur-Namma's son Šulgi. All of them were peg-shaped and depicted the king with a basket on his head.

The foundation deposits and the figurines were first quoted and the images published in the reports of the fifth and sixth excavation campaigns between 1955 and 1959 (Crawford 1958, 1959; Goetze 1956; Haines 1955, 1956, 1958; Weidner 1957–1958, 1959–1960). Since then, several comprehensive lists have been published (Frayne 1997, 59–60, 128–29; Rashid 1983, 25, 29–30). A review of some of these publications reveals that at least nine Nippur foundation figurines had textile remains still adhering to them when they were recovered: two found at the Ekur (IM 59586 and OIM A30553) and all seven figurines found at the Inanna temple (IM 59587, IM 59588, IM 59589, IM 61403/I, OIM A31017, MMA 59.41.I, and 961.162.1/ROM2004_1044_4). Moreover, some publications note that all the figurines were wrapped in cloth (Ellis 1968, 68; Zettler 1992, 248, 250–51).

As with the Tello figurines already described, the arrangement of the textile fragments that have survived indicates that the figurines were originally entirely wrapped, since traces of cloth remain around the neck and the arms. It is likely that part of the fabric was removed during fieldwork or during cleaning of the figurines for exhibition. It is not possible without further analysis to determine whether the fibres found attached to both groups of figurines are of animal or plant origin, although some hypotheses have been put forward (Garcia-Ventura 2008, 249–52; for a discussion of the use of wool and linen in cultic contexts, see Zawadzki 2006, 23). Judging from both the first impressions of the excavators and the catalogues which mention cloth adhering to the figurines, it seemed that the remains on the Tello figurines were probably of wool (de Genouillac 1936, 90) and the ones on the Nippur of linen (Basmachi 1972, 471). Given that recent analyses of the textile remains of the Tello figurine AO 76 have established that they are plant stem fibres (Thomas 2012, 153), linen seems more likely.

Contents and Containers

What was the relationship between the content and their containers? And what were their purpose and their significance? In both our examples, the content is made of durable, resistant materials—clay in the case of the tablets and metal in the case of the figurines; the container is usually made of a perishable material, a textile. As a result, only small pieces of textile or textile imprints now survive on the tablets and figurines. Clearly, therefore, the textile wrappings did not provide these materials with long-term protection. Textiles can offer good protection only temporarily and so may well have been considered suitable for preserving cuneiform tablets during, for example, a journey or storage, but they cannot protect a clay tablet in the same way that a clay envelope would; they protect the surface but guarantee neither safety nor privacy. Perhaps weight was a factor in their favour: when a large number of tablets had to be transported from one place to another, fabrics would have been preferable to clay. Textile wrappings, moreover, could be used when the tablets were still wet, whereas clay ones could be used only after they were dry. In other words, textiles might have been preferred because they could be applied more quickly. And opting for a clay envelope to wrap a wet clay tablet would have erased part of the writing.

But what about the foundation figurines? In this case, protection would not have been a priority. As already mentioned, the figurines are part of foundation deposits and were wrapped in a textile (the primary packaging, in contact with the object) before being buried in a brick box (the secondary packaging, guaranteeing survival over the ages) and finally placed in the earth itself (the tertiary packaging). Here, the function of the textiles must be symbolic rather than protective because textiles (the containers) are more delicate than metal figurines (the contents). This point is discussed later.

Finally, the use of a textile wrapping adds new meanings and value to both tablets and figurines. Different societies have considered different objects to be worthy of wrapping. When materials such as textiles, which are not especially long lasting, are used, the 'added value' factor comes into play. Nowadays, fragile objects are often protected with specially designed paper or plastic. But wrappings are often used to decorate rather than to protect; and often an object's value can be increased by the importance attached to its wrapping. The wrappings highlight the interesting and sometimes paradoxical relationship that exists today between the value of content and container. Some containers, such as plastic ones, for example, contain contents (for example, soap) that are less valuable than the containers in economic terms, because the contents are cheaper to produce than the container (for these contemporary paradoxes, see Cummings & Lewandowska 2000, 154–55). However, it is the contents that are needed. The opposite is of course true of the Mesopotamian tablets and figurines: the contents were more valuable and durable than the containers.

It is impossible at present to be certain that deposits with wrapped figurines were distinctly different from those with unwrapped ones. As has already been mentioned, wrappings have been neither preserved nor identified on many of the figurines, and it is therefore quite possible that more figurines than those presented here were originally wrapped at the time of their burial. Thus it is difficult to hypothesise about their number—although it is interesting to examine the type of goods that a different society chose to wrap in order to enhance meaning and value.

In Mesopotamia, cuneiform tablets and foundation figurines were both associated with rulers and institutions such as the temples and palaces. Mesopotamian societies produced both written registers and figurines to commemorate these buildings. Both, therefore, are tangible objects of power.

Wrapping with Textiles

Depositing the Pieces: Rituals and Wrappings

Figurines and tablets are found together in the deposit foundations of temples, and both types of object are used as foundational pieces. This section examines the steps leading up to their wrapping and deposition. Some texts describe rituals in which sculptures were ceremonially clothed (cf. *lubuštu* ceremonies in which the statues of gods are dressed, Oppenheim 1949; published more recently, for Old Babylonian texts, see Matsushima 1993; for Neo-Babylonian texts, see Zawadzki 2006). Although our foundation figurines seem to have been wrapped rather than actually clothed, the relationship between the content (statue, sculpture, figurine) and the container (textile, fabric) is clearly comparable in the two cases. In clothing ceremonies, the process of clothing is as important as the end result of being clothed; and, despite the lack of information about this wrapping process, it is possible to speculate that the same would hold true for the foundation figurines. The texts explain how each activity of the gods (as sculptures) was accompanied by particular rituals overseen by a huge number of high priests, musicians, and 'specialists' (Matsushima 1993, 215). Thus it seems likely that the act of wrapping would have been ritualised as well. And, if we consider the rites involved in clothing the sculptures, it seems possible that the act of wrapping, too, would have been in hands of the priests or even of members of the royal family.

Two features indicate the important role of textiles in relation to the foundation figurines. First, the figurines are decorated: the kneeling gods wear a kind of triangular hat, and the peg-shaped ones hold baskets on their heads. Second, and even more striking, the wrappings can be considered to be a special type of clothing for the figurines that reflects the secretive nature of both the act of deposition and of the figurine itself. It is conceivable that ritual performances may have played a role in creating these foundation tablets and figurines as well; the Neo-Assyrian texts explain how the materials with which figurines were made had to be crafted accompanied by certain rituals (Nakamura 2005, 29). It is also plausible that the king figurines with baskets were themselves representing some kind of ritual. Sumerian texts speak of kings participating in building rituals: kings carried the clay to mould, and the mortar to lay the bricks, in baskets on their heads (Ellis 1968, 23). Suter also noticed that 'the context in Gudea's Cylinder Inscriptions suggests that the basket was used for removing earth in the process of digging the foundation' (Suter 2010, 320–21). Furthermore, the texts also explain how the Mesopotamians performed rituals when laying the first stone of a building (Ambos 2004, 5; Hruška 1999), although the archaeological data to support these written sources are lacking. However, to quote Ellis (1968, 31), 'the initiation of the actual construction of a building was understandably an event of particular symbolic importance. It is the event most commonly mentioned in ancient building inscriptions'.

No matter what rituals were performed before the wrapping of the materials and their burial, one must consider not just the actors and the audience but also the order of events marking a deposition. Our information is, unfortunately, limited in this respect, but it is nevertheless important to mention these two ideas so as to support, and contextualise, the processes of wrapping and depositing. Understanding foundational rituals as performances implies the presence of either an active or a passive audience (Inomata & Coben 2006, 15). One can argue that the audience was likely to have been a restricted one because only a small number of specialised individuals (priests) and members of the elite (royal families) had access to specific areas of temples and palaces. The pieces may have been wrapped and buried by this select group, because these people were the only members of the community allowed to participate in such foundation rituals. These activities of selection and withdrawal may even have gone one step farther, since the materials deposited were never seen again once the boxes had been closed; they may only ever have been seen again, in a symbolic sense, by the divinities themselves. The same suggestion may apply to the arrangement of inscribed bricks, whereby their inscriptions are in contact with other bricks but invisible to anyone looking at the final built wall.

Three steps mark the importance of hiding and protecting the foundation deposits: wrapping the figurines and tablets; putting them in a brick box; and, finally, burying them in the earth. These three ritual steps transform the figurines from the corporeal to the symbolic realm just as the practice of wrapping reinforces the protective and secretive nature of the figurines. Following from Mitchell (2006, 387), therefore, the rituals carried out before wrapping and depositing could be labelled as rituals of separation (from the living world to another one), and the act of wrapping could be seen as a ritual of incorporation into other worlds. The rituals put emphasis on the 'performance' aspect (as understood in terms of transformation) of not only the wrapping of the figurines and tablets but also their concealment in boxes buried in the earth. In short, the act of deposition might be full of ritual significance, demonstrated by the different ritual steps and the care taken in the deposition. This process would be entirely understandable given that the objects buried are magical ones that might require some form of ritual activation, such as the act of wrapping, to trigger their prophylactic role.

Bodies and Wrapping

In this section, the focus turns to figurines and the ritual and symbolic implications of their wrapping. We begin by putting into context two theoretical, and interconnected, aspects: the concept of bodies and the concept of personhood (see López-Bertran 2007, 14–17 for a more detailed presentation). It is assumed that bodies and their representations are socially constructed and that human bodies are represented according to specific ways of understanding and perceiving corporealities (Boric & Robb 2008; Csordas 1994; Joyce 2005; Montserrat 1998). Such an approach emphasises the role of bodies as agents and not as mere instruments of the mind, a Cartesian idea that was entirely alien to ancient societies (cf. Nakamura 2005, 38). The Mesopotamians did not distinguish between brain and mind; in fact, the Sumerian language has a single word, šà, to denote mind, body, and heart (Asher-Greve & Asher 1998, 39–40). It is interesting to note here that they had a specific word, alan ('representation' or 'image'), that they used to refer to (among other things) figurines such as those analysed here (see Assyrian Dictionary of the Oriental Institute of the University of Chicago definition for the Akkadian term *ṣalmu* and remarks about this definition by Irene Winter in 1992, 36, note 5).

The first characteristic that draws our attention to the body and corporality is that a wrapped body is a body that has been deprived of the power to gesture. The elimination of this power may well be a deliberate act. Indeed, the bodies of the Nippur figurines undergo a transformation even before being wrapped, because they are peg-shaped—they are bodies without legs, and the lower part of the body is longer than the trunk. Unlike other divine representations that portray sensuous experiences such as eating, drinking, dancing, or dressing—all the actions of real living beings (about the mouth-opening ritual, see Winter 1992, 22–24)—the ritual performance of wrapping deprived these figurines of any movement, gesture, or sensation. They were transformed or moved to other worlds where their wrapping would prevent them from touching, seeing, hearing, smelling, or tasting. The practice of wrapping is performative as it transforms the corporeality of the figurines. In her study of Neo-Assyrian figurines, Nakamura states that once these materials are buried they are removed from the sensuous experience of the human-object relationship; they remained still and concentrated on warding off evil spirits (Nakamura 2005, 38). Thus changes in appearance imply changes in identity, and, it is suggested, such is the case with these figurines.

Wrapping up the figurines transforms them from being physically active in rituals to being deprived in terms of corporality and senses. However, this state does not negate the ideas expressed here. As already said, it is possible to recognise only the final step in the living process of the figurines. It is therefore quite possible that figurines, especially the ones holding baskets on their heads, were kinetic or active in performing rituals before being wrapped. In addition, the absence of corporealities does not equate with uselessness. These foundation deposits, it must be remembered, were intended to function in a magical, protective sense.

This line of reasoning leads to a consideration of the significance of the multiple personhoods that lie beneath the peg shapes and the human forms. Both kinds of figurines offer clear examples of what is termed 'dividuality', as opposed to 'individuality' (see Fowler 2004 for an insightful analysis). Dividuality means that people 'were the constantly changing products of social interactions between them and the others'; people who are dividual are formed by the substances and the actions of others (Fowler 2004, 25–26). These statements have two implications for this discussion. First, the Nippur figurines are examples of one of the multiple ways of creating, understanding, and representing kings. By wrapping them and depositing them in boxes, humans reinforce one aspect of these kings, their protective function, and eliminate others related to their kinetic corporeality. So, the function and physicality of these figurines of kings depend on the intentions of their producers.

Second, some of these pieces are peg-shaped and therefore 'non-anthropomorphic'. This typology reinforces the argument that dividual and multiple personhoods can be connected not only with other beings but also with other objects. These pieces are kings and pegs at the same time: in other words, pegs become human beings, and, simultaneously, kings become the foundations of the temples they commissioned and in which they are buried. The one cannot be conceived without the other, which is why they are represented together, creating a hybrid living being that has lost its human physical features not only because of its wrapping but also because of its shape. The same idea can be applied to the gods holding pegs. Gods are conceived and represented as people and thus share with them the dividual dimension; Ur III kings were also deified (on this occasional phenomenon in Mesopotamian kingship, see Suter 2010, 319, 348–49, with previous references). In both cases, wrapping the pieces reinforces the idea of the figurines as living beings. The wrapping in foundational deposits may represent exactly the same idea that the ceremonial clothes of kings and divinities represent in other rituals.

The act of burial also reinforces the idea of the living, human dimensions of the pieces. Putting the figurines inside boxes has been interpreted as a way of providing houses for deities (Frankfort 1978, 267). Furthermore, the act of depositing suggests that objects share the same qualities as people: they are born, they live, and they die (Fowler 2004, 52). Unfortunately, it is possible to reconstruct only the final of all the steps in the creation of the figurines: their burial in the foundational deposits. In this context, it is also possible that the act of wrapping up the figurines might be conceived as a funerary ritual for them. Although information is lacking about contemporary Mesopotamian funerary rituals, it seems likely that the wrapping might work as a kind of shroud. Far from signifying the end of their function and life, their burial and their wrapping would then represent exactly the opposite: their transformation and the importance of their protective role, as discussed earlier.

Conclusion: Power, Memories, and Wrapping

Textile remains may be as important as the goods they contain or wrap. Southern Mesopotamia, in particular, produced textiles not only for domestic consumption but for export as well. Textiles were a key item of trade and are as relevant as other archaeological remains. But these textile remains are fragile and scarce in Ancient Mesopotamia; thus it is essential for them to be preserved and analysed.

This chapter argues that textiles have not only a practical use but also, and more important, a symbolic one. As well as protecting objects, they endow them with added value, since both tablets and figurines are images and symbols of institutional power. This power is clearly linked to the aim of preserving selected memories as a means to construct a past:

> In Mesopotamia burial constituted a pervasive and important ritual idiom; people buried valuables, sacrifices, foundation offerings, caches of various materials, and their dead. . . . In a basic sense, burial can mean to store, preserve, and put the past on hold. This concept of burial holds purchase in the way in which protection relates to memory. . . . Burial keeps things hidden and protected such that preservation binds memory to a specific locality, from which it can be retrieved in the future as a given past. (Nakamura 2005, 36–37)

The practices of wrapping and burying certain objects of value and power—gods, kings, and tablets—share many similarities. Wrapped figurines are the product of a ritualised deposition process, and they have a function even while buried and hidden underground. The act of wrapping was used both to preserve the past and to select specific items to be remembered in the future; and this transformation has corporeal and bodily consequences.

Acknowledgements

We wish to thank the curators and researchers who helped us to find the figurines cited, which were scattered in collections and museums: Susan Allison (The Oriental Institute Museum of the University of Chicago), Benjamin R. Foster and Ulla Kasten (Yale Babylonian Collection), Richard L. Zettler (University of Pennsylvania Museum, Philadelphia), and Claudia Suter. We would also like to thank those who helped us to get the permissions to publish some of the images: Steve Tinney (University of Pennsylvania Museum, Philadelphia) and the late Irene Good (The Metropolitan Museum of Art, New York). We also thank Friedhelm Pedde for always encouraging us to go farther with our study of wrapped-up figurines. We are also indebted to the two anonymous reviewers for their insightful comments and to the editors of the volume for giving us the opportunity to include our contribution.

References

Ambos, C. 2004. *Mesopotamische Baurituale aus dem 1. Jahrtausend v. Chr.* Dresden: Islet.

Asher-Greve, J. M., & Asher, A. L. 1998. From Thales to Foucault . . . and Back to Sumer. In J. Prosecký, ed., *Intellectual Life of the Ancient Near East. Papers Presented at the 43rd Rencontre Assyriologique Internationale. Prague, July 1–5, 1996.* Prague: Academy of Sciences of the Czech Republic Oriental Institute, pp. 29–40.

Azara, P., Wunenburger, J. J., Subías, E., Mar, R., & Margueron, J.-C. 2000. *La fundación de la ciudad. Mesopotamia, Grecia y Roma.* Barcelona: Centre de Cultura Contemporània de Barcelona/Institut d'Edicions de la Diputació de Barcelona.

Basmachi, F. 1972. *Treasures of the Iraq Museum, Baghdad.* Baghdad, Republic of Iraq: Ministry of Information, Directorate General of Antiquities.

Boric, D., & Robb, J. (eds.) 2008. *Past Bodies: Body-Centered Research in Archaeology.* Oxford: Oxbow Books.

Cartwright, C. & Taylor, J. 2011. Investigating Technological and Environmental Evidence from Plant Remains and Molluscs in Cuneiform Tablets. *The British Museum Technical Research Bulletin* 5, pp. 67–72.

Chen, H. L., Jakes, K. A., & Foreman, D. W. 1998. Preservation of Archaeological Textiles through Fibre Mineralization. *Journal of Archaeological Science* 25, pp. 1015–21.

Crawford, V. E. 1958. Report of Director of the School at Bagdad. *Bulletin of the American Schools of Oriental Research* 152, pp. 7–9.

———.1959. Nippur, the Holy City. *Archaeology* 12, pp.74–83.

Cros, G. 1910. *Nouvelles fouilles de Tello.* Paris: Ernest Leroux.

Csordas, T. J. 1994. Introduction: The Body as Representation and Being-in-the-World. In T. J. Csordas, ed., *Embodiment and Experience: The Existential Ground of Culture and Self.* Cambridge: Cambridge Studies in Medical Anthropology, pp. 1–26.

Cummings, N., & Lewandowska, M. 2000. *The Value of Things.* Basel: Birkhäuser–August Media Ltd.

Cuneiform Digital Library Initiative (CDLI), http://cdli.ucla.edu/, accessed July 30, 2013.

de Genouillac, H. 1936. *Fouilles de Telloh: Époques d'Ur III Dynastie et Larsa.* Paris: Mission Archéologique du Musée du Louvre et du Ministère de l'Instruction Publique, Paul Geuthner.

de Sarzec, E., & Heuzey, L. 1884–1912. *Découvertes en Chaldée.* Paris: Ernest Leroux.

Ellis, R. S. 1968. *Foundation Deposits in Ancient Mesopotamia.* New Haven, CT: Yale University Press.

———. 2001. Mesopotamian Foundation Ceremonies and Deposits. In P. Azara, R. Mar, E. Riu, & E. Subías, eds., *La fundación de la ciudad: Mitos y ritos en el mundo antiguo.* Barcelona, Actes del col.loqui internacional (8/9/10 de juny de 2000, Barcelona), Museu d'Arqueologia de Catalunya, Ediciones UPC, pp. 57–64.

Fowler, C. 2004. *The Archaeology of Personhood: An Anthropological Approach.* London: Routledge.

Frankfort, H. 1978 [1948]. *Kingship and the Gods: A Study of Ancient Near Eastern Religion as Integration of Society and Nature.* Chicago: University of Chicago Press.

Frayne, D. R. 1997. *Ur III Period (2112–2004): The Royal Inscriptions of Mesopotamia. Early Periods (RIME 3/2)*, Toronto: University of Toronto Press.

Garcia-Ventura, A. 2008. Neo-Sumerian Textile Wrappings: Revisiting Some Foundation Figurines from Nippur. *Zeitschrift für Orient Archäologie* 1, pp. 246–54.

———. 2012. The Emperor's New Clothes: Textiles, Gender and Mesopotamian Foundation Figurines. *Altorientalische Forschungen* 39(2), pp. 235–53.

Goetze, A. 1956. Nippur Foundation Boxes. *Archaeology* 9, pp. 216–17.

Haines, R. C. 1955. The Latest Report on the Progress of the Excavations at Nippur. *Sumer* 11, pp. 107–09.

———. 1956. The Temple of Inanna at Nippur. *The Illustrated London News*, 18th August, pp. 266–69.

———. 1958. Further Excavations at the Temple of Inanna. *The Illustrated London News*, 6th September, pp. 386–89.

Heuzey, L. 1902. *Catalogue des antiquités chaldéens du Musée du Louvre*, Paris: Librairies-imprimeries réunies.

Hruška, B. 1999. Zum Gründungsritual im Tempel Eninnu. In B. Böck, E. Cancik-Kirschbaum, & T. Richter, eds., *Munuscula Mesopotamica: Festschrift für Johannes Renger.* Münster: Ugarit-Verlag, pp. 217–28.

Inomata, T., & Coben, L. S. 2006. *Archaeology of Performance: Theaters of Power, Community and Politics.* Lanham, MD: AltaMira Press.

Joyce, R. A. 2005. Archaeology of the Body. *Annual Review of Anthropology* 34, pp. 139–58.

López-Bertran, M. 2007. *Ritualizando cuerpos y paisajes: un análisis antropológico de los ritos fenicio-púnicos*, Barcelona, Ph.D. Dissertation, Universitat Pompeu Fabra, http://www.tesisenred.net/TDX-0513108-170353, accessed July 30, 2013.

Matsushima, E. 1993. Divine Statues in Ancient Mesopotamia: Their Fashioning and Clothing and Their Interaction with the Society. In E. Matsushima, ed., *Official Cult and Popular Religion in the Ancient Near East: The City and Its Life Held at the Middle Eastern Culture Center in Japan, Mitaka, Tokyo, March 20–22, 1992.* Heidelberg, pp. 209–19.

Mitchell, J. P. 2006. Performance. In C. Tilley, W. Keane, S. Kuechler-Fogden, M. Rowlands, & P. Spyer, eds., *Handbook of Material Culture.* Thousand Oaks, CA: Sage, pp. 384–401.

Montserrat, D. 1998. Introduction. In D. Montserrat, ed., *Changing Bodies, Changing Meanings: Studies on the Human Body in Antiquity.* London: Routledge, pp. 1–9.

Nakamura, C. 2005. Mastering Matters: Magical Sense and Apotropaic Figurine Worlds of Neo-Assyria. In L. Meskell, ed., *Archaeologies of Materiality.* Oxford: Blackwell, pp. 18–45.

Oppenheim, A. L. 1949. The Golden Garments of the Gods. *Journal of Near Eastern Studies* 8, pp. 172–93.

Parrot, A. 1948. *Tello: vingt campagnes de fouilles (1877–1933).* Paris: Albin-Michel.

Postgate, J. N. 1994. *Early Mesopotamia: Society and Economy at the Dawn of History.* London: Routledge.

Rashid, S. A. 1983. *Gründungsfiguren im Iraq.* München: Beck.

Sallaberger, W. 2004. Relative Chronologie von der späten Frühdynastischen bis zur altbabylonischen Zeit. In J.-W. Meyer & W. Sommerfeld, eds., *2000 v. Chr. Politische, Wirtschaftliche und Kulturelle Entwicklung im Zeichen einer Jahrtausendwende.* Berlin, 3. Internationales Colloquium der Deutschen Orient-Gesellschaft 4–7, April 2000 in Frankfurt/Main und Marburg/Lahn: Saarbrücker Druckerei und Verlag, pp. 15–43.

Schmandt-Besserat, D. 1981. From Tokens to Tablets. *Visible Language* 15, pp. 321–44.

Suter, C. E. 2000. *Gudea's Temple Building: The Representation of an Early Mesopotamian Ruler in Text and Image.* Groningen: STYX Publications.

———. 2010. Ur III Kings in Images: A Reappraisal. In H. D. Baker, E. Robson, & G. Zólyomi, eds., *Your Praise Is Sweet: A Memorial Volume for Jeremy Black from Students, Colleagues and Friends.* London: British Institute for the Study of Iraq, pp. 319–49.

Thomas, A. 2012. Restes textiles sur un clou de fondation de Gudea. Étude préliminaire. *Paléorient* 38(1–2), pp. 149–57.

Van de Mieroop, M. 2004. *A History of the Ancient Near East, ca. 3000–323 BC.* London: Blackwell.

Waetzoldt, H. 1972. *Untersuchungen zur neusumerischen Textilindustrie.* Roma: Centro per le Antichità e la storia dell'arte del Vicino Oriente.

Weidner, E. F. 1957–1958. Ausgrabungen und Forschungsreisen. *Archiv für Orientforschung* 18, pp. 173–74.

———. 1959–1960. Ausgrabungen und Forschungsreisen. *Archiv für Orientforschung* 19, pp. 198–200.

Winter, I. 1992. 'Idols of the King': Royal Images as Recipients of Ritual Action in Ancient Mesopotamia. *Journal of Ritual Studies* 6(1), pp. 13–42.

Zawadzki, S. 2006. *Garments of the Gods: Studies on the Textile Industry and the Pantheon of Sippar According to the Texts from the Ebabbar Archive.* Göttingen: Academic Press Fribourg—Vandenhoeck & Ruprecht Göttingen.

Zettler, R. L. 1992. *The Ur III Temple of Inanna at Nippur.* Berlin: Dietrich Reimer Verlag.

12 Wrapped in Images: Body Metaphors, Petroglyphs, and Landscape in the Island World of Rapa Nui (Easter Island)

Karina Croucher and Colin Richards

Rapa Nui is known for its remoteness, often being described as the one of the most isolated places on the planet. This is due to its South Pacific location at the eastern tip of the Polynesian triangle, c. 2,300 miles west of the South American mainland and c. 1,300 miles east of its nearest neighbour Pitcairn Island (Figure 12.1). Despite earlier claims to the contrary (for example, Heyerdahl 1941, 1951), a wide array of evidence, including cultural traditions, language roots, and osteological evidence, clearly establishes a firm Polynesian context for the prehistoric inhabitants of Rapa Nui (for instance, Baker & Gill 1997, 54; Finney & Alexander 1997; Golson 1965; Lee 1997, 8; Swindler et al. 1997, 167; Van Tilburg 1994). The fame of Rapa Nui is not, however, predicated on its remoteness but on the dramatic scale of monumentality that is present across the island. Dotted around the coastline are a series of raised stone platforms (*ahu*) on which once stood large stone statues known as *moai*. The *moai* represent one of the most iconic images of Polynesian monumentality (Figure 12.2). To emphasise their extraordinary scale, the heads of the *moai* were frequently adorned with cylinder-shaped red stone topknots known as *pukao*.

The *ahu* and *moai* are not the only outstanding features of the Rapa Nui past. The large number of petroglyphs on the island stand out in the broader context of Pacific rock-art in terms of their scale, quality, and diversity (Lee 2001, 583; Lee & Stasack 1999, 165–66). In technique, the petroglyphs are incised,

Wrapping and Unwrapping Material Culture: Archaeological and Anthropological Perspectives by Susanna Harris & Laurence Douny, 209–228 © 2014 Left Coast Press, Inc. All rights reserved.

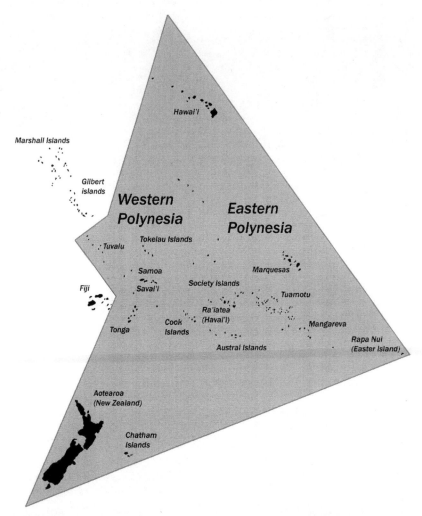

Figure 12.1 Position of Rapa Nui within the Polynesian triangle (map adapted by Colin Richards)

grooved, bas-relief, and painted, sometimes being carved in a truly exquisite manner. They occur on a variety of media, ranging from flat lava flows (*papa*) to large rounded boulders and to the surfaces of *moai* and *pukao*. Their depiction is broad and includes sea creatures, human faces, birdmen, canoes, and so forth (Lee 1992, 1997, 2004).

Although the monuments have begun to be placed in a 'landscape' context (for example, Hamilton et al. 2008), petroglyphs continue to inhabit a totally different realm of archaeological interpretation. In this chapter we argue that

Figure 12.2   Inland facing *moai* standing on *ahu* Nau nau, Anakena Bay (photo by Colin Richards)

not only is such a disjunction prohibitive to understanding the role and nature of 'rock-art' in prehistoric Rapa Nui but also that petroglyphs actually provide an essential interpretative route into prehistoric Polynesian understandings of landscape (or islandscape) as cosmology.

We draw on fieldwork undertaken in 2009 (Cristino et al. 2009) and investigate the deployment of petroglyphs within a particular landscape context and show that through the heuristic of 'wrapping', and metaphorical extension of the tattooed body, it is possible to provide an interpretation of the Rapa Nui islandscape as a 'living' cosmological construct. This is a complex and substantial topic, so here our analysis is restricted to an examination of the large extinct volcano of Rano Kau situated on the southwest corner of the island.

Wrapping Things

Wrapping things is an activity familiar to everyone. A pile of wrapped gifts lying beneath the tree on Christmas Eve presents a comforting and emotive image of the festive season. However, the idea of wrapping is not restricted merely to presents and presentation; as a mode of practice it has also been described as constituting a structuring or ordering principle of society (Hendry 1993, 1; Moeran 1990, 2), or as a 'stimulating analytical metaphor' (Ben-Ari 1990, 225). Although the practice of wrapping is almost universally employed, as a social strategy it takes on quite different connotations in particular societies, a situation that is aptly demonstrated in Hendry's analysis of Japanese society (1990, 1993).

Binding or wrapping represents a potent mode of analogical practice in a Polynesian context as a strategy of containment and protection. This role is most potently manifest in ritual contexts. In many societies, there is a fundamental categorical difference between gods and the living—it is never possible for them to come into direct contact. However, in Polynesian cosmology, there is no differentiation. Rather than being dichotomous, the relationship between deities and the living is one of points along a continuum, fused within genealogies (Shore 1989, 164). However, deities remain sacred and, more important, are the source of *mana*. *Mana* is genealogically passed from deities to people, through ancestral lines of ascent. Hence, *mana* is contained within, and articulated through, people and is essential for potency and social reproduction. The efficacy of *mana* is realised only in action and event. Consequently, there is a dependency on ritual transactions for the transference of *mana* for social reproduction. Because of the lack of categorical distinction between deities and living people, such exchanges are highly dangerous and so need to be contained, structured, and controlled through *tapu*. Through prescriptive rules and practices, *tapu* effects a state that demarcates, controls, and channels *mana*. This control is absolutely necessary, because such transactions also represent a breach between the cosmological realms of *Ao* (the everyday world of light and the living) and *Po* (the sacred domain of the ancestors).

In such contexts, wrapping or binding is a vital organ of *tapu*, since it is a technology of protection and containment. A consequence of thinking about the process of wrapping is that it stresses the critical importance of interfaces, skins, and membranes. This in turn broadens the possibilities of wrapping beyond protection and containment to include:

1. Concealment (allowing the potential of disclosure)
2. Unification
3. Re-presentation

Thinking about skins and membranes as forms of wrapping is important for a number of reasons. First, the emphasis is on practice: the wrapping of something, which leads directly to the converse possibility of unwrapping as a practice of disclosure and revelation. This practice also places greater interest on the mode and manner of wrapping, which is not merely something that separates or divides but that constitutes a skin or membrane that holds significance in its own form and materiality.

Skins or membranes are potentially paradoxical entities in that, although physically containing and concealing, they also advertise and draw attention to that being concealed. This paradox can be best described as wrapping as a mechanism of *indication*, whereby that which is being indicated is also necessarily hidden or obscured. Perhaps under such circumstances wrapping may additionally be conceived as an *embrace* of that concealed. This wrapping propagates a conjunction and intimacy between the practice, form, and materiality of wrapping and what it is that is being wrapped.

From *Ao* to *Po*: Tattooing as a Protective Membrane

Both Kaeppler (1988) and Gell (1993) have provided analyses of Polynesian tattooing with the basic thesis being that the tattoo acts as a second skin, a membrane of *tapu* reduction. Although such a 'skin' is acquired differently throughout Polynesia, in principle it relates to a barrier providing a sacred level of protection. Additionally, Kaeppler (1988, 66) details how tattooing was used for spiritual and physical protection on body areas not covered by the woven or feather cloak or, in the case of Rapa Nui, a barkcloth (*tapa*) cloak (2001, 35). Moreover, the cloak, *tapa* cloth, and tattoos bound and wrapped the body, adding to the genealogical, symbolic, and sacred protection of the wearer during essential but hazardous transactions between people and deities. Thus the tattoo can be said to operate as a function of the *tapu* system (for example, Allen 1997, 341). This protective function is particularly well attested to in relation to the practice of tattooing the female right hand in the Marquesas (Handy 2008 [1922], 5). This is precisely the hand that not only comes into direct contact with a corpse through the application of coconut oil but also is employed in the serving of the fermented breadfruit *popoi* from a bowl (ibid.; Gell 1993, 215). A similar protective role has been ascribed to the tattooed female hands of ancient Hawai'i (Allen 1997, 343).

Polynesian ritual transactions involving transformation and social reproduction are necessarily homologous to the original cosmogonic event. Generally speaking, the creation of the Polynesian world occurred with the brief fusion of the complimentary and antagonistic opposites *Po* (dark, underworld, inner, earth, female) and *Ao* (light, upperworld, outer, sky, male) (for example, Goldman 1970, 37; Handy 1927, 34–39). Subsequently, they remained 'cosmic principles constituting the dual order of the universe' (Bausch 1978, 175). The manifestation of *Ao* and *Po* is complex. For example, Handy muses on the way *Po*, recognised as both sacred and an underworld, was frequently associated with a gender and locality or place (1927, 34–35), such as *Hawaiki*, but ultimately concludes that 'it should be regarded more properly as signifying a state of existence' (ibid., 69). This interpretation of the nature of *Po* is effective in portraying the ambiguity and relational nature of cosmological structures. For instance, in Hawaiian cosmology, the inner body as a container of *Po* is separated from the external world (*Ao*) by the tattooed skin (Sowell 1998). Such identification is directly linked back to cosmogony, as in the Maori belief that the 'dark womb is identified with *Po* and seen as a space serving as the location for a creation' (Bausch 1978, 174).

Polynesian social reproduction as a consequence of *mana* therefore required the conjunction of one realm with the other—the 'irruption' of *Po* into *Ao* (Gell 1993, 126). Obviously, for this irruption to occur a conduit was required between the two realms. In the context of the body, 'orifices were important in Polynesian thought because they played a central role in the channelling of *mana* between the realms of *Ao* and *Po*' (Shore 1989, 147). Linkage between *Ao* and *Po* was therefore manifest in the flow of substances via bodily orifices or transgressions of the skin, including tattooing (Sowell 1998, 338). Such a process is fraught with danger, requiring great protection through *tapu* in the form of wrapping and binding. This is precisely the role of the tattoo, in both execution and function; the process of tattooing opens a pathway for the transference of *mana* (ibid., 338). As Sowell notes, 'by merging the spiritual and physical self, the resulting tattoo protected, defined and spiritually enhanced the person' (ibid., 339).

Given this role, it is of little surprise that in several locations in east Polynesia and Aotearoa (New Zealand) tattooing focuses on facial orifices. In the literature on Polynesian tattooing much discussion has centred on male tattooing (for example, Gell 1993; Handy 2008 [1922]). Nonetheless, as Gell (1993, 204–05) declares, there are clear differences in the nature of male and female tattoos and tattooing. This differentiation we suggest is a manifestation of the differential status of women accorded by Hanson (1982) as attracting deities and representing a passageway between the sacred and human realms of existence. This situation gave women a status that is both powerful and dangerous (Arredondo 2000, 46), capable of destroying *mana* and removing taboos (Arredondo 2003, 24). In the context of a potential conduit between the realms of *Ao* and *Po*, the association of the 'female principle' with the more sacred *Po* as a state of existence takes on greater import. As Thomas observes, the vagina, through menstruation and childbirth, was the most potent of these channels, acting 'like *other* orifices, as a conduit between this world and the other' (1990, 70, our italics). Unlike the vagina, which is covered, wrapped, and bound by clothing, other orifices such as the mouth, ears, and nose are revealed and unprotected.

Female facial tattoos of east Polynesia and Aotearoa tend to focus on the mouth (Figure 12.3). For example, Maori female tattooing was known as *taanga ngutu* ('lip-weaving') (Best 1904, 170). Women's tattoos of the mouth were not restricted to the outer lips but were also applied on the inner lips up to the gums (Robley 1896, 33–47). The application of tattoos to the lips and ears was also a feature of women's tattooing in the Marquesas. The designs of the lips were called *koniho*, resembling teeth (*niho*); and those of the ears, *omua puaina* (Handy 2008 [1922], 28). Thomson (2007 [1891], 466) observed that on Rapa Nui women were tattooed with more elaborate designs and 'the lips were freely tattooed after the manner of the Maoris, with lines curving around the chin and extending to the cheekbones' (ibid., 467).

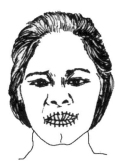

Figure 12.3 Female facial tattoos in the Marquesas (after Handy 1922, Plate VI, A)

At a general level, we can agree with Kaeppler (1988) and Gell (1993) that tattooing in east Polynesia was a process of inscription on the skin that acted as an additional protective membrane. Since it is the connectivity between people and deities that is at issue, orifices, as conduits between *Ao* and *Po*, are particularly ambiguous and dangerous features. We suggest this vulnerability seems to be of greater potency for Polynesian women (cf. Hanson 1982) and consequently female tattooing concentrated on uncovered body orifices, particularly the mouth and lips. A further link between women and tattooing lies in Rapa Nui mythology, which describes how female spirits introduced the practice of tattooing, with the process of beautification through tattooing also believed to ascribe the wearer with *mana* (Arredondo 2000, 42; Kaeppler 2001, 37).

We now extend the themes outlined in this discussion of tattooing in order to provide an insight into how the Polynesian inhabitants of Rapa Nui necessarily created landscape as cosmology.

Volcanoes, Caves, and Petroglyphs: Rapa Nui Doorways to Another World

In size, Rapa Nui is actually very small, comprising an area of only c. 64 square miles. The island has a triangular shape, having been formed by the sequential eruption of three great volcanoes, Poike, Rano Kau, and Terevaka (Fischer & Love 1993, 1–3). These are now extinct, but their volcanic cones effectively define and dominate each corner of the island, with spectacular sea cliffs up to 300 m in height forming the seaward sides of both Rano Kau in the southwest and Poike in the east (Figure 12.4). Of the three formative volcanoes, only Rano Kau retains a large crater or caldera, c. 1.6 km in diameter, which today contains a freshwater lake (Figure 12.5). Rano Raraku, the famous *moai* quarry, is the only other extinct volcano on the island comparable to Rano Kau in terms of either crater size or the presence of a sizable internal freshwater

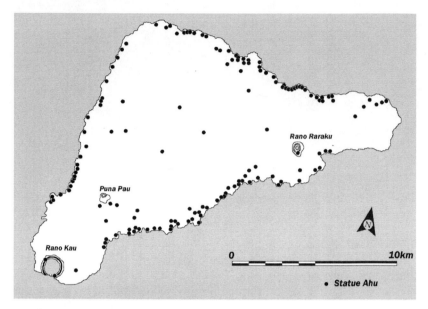

Figure 12.4 The location of Rano Kau and distribution of monumental *ahu* triangle (map adapted by Colin Richards)

lake (Figures 12.4 and 12.6). Inland, several smaller extinct volcanic cones project skywards effectively punctuating views across the land.

The open, barren appearance of the island interior today is mainly illusory in respect to the prehistoric past. Lush palm-tree cover greeted the arrival of the first Polynesians when they stepped ashore (for example, Flenley 1993; Flenley & Bahn 2002, 78–88; Flenley et al. 1991). Through this vegetation cover, the volcanic hills and cones would have projected above the tree line.

Because of its volcanic origins and the presence of numerous lava tubes, Rapa Nui is also an island of caves. Caves abound in both inland and coastal areas, providing a honeycomb of subterranean passages. In size, the caves vary dramatically. Some are large, open-mouthed, and cavernous, such as Ana Kai Tangata on the southwestern shore and the inland cavern of Ana Te Pahu. Others are much smaller, with narrow concealed entrances and restricted chambers, a situation so vividly and claustrophobically described by Thor Heyerdahl (1958) in his book *Aku Aku*. Consequently, concealed below the bright, hot, rocky, surface of the island is a dark, cool, and secret subterranean world.

Together, these natural features constituted the lived and experienced island world of the prehistoric people in Rapa Nui. However, at the end of a person's life it was time for the soul to leave the island and to travel back to *Hiva*, the Rapa Nui equivalent of *Hawaiki*. To gain access to *Hiva* necessarily involved passing into the realm of *Po*. Throughout Polynesia 'it was generally

Figure 12.5   The caldera of Rano Kau (photo by Colin Richards)

Figure 12.6   Sea creatures swirling around the large boulder at Hau Koka (photo by Colin Richards)

believed that there was a definite route or path taken by souls of the departed on their way to the next world' (Handy 1927, 71). To access this ancestral realm generally involved travelling along a road (*ara*) in a westerly direction to a coastal location where the spirit 'jumped off' into the depths of the ocean to continue its journey westward and downward (see Richards et al. 2011 for further discussion of ancestral *ara*). Passage along the spirit *ara* was punctuated by a number of 'stopping or gathering places' where the ultimate fate of the spirit was negotiated (for instance, Handy 1927, 71–74; Williamson 1937, 275). Consequently, the spirit *ara* is an uncertain path to follow:

> The souls of the Marquesans passed along the high mountain ridge that forms the backbone of the main island of their group to the high promontory at the west called Kiukiu. As they marched along the path of souls, the ghosts could be seen dressed in their white garments (mortuary wrappings), avoiding the valleys lest they be caught in the bush. . . . On their way the souls (or ghosts) strengthened themselves for their coming ordeals by bathing in a cool pool of water. Below the promontory was a rock. When the souls clapped their hands this opened, the sea rolled back, and the soul entered the nether world. (Handy 1927, 72)

The journey of the soul along the spirit *ara* in Aotearoa (New Zealand) is essentially identical in that it followed the mountain ranges north to Te Reinga, near the North Cape, where on the rocky cliff face 'there grew an ancient pohutukawa, and from this tree the souls leapt to a cave in the water below' (Hiroa 1958, 429; Orbell 1985a, 78).

These accounts of the passage taken by the soul back to *Hawaiki* are illuminating. They each involve both entering the ocean and a cave. This duality reverses the qualities and necessities of birth, embracing both the transformatory qualities of voyaging to *Hawaiki* (see Richards 2008) and the passage into the sacred subterranean world of *Po*. Frequently, the duality of the journey of the soul is also manifest in the treatment of the physical body after death. For example, there is extensive evidence of subterranean burial in caves from across eastern Polynesia, including Aotearoa (Orbell 1985b, 84–85) and Rapa Nui (for instance, Métraux 1940, 118; Shaw 2000). In some places, such as Hawai'i and the Marquesas, the corpse was actually placed in or with a canoe (for example, Handy 1923, 108; Kirch 1985, 175–77, 218–19), facilitating the journey to *Hawaiki*.

On Rapa Nui, Rano Kau has been suggested to be a similar 'jumping-off point' (Barthel 1978, 219; Lee 1992, 130). Rano Kau is undoubtedly a spectacular volcanic cone; its lip is composed of a series of strikingly shaped, black basalt outcrops punctuated by grassy patches. Internally, the walls of the crater or caldera plunge down to an area of vegetation encircling a large freshwater lake (Figure 12.5). At a general level, Rano Kau conforms to the Polynesian identification of extinct volcanic craters being conduits to the underworld *Po* (for instance, Bausch 1978, 175; Williamson 1933, 362). More specifically, Rano Kau is the place where the mythical leader of the first Polynesians to settle on

Rapa Nui, Hotu Matu'a, selects for his death (Métraux 1940, 68). It is at Maea Hono, a striking 3-m-high pillar of rock on the rim of Rano Kau, that according to McCoy (1968), Hotu Matu'a shouts his last words to *Hiva*. Conversely, Barthel (1978, 219–20), following Routledge (2005 [1919], 280), presents an account of Hotu Matu'a shouting his last words on the western rim of Rano Kau at Orongo.

That the crater Rano Kau was the 'jumping off place for souls' is suspected by Barthel (1978, 223), and he notes that the crater was originally named Poko Uri, which translates as 'dark hole, black night, dark underworld' (ibid.). Lee (1992, 130) agrees with this designation, adding that Rano Kau is the westernmost point of Rapa Nui, typical of Polynesian jumping off places and, as such, represents one of the most important features on the island. Taken together the evidence is compelling.

Hidden in dense vegetation at the base of the crater is Hau Koka, a cluster of rocks covered by 'the most impressive collections of petroglyphs on the island' (Lee 1992, 164). The arrangement of decorated rocks is instructive. The most famous is a beautifully decorated rounded boulder set back c. 10 m from the edge of the lake. In terms of composition and application 'there is . . . nothing equal to it in all of Polynesia' (ibid.). Overall, the boulder measures c. 3 m in diameter and is decorated over its surface with a series of amazing sea creatures, one of which has a human head (Figure 12.6). A series of smaller decorated rocks run down toward the lake, where a single large rock acts as a natural platform adjacent to the water's edge (Figure 12.7). This rock

Figure 12.7   The decorated rock at the water's edge at Hau Koka; the point of entry into *Po* (photo by Colin Richards)

is decorated with a series of petroglyphs, including three carved bowls. The question arises as to why some of the most amazing petroglyphs in Rapa Nui are inscribed on a concealed series of boulders and rocks adjacent to the lake edge at the base of the Ran Kau crater. We suggest that there can be little doubt that this is the final jumping place into the crater lake to enable the entry of souls down to the underworld realm of *Po*.

The petroglyphs wrap around the boulders and stones at Hau Koka in a most comprehensive and emphatic manner. There are other petroglyphs recorded at another fourteen points within the crater (McCoy 1968), including a cave high up on the southwest slope. However, none compare with the outstanding adornment of Hau Koka (Lee 1992, 165). The passage of the dead is an ambiguous and fearsome event, because it constitutes the return of persons to the sanctity of *Po*. Here we follow Rainbird (2002, 2008) in relating the tattooing of the skin with ink and images to the tattooing of the land with paint and petroglyphs. Just as the tattooing of the female right hand in the Marquesas (Handy 2008 [1922], 5) effected a protective membrane to the pollution of touching the dead, so the tattooing of the rocks with petroglyphs at Hau Koka provided protection against the souls of the dead. This *tapu* was essential, since such a metamorphosis represented the 'irruption' of *Po* into *Ao* (Gell 1993, 126). Rano Kau acted as the main conduit from the inhabited realm of *Ao* to the sacred underworld *Po*. It is therefore essentially an orifice or passage between the two states (Bausch 1978, 175). At particular moments, a conjunction or irruption occurs, caused perhaps by the passage of souls or other forms of ritual transaction taking place at Hau Koka.

During the extensive archaeological survey undertaken by McCoy (1968, 1976), and subsequent rock art surveys by Lee (for example, 1992, 1993), substantial numbers of petroglyph sites were discovered around the rim of Rano Kau. As Lee (1992, 158) notes, their scattered distribution reflects the availability of appropriate rock outcrops, although it is notable that not all rock surfaces were chosen for inscription. One site in particular on the west side of the caldera, at Mata Ngarau, Orongo, is world famous for its spectacular birdman petroglyphs. However, other less known petroglyph sites are present on rock outcrops around the volcano rim (Figures 12.8 and 12.9). Some of these sites, such as Vai Atare and Te Vare, are also extensive and contain a range of well-executed designs, including, birdmen, makemake faces, fish, comet-tails, cup-marks, and lines. An intriguing aspect of some of these sites is that the petroglyphs are cut into inaccessible rock faces on the very lip of the crater. As Lee perceptively comments: 'this placement indicates that the designs were not created for general viewing but more likely were offerings for the gods; another possible explanation is that the act of their creation was more important than their being seen' (ibid., 159).

These are not mutually exclusive interpretations. Again, the distribution of these petroglyphs can be likened to the female facial tattoos of east Polynesia

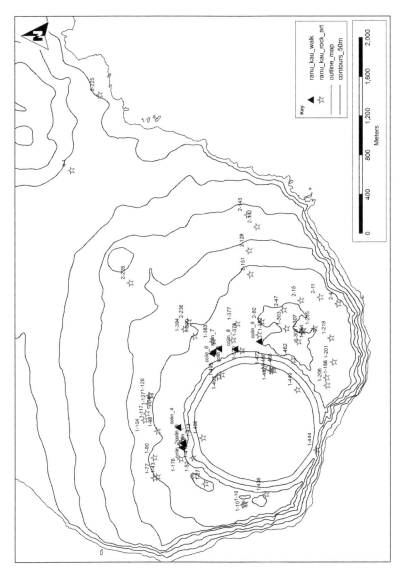

Figure 12.8 Distribution of petroglyphs around the caldera of Rano Kau (figure courtesy of Kate Welham).

Figure 12.9   Petroglyphs at Te Vare on the northwestern rim of the Rano Kau caldera (photo by Colin Richards)

and Aotearoa, which tend to centre on the mouth. Recall also that women's facial tattoos were not restricted to the outer lips but were also applied to the concealed areas within the mouth, such as the inner lips up to the gums (Robley 1896, 33–47). The observation of women's facial tattoos has interesting implications for gendered aspects of landscape. Note, however, that in the deployment of rock-art at Rano Kau we are witnessing a homology between the tattoos of the mouth and the petroglyphs of the volcano. In this instance, a Polynesian landscape is cosmologically constituted in the same way as the human body.

Let us now consider Lee's second line of interpretation for a moment, that of the importance of the practices of petroglyph creation. The process of carving and tattooing is often viewed as bringing on ancestral benevolence (Coward & Gamble 2010; Henare 2005); the processes of making are thus not simply for the achievement of the final design or tattoo. The process of tattooing, argues Gell (1993, 304), involves three stages: incision, healing, and the final image, the last being permanently marked on the body. It is also apparent that these stages are replicated in the production of rock-art on the black basalt of Rano Kau. Apart from bas-relief carving, petroglyphs are incised or pecked into the rock. The eventual darkening and 'healing' of the image follows an intermediate period of fresh scarring, white against the black.

Just as tattoos wrap the bodies of people, so petroglyphs wrap the land and *ahu* wrap the island. The practices of tattooing and rock-art create openings, or *ara*, channelling *mana* between the realms of *Ao* and *Po*. Spoken chants are captured within the openings and sealed in through the healing process (Gell 1993, 57; Kaeppler 1989, 168); thus the processes of rock-art and tattooing may have been equally wrapped by sound. The production of sound, through pecking into the rock, has been recognised as an important aspect of petroglyph production (cf. Ouzman 2001; Rainbird 2002) and may account for small rock-carved cupules. The practice of tattooing is highly dangerous and controlled and contained by *tapu*. Just as restrictions are placed on tattooer and tattooed alike, both during the penetration of the skin and during the subsequent healing period (for example, Sowell 1998, 339), so similar sanctions and restrictions could accompany the creation of rock-art. In short, we can concur with Lee (1992, 159) in suggesting the practices of rock-art production were equally important as the final petroglyph.

The evidence suggests that beyond the image-wrapped Rano Kau, other conduits to the underworld may exist, through caves. There are several cave entrances that have been inscribed with rock-art; frequently these feature makemake faces or komari, the latter symbol particularly associated with protection (Lee 1987, 52; 1992, 195). For the Rano Kau crater, McCoy observed rock-art both in a cave located on the exterior edge of the volcano crater, containing a komari motif (McCoy 1968, 1–27), and in another cave on the interior slope containing makemake faces and birdman motifs, which McCoy describes as indicating an 'important site' (1968, 1–438). Rock-art has also been documented in caves around the coastal regions of poike, the north shores above Anakena, and the small islands of Motu Iti and Motu Nui. Additional discoveries are undoubtedly yet to be made; a recent survey of 314 of Rapa Nui's caves have documented petroglyphs, including the makemake, the birdman, and komari motifs, as well as depictions of fish and plants (Ciszewski, Zdzislaw, & Szelerewicz 2010, 90). Further survey and research promises to reveal additional evidence for the wrapping of these features in motifs as conduits to the underworld.

Cosmological Landscapes: Petroglyphs as Tattooing and Wrapping the Land

Although there have been extensive research concerned with Rapa Nui petroglyphs (for example, Lavachery 1939; Lee 1992, 1993, 2000), there is a tendency, as with rock-art studies more generally, for such art to be viewed almost independently of other archaeological evidence (see, however, Van Tilburg & Lee 1987). There are numerous reasons for this cleavage, not least because of the notorious difficulties of establishing accurate absolute or relational chronologies. Moreover, a concern with both the aesthetic and communicative aspects of rock-art has led to an almost subdisciplinary status for rock-art studies in archaeology. This general trend is certainly visible in studies of Rapa Nui prehistory. Because the prehistory of Rapa Nui is represented as 'phased' chronological units (for instance, Martinsson-Wallin 1994, 83–84; Skjølsvold 1993, 94; Smith 1961, 212; Van Tilburg 1994), 'period' disjunction inevitably occurs. The majority of petroglyphs are often consigned to a date or phase later than the classic period of *ahu* and *moai* monumentality, thereby by default decreasing their importance.

The petroglyphs of Rapa Nui, however, are not confined to a later prehistoric date (cf. Van Tilburg & Lee 1986). Lee demonstrates that, in some contexts, a process of superimposition occurs, effectively revealing their continual application throughout prehistory. For instance, the komari and ship motifs consistently appear to postdate images of the birdman and makemake (Lee 1987, 52; 1992, 195). Nor should petroglyphs be considered as some form of aesthetic epiphenomenona, that is, as something that is merely decorative in content and, in the absence of social context, essentially impossible to interpret meaningfully. On the contrary, we suggest that while petroglyphs may be understood in terms of aesthetics and communication, they also constitute a form of inscriptive practice that is transformative in nature. Moreover, when considered alongside other forms of inscriptive technologies, especially of the body, the rock-art of Rapa Nui assumes paramount significance in our understanding the construction and constitution of apparently alien Polynesian worlds and landscapes.

Tattooing and rock-art wrap the body and the landscape and are a necessary component of *tapu*, mediating the transference of *mana*. Protection is needed to negotiate the danger associated with *Man* and states of *Tapu*, and this protection is provided through wrapping in images during the processes of tattooing and rock-art. Uncovered orifices, as apertures between the realms of *Ao* and *Po* and conduits to the underworld, require extra protection. Such orifices include the human mouth on females, regarded as potent and potentially dangerous, the volcano craters, and caves. The body and the landscape are wrapped through these inscriptive practices of protection.

In this chapter we have investigated how the concept of wrapping can be used as an interpretative device for understanding the processes of marking the body and the land on Rapa Nui. Further research will elucidate the role of wrapping beyond the Rano Kau volcano focused on here by exploring these themes for the rest of Rapa Nui and by setting them within broader Polynesian cosmological beliefs.

Acknowledgements

Foremost we wish to thank CONAF, especially Susana Nahoe and Enrique Tucki, for permission to visit the Rano Kau sites. We are grateful to Tamsin Parish, Tiki Paoa, and Kate Welham, who participated in the 2010 fieldwork season, for their discussion of many of the themes within this chapter. We also thank Georgia Lee for her generosity with information and enthusiasm for this research, which forms part of a broader project: Rapa Nui: Landscapes of Construction Project, directed by Sue Hamilton, Susana Nahoe, Colin Richards, and Francis Torres H. We also thank the Museo Antropologico P. Sebastian Englert on Rapa Nui for access to resources, including McCoy's original survey. We also wish to thank Susanna Harris and Laurence Douny for their invitation to participate in this volume and the preceding conference.

References

Allen, T. 1997. The Tattooed Hand in Hawai'i. In C. M. Stevenson, G. Lee, & F. J. Morin (eds.), *Easter Island in the Pacific Context*. South Seas Symposium, Proceedings of the Fourth International Conference on Easter Island and East Polynesia. Los Osos, CA: The Easter Island Foundation, pp. 341–45.

Arredondo, A. M. 2000. The View of Women in Rapanui Society, Part 1: Women in Myths and Legends. *Rapa Nui Journal* 14(2), pp. 42–46.

———. 2003. Lifehistories of Women in Rapanui Society in the First Half of the Twentieth Century. Gender Studies Part 3. *Rapa Nui Journal* 17(1), pp. 15–33.

Baker, S. J., & Gill, G. W. 1997. A Modification of Results of the Osteological Analysis of the Norwegian Expedition to Easter Island. *Rapa Nui Journal* 11(2), pp. 53–59.

Barthel, T. S. 1978. *The Eighth Land: The Polynesian Discovery and Settlement of Easter Island*. Honolulu: University Press of Hawai'i.

Bausch, C. 1978. Po and Ao, Analysis of an Ideological Conflict in Polynesia. *Journal de la Société des Océanistes* 34(61), pp. 169–85.

Ben-Ari, E. 1990. Many Voices, Partial Worlds: On Some Conventions and Innovations in the Ethnographic Portrayal of Japan. In E. Ben-Ari, B. Moeran, & J. Valentine (eds.), *Unwrapping Japan: Society and Culture in Anthropological Perspective*. Manchester: Manchester University Press, 104–20.

Best, E. 1904. The Uhi-Maori or Native Tattooing Instruments. *Journal of the Polynesian Society* 13(2), pp. 164–72.

Ciszewski, A., Zdzislaw, J. R., & Szelerewicz, M. 2010. *Las Cuevas de la Isla de Pascua: El Mundo Subterraneo de Rapa Nui*. Krakow: AGH University of Science and Technology.

Coward, F., & Gamble, C. 2010. Metaphor and Materiality in Earliest Prehistory. In L. Malafouris & C. Renfrew (eds.), *The Cognitive Life of Things: Recasting the Boundaries of the Mind*. Cambridge: McDonald Institute for Archaeological Research, pp. 47–58.

Cristino, C., Downes, J., Hamilton, S., Nahoe, S., Nunn, R., Kirkpatrick, D., Pollard, J., Richards, C., Seager, M., Thomas, A., Stanford, F., Torres, H., Vargas, P., Welham, K., & Whitehouse, R. 2009. *Rapa Nui Landscapes of Construction Project: Excavations at Puna Pau 2009*. Rapa Nui: Structures Report for CONAF.

Finney, J. C., & Alexander, J. D. 1997. The Rapa Nui Language of Easter Island: Where Does It Fit in the Polynesian Family Tree? In *Easter Island in Pacific Context South Seas Symposium, Proceedings of the Fourth International Conference on Easter Island and East Polynesia*. Los Osos, CA: Easter Island Foundation, pp. 20–32.

Fischer, S. R., & Love, C. M. 1993. Rapanui: The Geological Parameters. In S. R. Fischer (ed.), *Easter Island Studies: Contributions to the History of Rapanui in Memory of William T. Mulloy*. Oxford: Oxbow Monograph 32, pp. 1–6.

Flenley, J. R. 1993. The Present Flora of Easter Island and Its Origins. In S. R. Fischer (ed.), *Easter Island Studies: Contributions to the History of Rapanui in Memory of William T. Mulloy*. Oxford: Oxbow Monograph 32, pp. 7–15.

Flenley, J. R., & Bahn, P. 2002. *The Enigma of Easter Island*. Oxford: Oxford University Press.

Flenley, J. R., Teller, J. T., Prentice, M. E., Jackson, J., & Chew, C. 1991. The Late Quaternary Vegetational and Climactic History of Easter Island. *Journal of Quaternary Science* 6, pp. 85–115.

Gell, A. 1993. *Wrapping in Images: Tattooing in Polynesia*. Oxford: Clarendon Press.

Goldman, I. 1970. *Ancient Polynesian Society*. Chicago: University of Chicago Press.

Golson, J. 1965. Thor Heyerdahl and the Prehistory of Easter Island. *Oceania* 36, pp. 38–83.

Hamilton, S., Nahoe Arellano, S., Richards, C., & Torres, H. F. 2008. Quarried Away: Thinking about Landscapes of Megalithic Construction on Rapa Nui (Easter Island). In B. David & J. Thomas (eds.), *Handbook of Landscape Archaeology*. Walnut Creek, CA: Left Coast Press, pp.176–86.

Handy, E. S. C. 1923. *Native Culture of the Marquesas*. Honolulu: Bernice P. Bishop Museum Bulletin 9.

———. 1927. *Polynesian Religion*. Honolulu: Bernice P. Bishop Museum Bulletin 34.

Handy, W. C. 1922. *Tattooing in the Marquesas*. Bernice P. Bishop Museum, Bulletin 1.

———. 2008 [1922]. *Tattooing in the Marquesas*. Mineola, NY: Dover Publications.

Hanson, F. A. 1982. Female Pollution in Polynesia. *Journal of the Polynesian Society* 91(3), pp. 335–81.

Henare, A. 2005. Ngo Aho Tipuna (Ancestral Threads): Maori Cloaks from New Zealand. In D. Miller & S. Kuchler (eds.), *Clothing as Material Culture*. Oxford: Berg, pp. 121–38.

Hendry, J. 1990. Humidity, Hygiene, or Ritual Care: Some Thoughts on Wrapping as a Social Phenomenon. In E. Ben-Ari, B. Moeran, & J. Valentine (eds.), *Unwrapping Japan: Society and Culture in Anthropological Perspective*. Manchester: Manchester University Press, pp. 13–25.

———. 1993. *Wrapping Culture: Politeness, Presentation and Power in Japan and Other Societies*. Oxford: Clarendon Press.

Heyerdahl, T. 1941. Did Polynesian Culture Originate in America? *International Science* 1, pp. 15–26.

———. 1951. *The Kon-Tiki Expedition: By Raft across the South Seas* (14th impression, June 1951). London: George Allen & Unwin.

———. 1958. *Aku-Aku: The Secret of Easter Island*. London: George Allen & Unwin Ltd.

Hiroa, T. R. 1958. *The Coming of the Maori*. Wellington: Whitcombe and Tombs.

Kaeppler, A. L. 1988. Hawaiian Tattoo: A Conjunction of Genealogy and Aesthetics. In A. Rubin (ed.), *Marks of Civilization*. Los Angeles: Museum of Cultural History, University of California, pp. 157–70.

———. 1989. Art and Aesthetics. In A. Howard & R. Borogsky, eds., *Developments in Polynesian Ethnology*. Honolulu: University of Hawai'i Press, pp. 211–40.

———. 2001. Rapa Nui Art and Aesthetics. In E. Kjellgren, ed., *Splendid Isolation: Art of Easter Island*. New York: The Metropolitan Museum of Art, pp. 32–41.

Kirch, P. V. 1985. *Feathered Gods and Fishhooks: An Introduction to Hawaiian Archaeology and Prehistory*. Honolulu: University of Hawai'i Press.

Lavachery, H. 1939. *Les Pétroglyphes de L'île de Pâques*. Anvers: de Sikkel.

Lee, G. 1987. Further Comment on Paul G. Bahn's 'No Sex, Please, We're Aurignacians'. *Rock Art Research* 4(1), pp. 51–55.

———. 1992. *The Rock Art of Easter Island: Symbols of Power, Prayers to the Gods*. Los Osos, CA: Institute of Archaeology, University of California.

———. 1993. The Rock Art of Rapanui. In S. R. Fischer, ed., *Easter Island Studies: Contributions to the History of Rapanui in Memory of William T. Mulloy*. Oxford: Oxbow Monograph 32, pp. 112–21.

———. 1997. Petroglyph Motif Distribution in East Polynesia. *Rapa Nui Journal* 11(1), pp. 5–9.

———. 2000. Rock Art of the Ceremonial Complex at Ahu Ra'ai. In C. M. Stevenson & W. S. Ayres, eds., *Easter Island Archaeology: Research on Early Rapanui Culture*. Los Osos, CA: Bearsville Publishers, pp. 45–52.

———. 2001. Oceania. In D. S. Whitley, ed., *Handbook of Rock Art Research*. Walnut Creek, CA: AltaMira Press, pp. 576–604.

———. 2004. Rapa Nui's Sea Creatures. *Rapa Nui Journal* 18(1), pp. 31–38.

Lee, G., & Stasack, E. 1999. *Spirit of Place: Petroglyphs of Hawai'i*. Los Osos, CA: Easter Island Foundation.

Martinsson-Wallin, H. 1994. *Ahu: The Ceremonial Stone Structures of Easter Island*. Uppsala: Societas Archaeologica Upsaliensis.

Métraux, A. 1940. *Ethnology of Easter Island*. Honolulu: Bernice P. Bishop Museum Bulletin 160.

McCoy, P. C. 1968. *Field Notes*. Manuscript on file in Museo Antropologico P. Sebastian Englert, Rapa Nui.

———. 1976. Easter Island Settlement Patterns in the Late Prehistoric and Proto-historic Periods. *Bulletin Five, International Fund for Monuments*. New York: Easter Island Committee International Fund for Monuments Inc.

Moeran, B. 1990. Introduction: Rapt Discourses—Anthropology, Japanism, and Japan. In E. Ben-Ari, B. Moeran, & J. Valentine, eds., *Unwrapping Japan: Society and Culture in Anthropological Perspective*. Manchester: Manchester University Press, pp. 1–12.

Orbell, M. 1985a. *Hawaiki: A New Approach to Maori Tradition*. Christchurch: University of Canterbury Publication No 35.

———. 1985b. *The Natural World of the Maori*. Auckland: Bateman.

Ouzman, S. 2001. Seeing Is Deceiving: Rock Art and the Non-Verbal. *World Archaeology* 33(2), pp. 237–56.

Rainbird, P. 2002. Marking the Body, Marking the Land: Body as History, Land as History—Tattooing and Engraving in Oceania. In Y. Hamilakis, M. Pluciennik, & S. Tarlow, eds., *Thinking through the Body: Archaeologies of Corporeality*. New York: Kluwer/Plenum, pp. 233–48.

———. 2008. The Body and the Senses: Implications for Landscape Archaeology. In B. David & J. Thomas, eds., *Handbook of Landscape Archaeology*. Walnut Creek, CA: Left Coast Press, pp. 263–70.

Richards, C. 2008. The Substance of Polynesian Voyaging. *World Archaeology* 40(2), pp. 206–23.

Richards, C., Croucher, K., Paoa, T., Parish, T., Tucki, E., & Welham, K. 2011. Road My Body Goes: Re-Creating Ancestors from Stone at the Great *Moai* Quarry of Rano Raraku, Rapa Nui (Easter Island). *World Archaeology* 43(2), pp. 191–210.

Robley, H. G. 1896. *Moko: The Art and History of Maori Tattooing*. London: Chapman & Hall.

Routledge, K. 2005 [1919]. *The Mystery of Easter Island*. Rapa Nui: Museum Press.

Shaw, L. C. 2000. Human Burial in the Coastal Caves of Easter Island. In C. M. Stevenson & W. S. Ayres, eds., *Easter Island Archaeology: Research on Early Rapanui Culture*. Los Osos, CA: Easter Island Foundation, pp. 59–80.

Shore, B. 1989. Mana and Tapu. In A. Howard & R. Borofsky, eds., *Developments in Polynesian Ethnology*. Honolulu: University of Hawai'i Press, pp. 137–74.

Skjølsvold, A. 1993. The Dating of Rapanui Monolithic Sculpture. In S. R. Fischer, ed., *Easter Island Studies: Contributions to the History of Rapanui in Memory of William T. Mulloy*. Oxford: Oxbow Monograph 32, pp. 89–95.

Smith, C. S. 1961. A Temporal Sequence Derived from Certain *ahu*. In T. Heyerdahl & E. N. Ferdon, eds., *Reports of the Norwegian Archaeological Expedition to Easter Island and the East Pacific*, Vol. 1: *The Archaeology of Easter Island*. London: Allen & Unwin, pp. 181–219.

Sowell, T. L. 1998. Light from Darkness: Hawaiian Concepts of *Ao* and *Po*, and the Mediating Role of Tattoo. In C. M. Stevenson, G. Lee, & F. J. Morin, eds., *Easter Island in Pacific Context: South Seas Symposium*, Proceedings of the Fourth International Conference on Easter Island and East Polynesia, University of New Mexico, Albuquerque, August 5–10, 1997. Los Osos, CA: Bearsville Press and Cloud Mountain Press, pp. 337–40.

Swindler, D. R., Drusini, A. G., Cristino, C., & Ranzato, C. 1997. Molar Crown Morphology of Precontact Easter Islanders Compared with Molars from Other Islands. In Georgia Lee, Christopher M. Stevenson, & F. J. Morin, eds., *Easter Island in Pacific Context, South Seas Symposium, Proceedings of the Fourth International Conference on Easter Island and East Polynesia*. Los Osos, CA: Easter Island Foundation, pp. 163–68.

Thomas, W. 1990. *Marquesan Societies: Inequality and Political Transformation in Eastern Polynesia*. Oxford: Clarendon Press.

Thomson, W. J. 2007 [1891]. *Te Pito Te Henua or Easter Island*. Hanga Roa: Rapa Nui Press.

Van Tilburg, J. A. 1994. *Easter Island: Archaeology, Ecology and Culture*. London: British Museum Press.

Van Tilburg, J. A., & Lee, G. 1987. Symbolic Stratigraphy: Rock Art and the Monolithic Statues of Easter Island. *World Archaeology* 19(2), pp. 133–49.

Williamson, R. W. 1933. *Religious and Cosmic Beliefs of Central Polynesia*, Vol. 1. Cambridge: Cambridge University Press.

———. 1937. *Religion and Social Organization in Central Polynesia*. Cambridge: Cambridge University Press.

Index

About the Authors

Johanna Banck-Burgess is employed at the Regierungspräsidium Stuttgart Landesamt für Denkmalpflege. She wrote her dissertation on the textiles preserved in the Hochdorf IV burial and presented her results in a landmark publication. She is an active member of the North European Symposium for Archaeological Textiles.

Karina Croucher is a Lecturer in Archaeology at the University of Bradford. She specializes in archaeologies of identity and the body, focusing on prehistoric contexts. Karina has recently completed a British Academy Postdoctoral Fellowship and is author of *Death and Dying in the Neolithic Near East*, Oxford University Press.

Laurence Douny is an honorary research fellow at University College London. Since 2008, she has conducted extensive research on wild silk and indigo in West Africa, funded by the Leverhume Trust in collaboration with The British Museum. Her work is based in Mali, Burkina Faso, Northern Ivory Coast, and Northern Nigeria, where she has been focusing on the materials, design, and techniques of wild silk indigo wrappers and embroidery.

Agnès Garcia-Ventura is Assistant Professor at the Universitat Autònoma de Barcelona. Her research focuses on textiles and gender in Mesopotamia with particular attention to the organisation of work as reflected in the Ur III administrative texts, performance, and visual imagery sources, such as foundation figurines.

Margarita Gleba is ERC Senior Research Associate, McDonald Institute for Archaeological Research, University of Cambridge. She has published extensively on archaeological textiles, including her well-received monograph *Textile Production in Pre-Roman Italy* and a major co-edited volume *Textiles* *and Textile Production in Europe: From Prehistory to* AD *400*, which provides a timely update of European textile research.

Susanna Harris is ERC Research Associate at the Institute of Archaeology, University College London. Her research focuses on the cloth and clothing of prehistoric Europe. Recent research includes an experimental approach to Mesolithic cloth types, the material properties of fibres used in prehistory, and the analysis of regional costumes represented on statue menhirs of the third millennium B.C.E.

Janet M. Johnstone studied Egyptian Archaeology at University College London, where she specialised in ancient Egyptian textiles and clothing. She is an independent researcher working as a clothing consultant focused on the interpretation and construction of ancient Egyptian clothing. Johnstone recently studied the Salakhana Trove, a cache of over 600 Ramesside stelae and other objects from Asyut. In this project she analysed the clothing as a means to date and categorise the professional and social status of donors portrayed on the stelae.

Mireia López-Bertran is a postdoctoral researcher at the Spanish Ministry of Education and Culture—FECYT and Honorary Research Fellow at the University of Glasgow. She specialises in the Phoenician and Punic sites of the ancient Mediterranean, with research interests in gender, embodiment, and ritual.

Nicolette Makovicky is Lecturer in Russian and East European Studies at Oxford University. She has conducted long-term fieldwork in Slovakia and Poland. She is the author of two forthcoming edited volumes: *Neoliberalism, Personhood, and Postsocialism: Enterprising Citizens in Changing Economies*, published with Ashgate, and *Economies of Favour after Socialism*, co-edited with David Henig and published with Oxford University Press.

Titika Malkogeorgou studied fine art and conservation and was awarded a Ph.D. in Anthropology by University College London in 2011. She studies material culture, construction, preservation, and transmission of cultural knowledge through the ethics and theory of conservation practice, and concepts of objectification and social transformation. She has conducted research with the National Trust and the Victoria and Albert Museum.

Colin Richards is Professor of World Prehistory at the University of Manchester. He specializes in architecture and monumentality and has conducted fieldwork in Orkney, Lewis, and Rapa Nui. He has published extensively on the Neolithic of Northwest Europe, with a special interests in the archaeology of Polynesia and Northern Scotland.

Nancy Ukai Russell is an independent researcher who recently received a degree in Media Anthropology at the School of Oriental and African Studies, University of London. She is studying contemporary babywearing and how the embodied practice of infant transport is evolving in contexts that have lacked such a cultural tradition and the material objects that support it.

Barbara Wills works as a conservator at the British Museum on a range of organic materials, specialising in the conservation of leather, basketry materials, human remains, and ancient Egyptian objects. She has recently completed a two-year project to study and stabilise a group of natural mummies from salvage excavations near the Fourth Nile Cataract in Sudan, which was supported by the Clothworkers' Foundation.